IMAGES
of America

REVERE BEACH

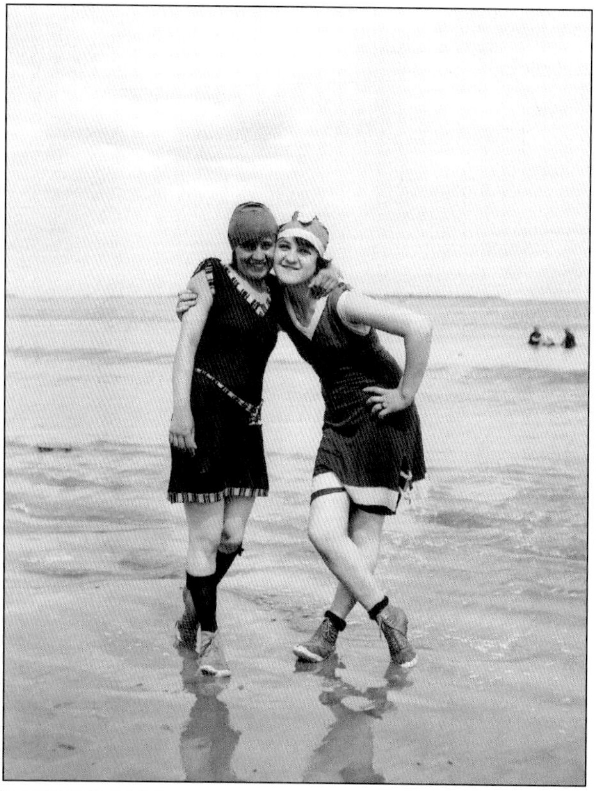

One afternoon in 1919, *Boston Herald-Traveler* staff photographer Leslie Jones immortalized on film these two playful young women, who appear eager to strike a whimsical pose for the camera, seeming to enjoy the unexpected attention. Sporting bathing caps and fashionable swim costumes, both of them also wear dark knee-length stockings and tightly laced aquatic footwear. (Courtesy Boston Public Library, Prints Department.)

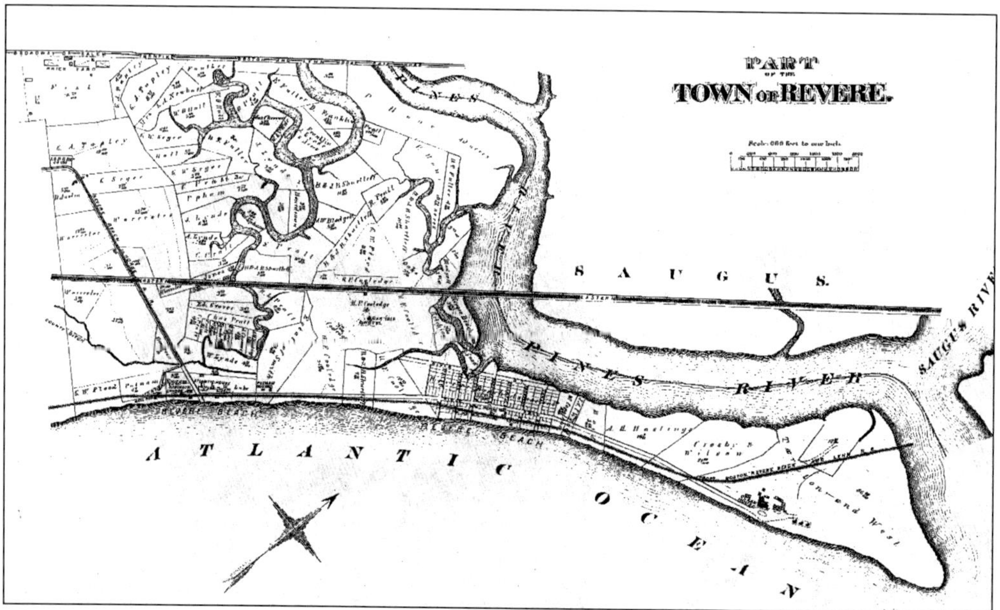

This 1874 map of coastal Revere showcases the graceful curve of the town's famed crescent-shaped beach. In fact, town officials voted in 1881 to designate the shore locale Crescent Beach. The Eastern Railroad bisects the section of town represented here, and tracks for the recently chartered narrow-gauge railroad run immediately along the crest of delicate shoreline. Later, in 1915, Revere received its city charter. (Courtesy Ann Kelleher.)

IMAGES
of America

REVERE BEACH

Leah A. Schmidt

ARCADIA
PUBLISHING

ISBN 978-0-7385-1030-9

Published by Arcadia Publishing
Charleston, South Carolina

Printed in the United States of America

Library of Congress Catalog Card Number: 2002102510

For all general information contact Arcadia Publishing at:
Telephone 843-853-2070
Fax 843-853-0044
E-mail sales@arcadiapublishing.com
For customer service and orders:
Toll-Free 1-888-313-2665

Visit us on the Internet at www.arcadiapublishing.com

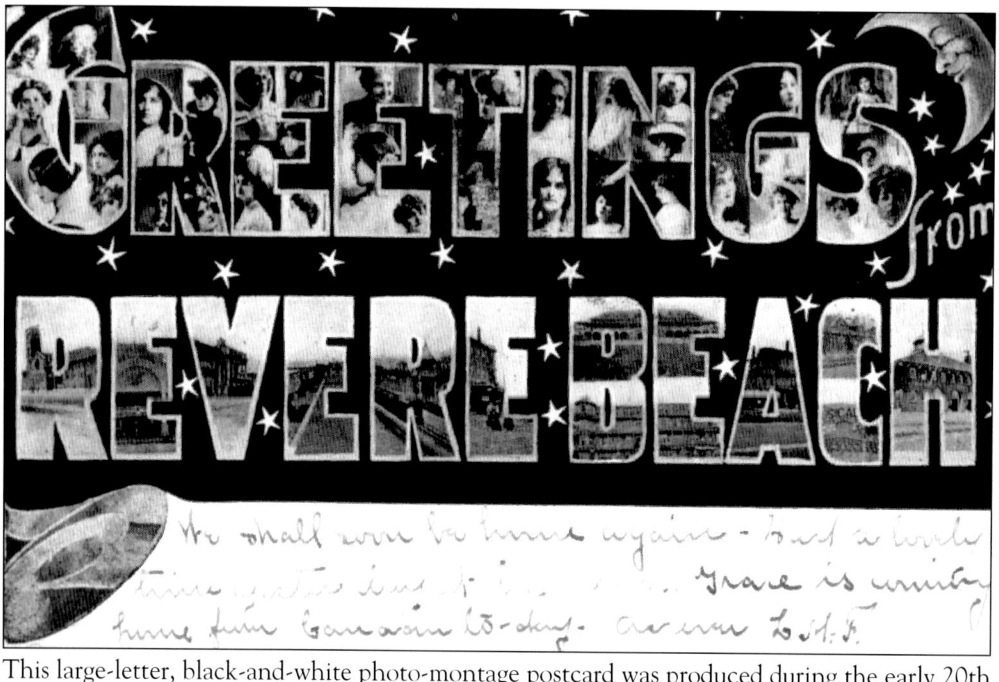

This large-letter, black-and-white photo-montage postcard was produced during the early 20th century. Set against a contrived evening sky, a jovial crescent moon smiles broadly as if in approval of the destination prominently emblazoned across the commercially produced card. The enormous letters at top include minute photographs of late-Victorian women. Pictures represented in the wording below concern local landmarks located along Revere Beach Boulevard. (Courtesy Leah Schmidt.)

Contents

ACKNOWLEDGMENTS

I extend my heartfelt thanks and immense gratitude to the following individuals and organizations who have contributed advice, research material, photographs and images, wisdom, and related assistance as I was preparing *Revere Beach* for publication: the Academy of Motion Picture Arts & Sciences; the Arnold Arboretum; Megan Dumm and Gail Sweeney of Arcadia Publishing; Jane Duggan and Aaron Schmidt of Boston Public Library's Prints Department; Jean Bennett; Beverly Historical Society; Robin Innes of Cedar Point Park; Nadine Mironchuk of Chelsea Historical Society; Weldon Brown of Chelsea Public Library; Jack and Miriam Cook; Lorraine Cousins; Sandra Stanger and Allan Kort of the *Daily Evening Item*; Mr. and Mrs. Lawrence C. Edwards; the Essex National Heritage Area; Sheila Farrell; Helen Fillmore; Carroll F. Gray; Dolores Hass; Ann Kelleher; Lynn Area Chamber of Commerce; Diane Shephard and Sandra Krein of the Lynn Museum; Bethany Cove of Lynn Public Library; Malden Public Library; Marblehead Public Library; Martha Clark of Massachusetts Archives; Brian McCarthy; Peter McCauley; Staley McDermet; Medford Historical Society; Sean Fisher of the Metropolitan District Commission; Calantha Sears of Nahant Historical Society; Edward and Frederick Nazzaro; Barbara Neiley and Patricia Romeo of North Reading Historical Commission; Michele Clark, Anthony Reed, and Mike Dosch of the Frederick Law Olmsted National Historic Site; George Ostler; Carol Morini of the Peabody Essex Museum; Martha Holden of the Peabody Institute; Bob Upton of reverebeach.com; Janice Corkhum of Revere Chamber of Commerce; Robert Furlong, Robert Marra, and Mayor Thomas Ambrosino of the city of Revere; Revere Historical Commission; Joshua Resnek and the *Revere Journal*; Revere Society for Cultural and Historic Preservation; Rev. Dr. Marlayna L. Schmidt; Benjamin Shurtleff; Diane McIntire of the Silent Majority; Robert Stanley; Swampscott Public Library; Adele Toro; Winthrop Chamber of Commerce; David Hubbard of Winthrop Historical Society; and Ann Gutting and Pete Solomon of Winthrop Public Library.

Introduction

Revere Beach's illustrious roots are firmly embedded in the Colonial period. Originally settled by Pawtucket Indians, the region known as Rumney Marsh, with its wide, crescent-shaped, natural barrier sand dune, was first traversed by European settlers during the 1620s. In 1634, Rumney Marsh was annexed by Boston, and some years later it became part of Winnisimmet (Chelsea). The area flourished as a prosperous farming community, and few structures existed on or in the general vicinity of what was known as Chelsea Beach.

In 1834, Solomon Hayes, formerly of Boston, purchased an ample parcel of land known as Point of Pines, located toward the beach's nothernmost point. Here, he constructed a tavern called the Robinson Crusoe House, which successfully operated for several decades. One year before the former Rumney Marsh split from Chelsea proper to create North Chelsea in 1846, Cornelius Ellis opened the Neptune House, later known as the Revere House, located approximately halfway between Point of Pines and Revere Street. By the 1850s, John Moran had erected the Atlantic House near Revere Street and a small establishment known as Gay's Saloon had been constructed near the foot of Beach Street. Within 15 years, the latter establishment had been renamed and relocated nearer the beach and a larger structure, which operated as the Pavilion Hotel, had been built. It was here on April 18, 1881, that town fathers gathered and voted to rename the shore locale Crescent Beach. On Sunday, July 8, 1883, the Pavilion Hotel reopened as the magnificent Vue de l'Eau. In 1889, the renowned structure was rechristened Hotel Strathmore. It operated for six additional years before it was destroyed by fire in April 1895.

Beginning in the late 1830s, commercial development occurred on both the land and seaward sides of the beach and increased remarkably as the decades advanced. In 1871, the town of North Chelsea adopted the name Revere in honor of the famed patriot and silversmith Paul Revere. By 1875, railroad trackage had been laid on the crest of the dune, which had been all but destroyed by ensuing seaward construction. The railroad greatly increased accessibility to throngs of visitors seeking seaside recreation and respite. In the early 1890s, the temporary Metropolitan Park Commission (MPC), spearheaded by renowned landscape architect Charles Eliot, advocated the establishment of a regional system of natural environs including hills, river basins, and saltwater beaches. Permanently established the following year, the Metropolitan Park Commission worked determinedly to acquire and set aside such reservations for the employment and enjoyment of the general public. Acquisitions commenced in Revere in 1895, and within one year three miles of shoreline had been claimed. From the outset, reclamation of Revere's gentle crescent posed an ambitious challenge—a challenge that was met with dogged determination by dedicated and farsighted individuals, Eliot included, who labored to reclaim the natural integrity of the beach and restore public access to one of Greater Boston's most profound natural environs. Indeed, achievement of Eliot's visionary design for Revere Beach Reservation ultimately required an expenditure of over $1 million, which allowed for, among other things, the relocation of the narrow-gauge railroad and the construction of a beachside driveway and promenade. Construction of a bathhouse, police station, eight paired pavilions, bandstand, and superintendent's house—all under the meticulous direction of architect William Austin—continued for a decade. Sea walls and additional shore protection were also introduced. Today, Revere Beach Reservation remains under the jurisdiction of the Metropolitan District Commission (MDC), which the MPC became in 1919, and proudly proclaims its title as America's first public ocean beach.

By the time Revere had received its city charter in 1915, its beach had achieved the coveted status of a premier New England seaside resort. A fledgling amusement industry had surfaced in the vicinities of Point of Pines and Oak Island Grove by the early 1880s, providing patrons with family-oriented entertainment including band concerts and fireworks displays. By the dawn of the 20th century, an increasing number of amusements had also appeared along the beachside driveway, providing an additional commercial element to the many scenic delights Revere Beach Reservation had to offer. In 1906, Wonderland Amusement Park opened and entertained multitudes of visitors with its myriad attractions and elaborate exhibits. During its five years in operation, the park delighted millions of eager guests with celebrity performers including swimmer Annette Kellerman, aviator Lincoln Beachey, and western entertainer Pawnee Bill. In 1909, Pres. William H. Taft's commutes along Revere Beach Boulevard to and from his summer home in Beverly attracted considerable media attention, as did presidential candidate Col. Theodore Roosevelt's commanding campaign address offered from the veranda of the Point of Pines Hotel in August 1912.

As the century advanced in years, Revere Beach increased in popularity. By the 1920s, thrilling amusements including the Cyclone and Derby Racer had replaced more timid rides, reflecting society's confidence and renewed sense of adventure. The unfolding decades were indeed memorable and profitable ones for Revere Beach. Its ballrooms hosted regional beauty pageants and dance marathons, and its aquatic facilities hosted Olympic tryouts. By the 1940s, respected trumpeter Louis Prima and his orchestra were making live national broadcasts from a popular area nightspot, and Hollywood's elite, including Gloria Swanson, Marlene Dietrich, and Carole Lombard, had discovered Greater Boston's seaside gem. While the beach's unprecedented popularity waned somewhat in subsequent decades, Revere Beach still maintained its irrepressible charm and remained a favorite warm-weather destination for visitors of all ages regardless of ethnicity or socioeconomic status. As the 1960s dawned, most of the large-scale amusements had been superseded by family-friendly attractions such as arcades, mild-mannered boat rides, and bowling alleys. The closing of the famed Cyclone in 1969 heralded an impending end to the once lucrative amusement industry along Revere Beach, a demise further hastened by a series of destructive mid-to-late-century storms, culminating in the malevolent Blizzard of 1978.

Today, few tangible vestiges of Revere Beach's illustrious past remain. The beach itself has been resanded, and the gracious paired pavilions and bandstand were carefully restored during the early to mid-1990s. On July 15, 1998, the Revere Beach Reservation Historic District was accepted for inclusion in the National Register of Historic Places, a coveted honor that attests to the locale's profound and rich history.

One

Revere Beach Reservation

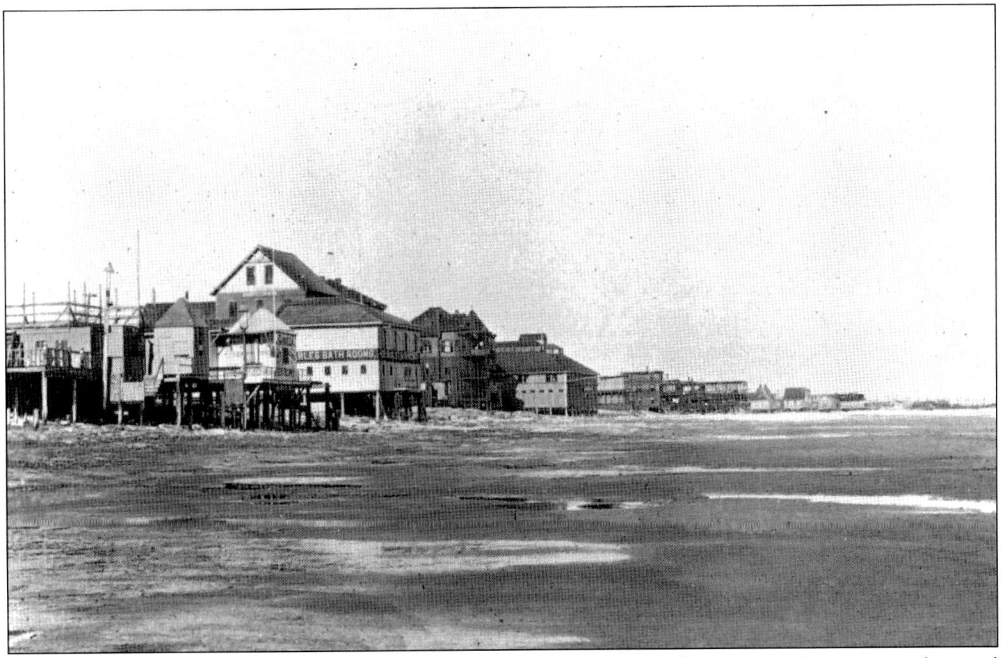

This 1892 Nathaniel L. Stebbins photograph shows the clutter of commercial structures located directly on Revere Beach that often obstructed the public's view of the shore. Following the acquisition of the beach by the Metropolitan Park Commission and the subsequent establishment of Revere Beach Reservation in 1895, commissioned landscape architect Charles Eliot directed the removal of more than 300 structures, 81 of which stood directly on the sand. (Courtesy MDC Archives, Boston.)

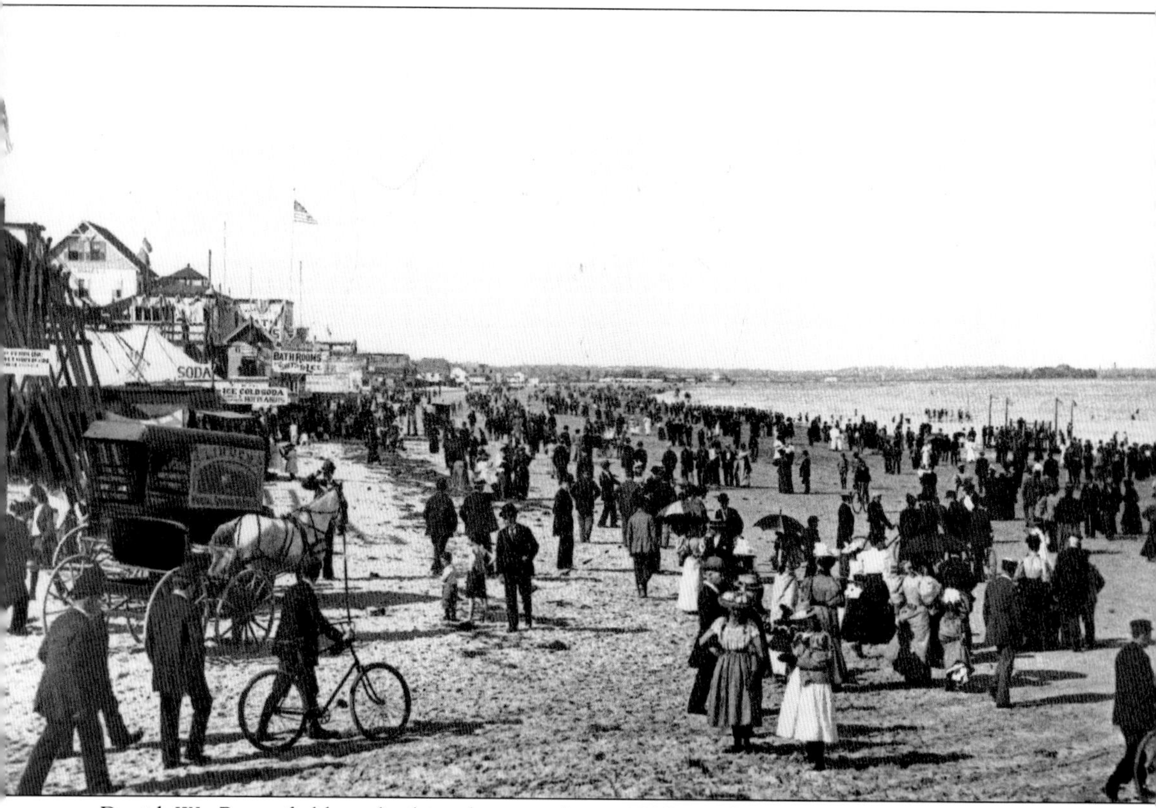

David W. Butterfield took this photograph in 1895 to showcase the crowded conditions created by private development located directly along the crest of newly created Revere Beach Reservation. Renowned landscape architect Charles Eliot deemed the location of these structures a "disgrace" and heartily advocated for their relocation in order to restore natural dignity to the beach and to provide the public with unobstructed access, as well as unimpeded views of the gently curved shore. Indeed, in a formal report submitted by the Metropolitan Park Commission to the state legislature in 1893, Eliot extolled the significant virtues of free access to unspoiled natural environs. With obvious conviction, he noted that "local breathing spaces, and the existence of pleasant features of natural scenery in the neighborhood, are . . . essential to the moral and physical health of a community." Removal of beachside structures began immediately upon the creation of Revere Beach Reservation two years later and continued for some time. Formation of the reservation represented the realization of Eliot's environmental vision and ultimately ensured for posterity unlimited free access to one of Greater Boston's finest natural resources. (Courtesy MDC Archives, Boston.)

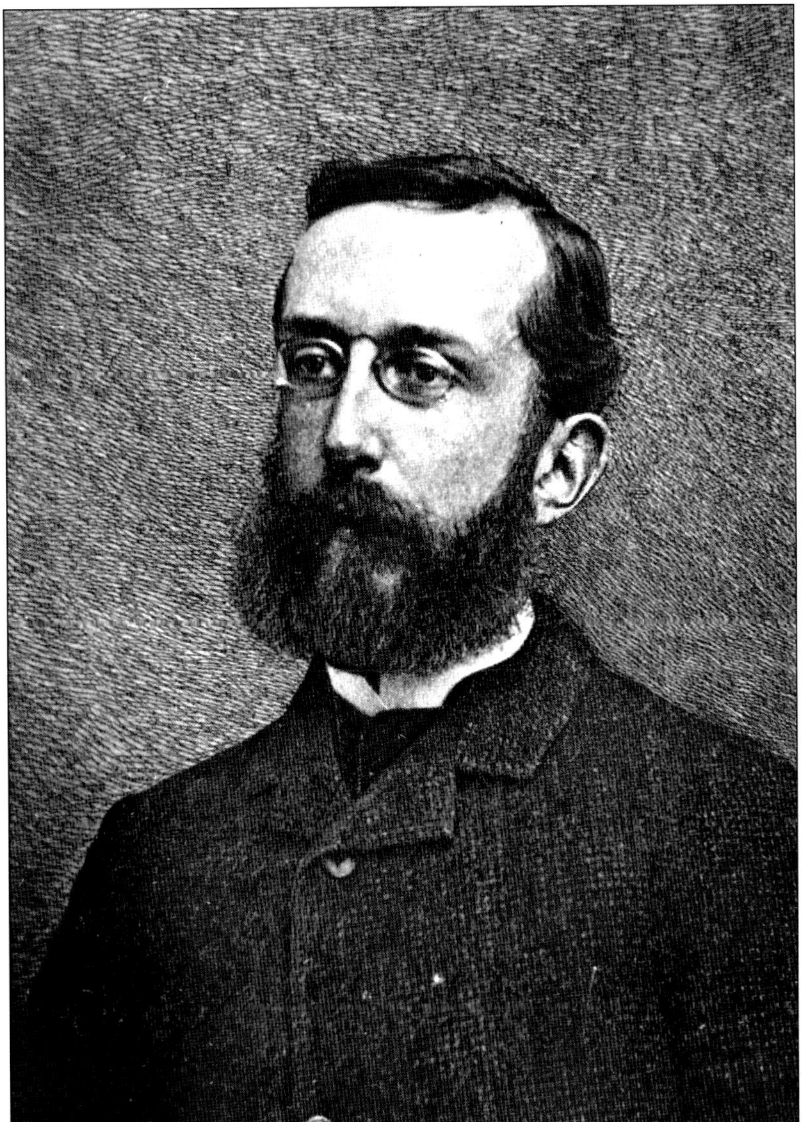

Forward-thinking landscape architect Charles Eliot believed that ordinary citizens were the guardians of natural scenery and that they should consider themselves true trustees of nature. A spirited fellow, Eliot served for a time as apprentice to Frederick Law Olmsted, who noted Eliot's passion for preservation of natural environs. Olmsted invited Eliot to join his prestigious firm and, in 1893, the firm of Olmsted, Olmsted and Eliot was formed. A noted critic, naturalist, and environmental historian, Eliot was soon employed as landscape architect for the fledgling Metropolitan Park Commission. He believed that the Metropolitan Park Commission should make acquisition of ocean areas a priority, and he toiled ceaselessly with officials to obtain, establish, and enhance the environs of Revere Beach Reservation. This formal photographic portrait of Eliot at age 35 was taken in 1895. Two years later, the visionary artist succumbed to spinal meningitis before many of his plans for Revere Beach were implemented. In 1898, Southern Circle was renamed Eliot Circle to honor both the architect and his profound contribution to the development of Revere Beach Reservation. (Courtesy National Park Service, Frederick Law Olmsted National Historic Site.)

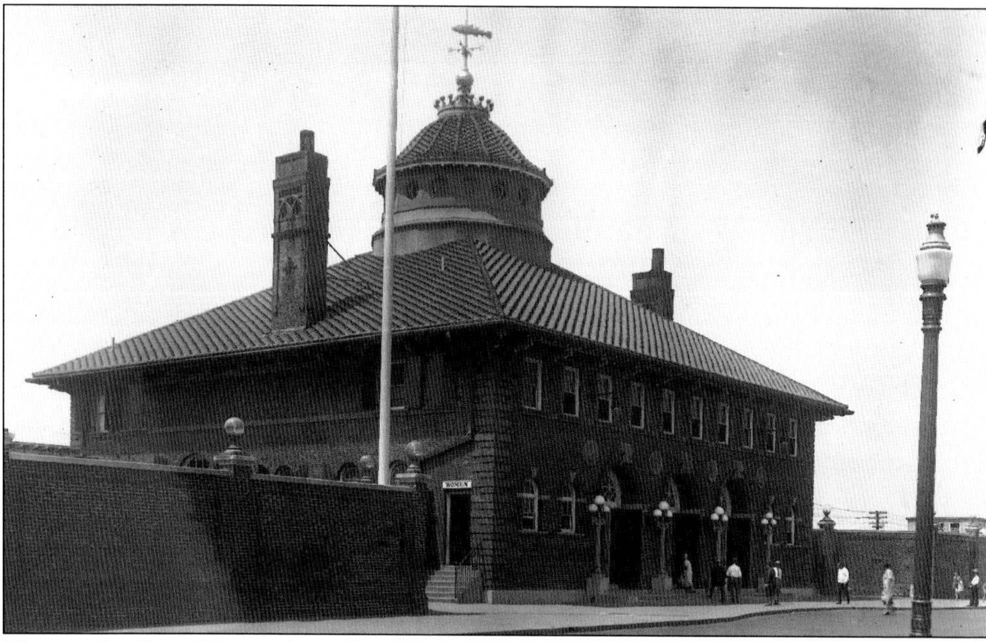

The resplendent Metropolitan District Commission Bath House, pictured in 1930, was designed by renowned Boston architect William Austin. Built in 1897 at the cost of $100,000, this magnificent Italian Renaissance building was constructed of brick and cement and featured an intricately detailed wooden interior, a terra-cotta tiled roof, and a multiwindowed central cupola. At the time of construction, the building was considered the largest public bathhouse in the United States. (Courtesy MDC Archives, Boston.)

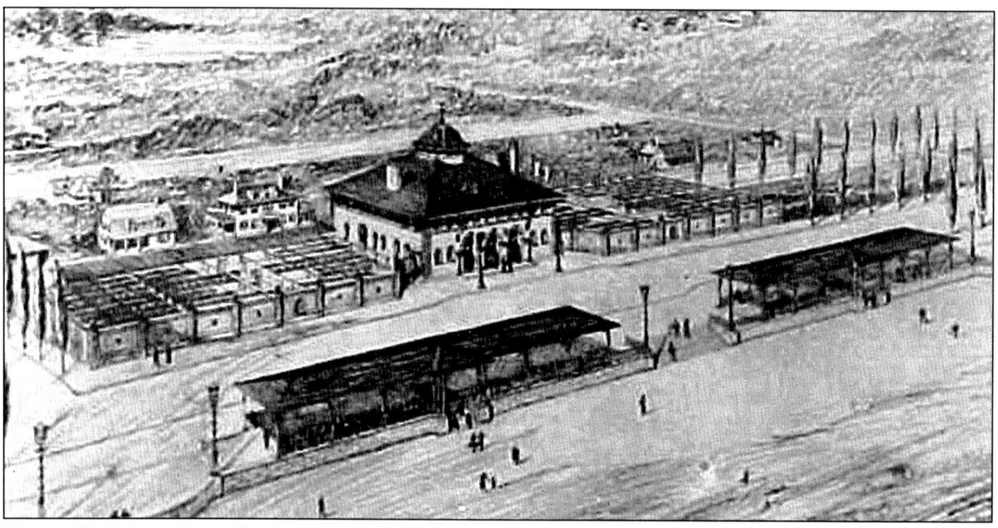

Centrally located on the newly completed beachside driveway later known as Revere Beach Boulevard, the majestic State Bath House contained a central administration building, an office, a laundry, a steam plant, a toilet room, and a detention area, as well as 1,000 gender-separated dressing rooms. In addition, a pedestrian tunnel that ran beneath the roadway connected the facility to the beach. Sadly, the building was razed in 1962 and the tunnel was infilled soon afterward. (Courtesy National Park Service, Frederick Law Olmsted National Historic Site.)

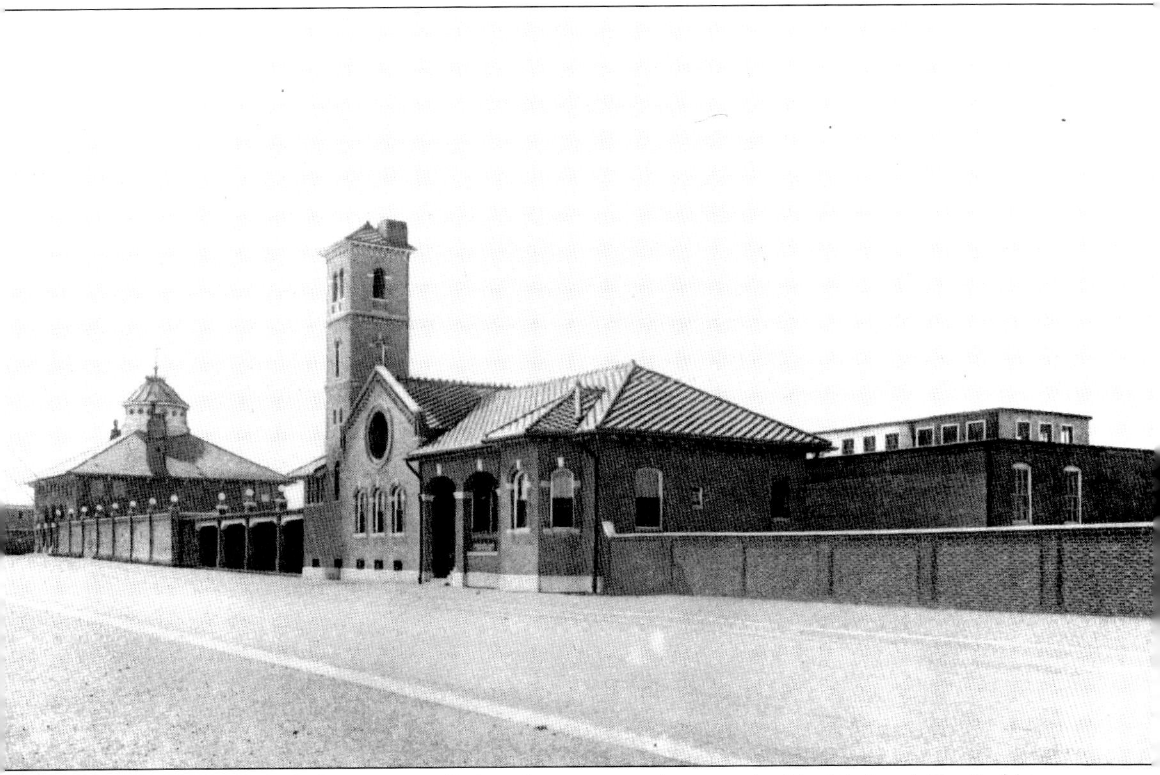

The Metropolitan Park Commission Police Station was photographed by Nathaniel L. Stebbins shortly after its completion in 1899. Designed by William Austin in the Italian Renaissance style, this baptistry-inspired, hip-roofed structure features an arcaded brick facade, a granite base course, an imposing 62-foot bell tower, and a molded terra-cotta tile cap. Several hundred yards to the south stands the grand State Bath House. The admirable architecture of both buildings made them the most stately structures along Revere Beach Reservation, a regal designation currently held solely by the police station. Located one-quarter mile from Revere Street, the structure endured an extensive renovation during the early 1980s. A six-foot-long copper codfish weathervane, which once graced the cupola of the bathhouse, surmounts the tower roof. The facility was used by the Metropolitan District Commission police until 1992, when the force merged with the state police. Today, the building is leased to the state police by the Metropolitan District Commission and remains a tangible reminder of the architectural grandeur that defined Revere Beach over a century ago. (Courtesy MDC Archives, Boston.)

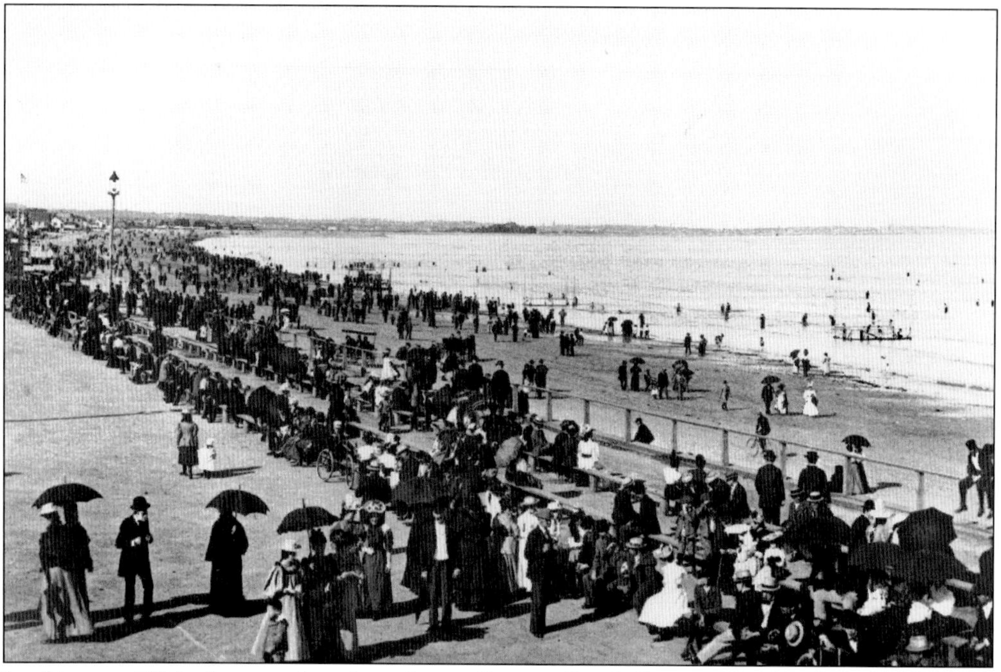

In this rare 1895 photograph, taken during Revere Beach Reservation's infancy, visitors sit on low benches located within and along a wooden-fenced promenade that divides land from shore. Offshore, aptly placed platforms provide welcome oases for surf-bound visitors. Onshore, strollers, bicycles, and horse-drawn carriages coexist and leisurely progress along the sand. At the left stands a recently installed lamppost, an early harbinger of the 20th century. (Courtesy MDC Archives, Boston.)

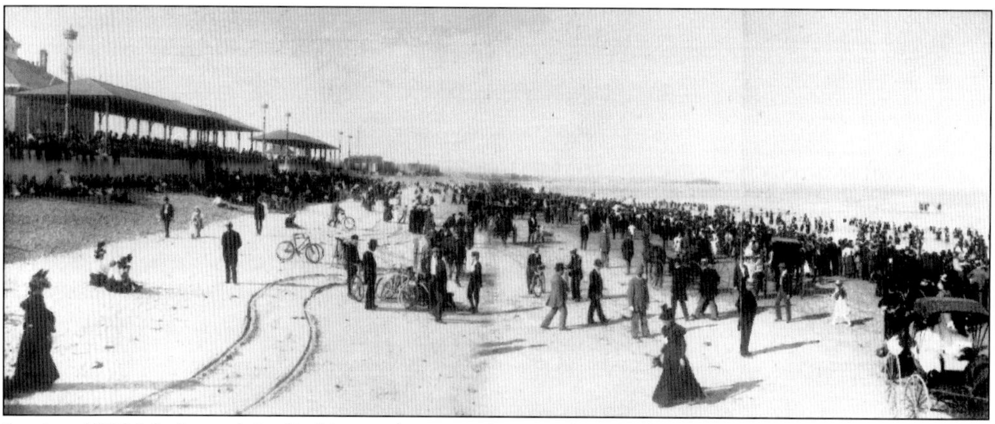

In this 1897 Nathaniel L. Stebbins photograph, people of all socioeconomic classes are seen enjoying the vast expanse of Revere's open shore. Photographed looking north from a central location upon the sand, carriage tracks etched in the granular terrain hearken back to a distant era when vehicles including horse-drawn transport were allowed to traverse the beach itself. Readily apparent at the left are the State Bath House and accompanying paired pavilions. (Courtesy MDC Archives, Boston.)

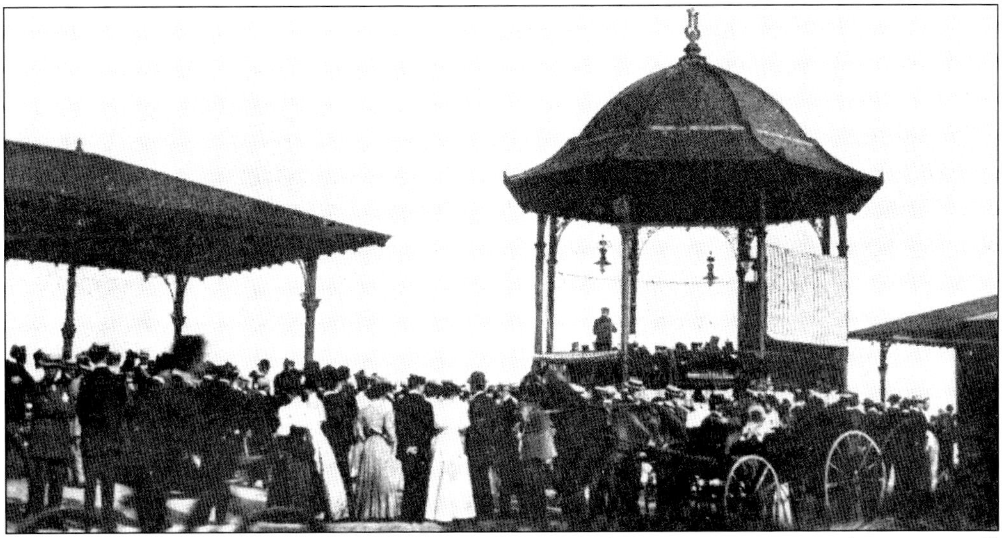

The Revere Beach Bandstand and accompanying pavilions were structures that were well used in fair weather, as evidenced by these 1906 photographs, which appeared in the *1907 Metropolitan Park Commission Annual Report*. Designed by William Austin of the acclaimed Boston design firm Stickney and Austin, the Victorian Eclectic bandstand and paired pavilions were constructed in 1897. These handsome structures feature simple scroll-and-circle iron brackets decorating cast-iron balustrades. They are topped by dark gray slate complete with copper roof flashing on wood boarding supported by wooden rafters. Located adjacent to Shirley Avenue, the Bandstand Pavilions are six bays in length, totaling 120 feet each. The gracious and ornate bandstand (above), with its swag motif embellishment, sports an octagonal design and a bell cast roof. A fanciful copper lyre surmounts the orchestral facility. In addition to the bandstand, all eight pavilions located along Revere Beach were meticulously restored in 1994. (Courtesy MDC Archives, Boston.)

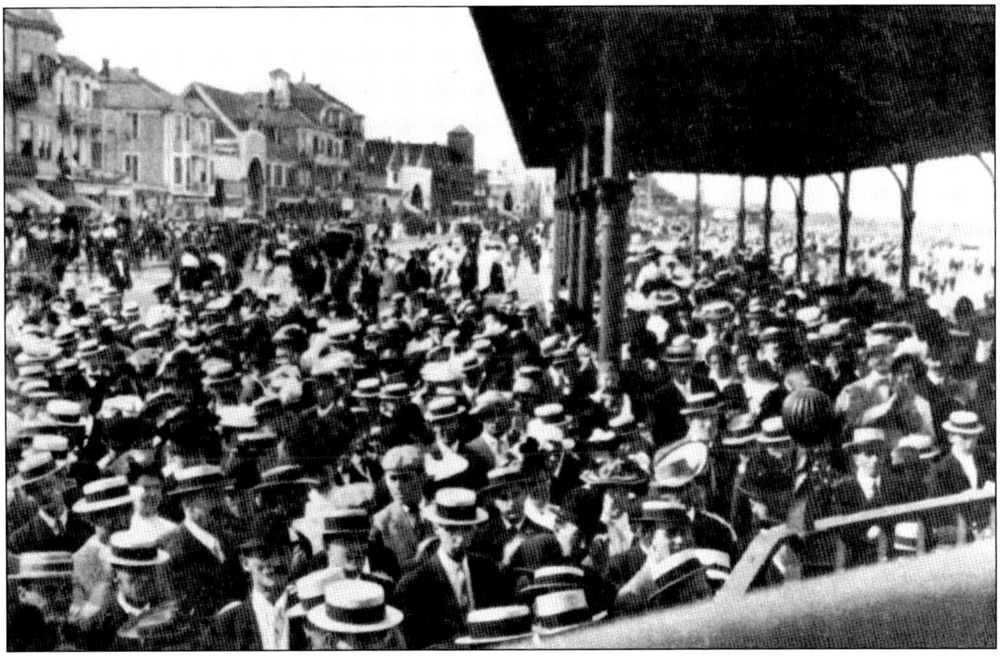

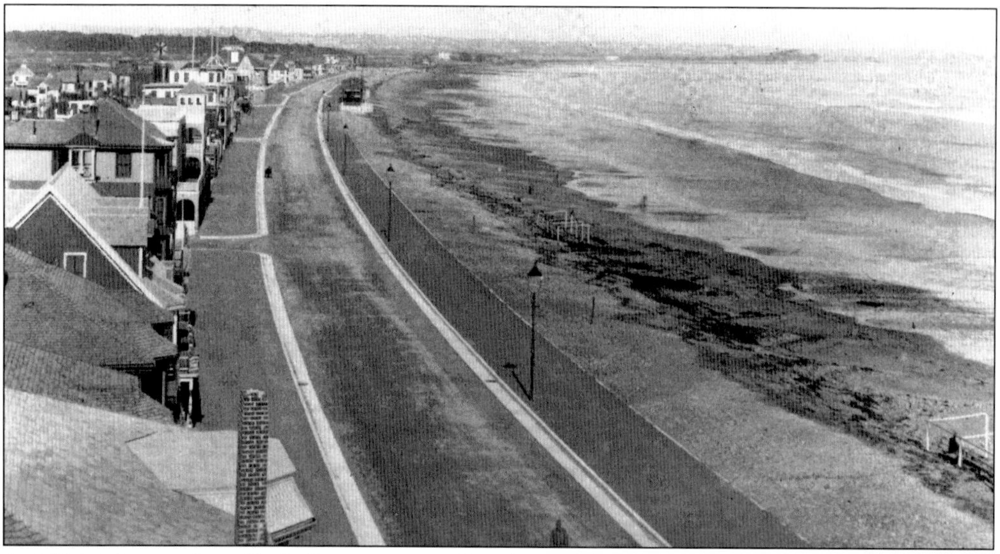

In 1894, Metropolitan Park Commission officials speculated that construction of a beachside driveway along Revere Beach Reservation would cost approximately $125,000. Formal plans were prepared in 1896. On May 12, 1897, John J. O'Brien & Company commenced construction of over one mile of southerly roadway, which was completed the following year. In 1904, E.W. Everson & Company received a $117,000 contract to complete the driveway from Revere Street to Northern Circle. (Courtesy MDC Archives, Boston.)

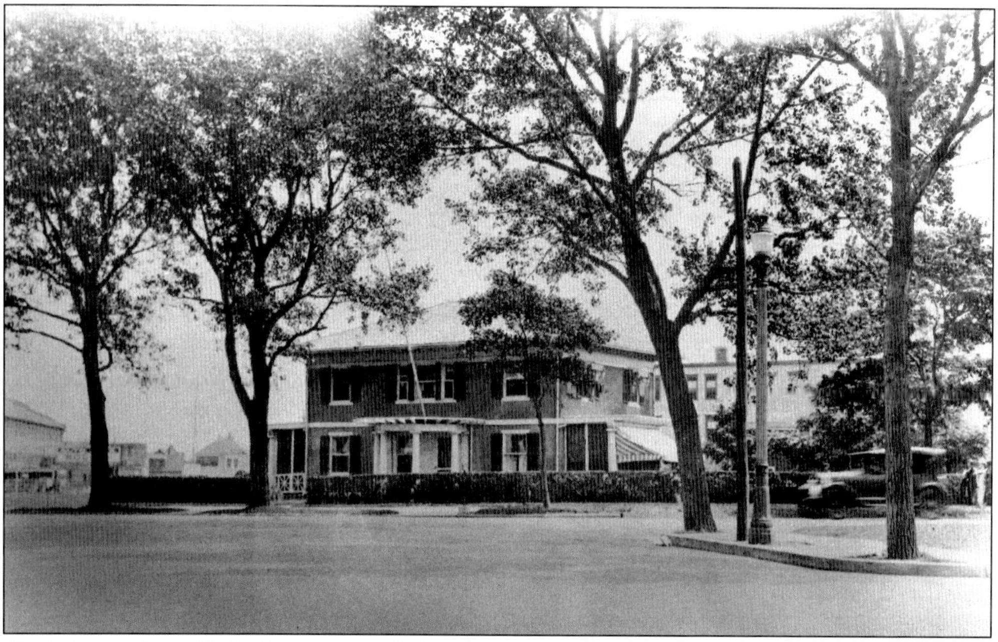

The Metropolitan Park Commission Police Superintendent's House still presides over Revere Beach Reservation from its One Eliot Circle location. Designed by William Austin, the Italianate-style residence was completed in 1905. Originally faced with concrete stucco, the building supported a molded ceramic tile roof and was home to Herbert W. West, acting police superintendent. Today, the former home lacks much of its earlier ornamentation and houses commission staff offices. (Courtesy Winthrop Public Library.)

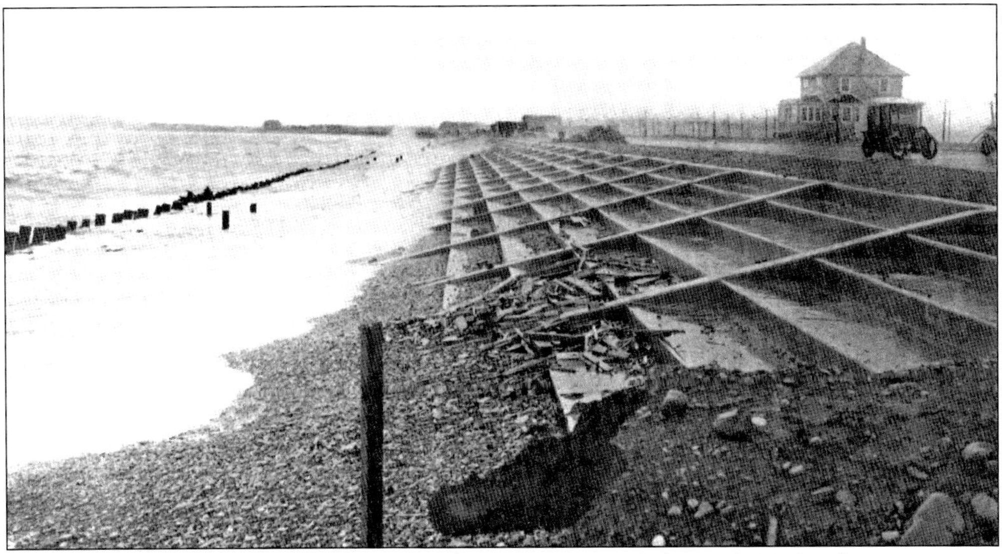

In 1914, a construction contract valued at $21,055 was awarded to M.J. McGawley to construct 30-foot-wide, bleacher-type concrete shore protection to run 1,500 feet along the northerly section of Revere Beach Reservation (above). The construction was completed the following year. This photograph, which appeared in a subsequent *Metropolitan Park Commission Annual Report*, clearly shows the gridlike sloped construction, which seems to stretch into infinity. Only two automobiles ply the roadway near a lone residence, suggesting that the photograph was taken during the popular resort's off-season. In 1915, another construction contract, this one valued at $19,853.80, was awarded to Coleman Brothers of Chelsea to construct similar shore protection between the bathhouse and Revere Street (below). This equally impressive photograph reveals the admirable scope of the project prior to completion. At the center is the elevated peak of the Thompson Scenic Mountain Railway, and to left of center rise the two towers of the Nautical Garden. The wooden pilings at the lower left of both photographs are visible today after powerful storms. (Courtesy MDC Archives, Boston.)

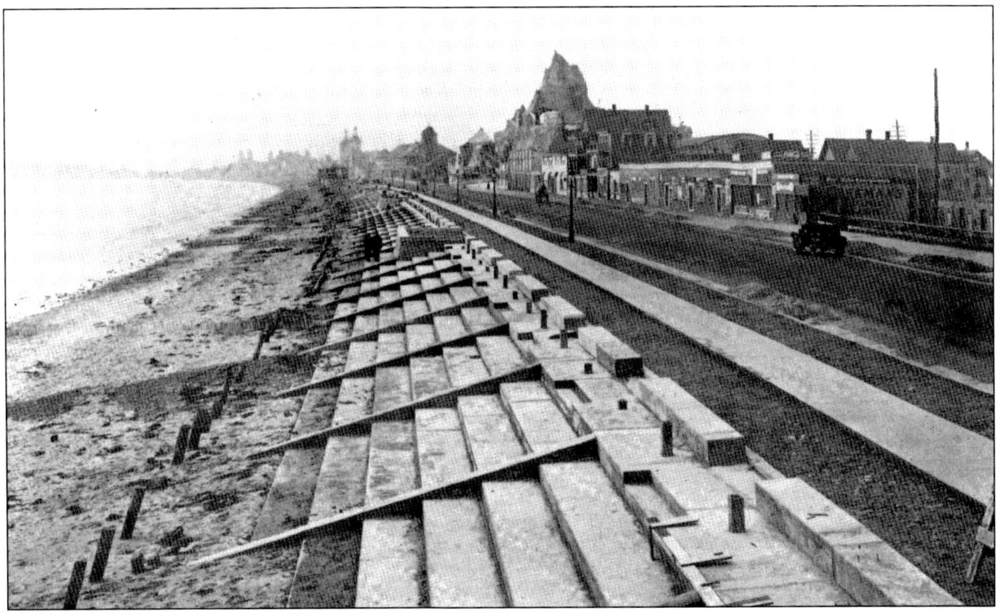

Commonwealth of Massachusetts.

METROPOLITAN PARK COMMISSION

RULES AND REGULATIONS

FOR THE GOVERNMENT AND USE OF THE

REVERE BEACH RESERVATION.

RULE 1. No person shall enter or leave the Reservation except at the regular designated entrances.

RULE 2. No person shall dig up, cut, break, remove, deface, defile, or ill-use any building, structure, fence, sign, bush, plant, turf, rock or other thing herein, belonging to the Commonwealth, or have possession of any part thereof.

RULE 3. No person shall throw any stone or other missile; or have possession of or discharge any destructive weapon, firearm, firecracker, torpedo or firework; or make a fire; or post, paint, affix or display any sign, notice, placard or advertising device; or, except with written authority from said Metropolitan Park Commission, engage in business, sell, or expose for sale, or give away any goods, wares, or circulars; or set a trap or snare; or injure or have possession of any wild animal or bird; or injure or disturb any bird's nest or eggs; or drop or place and suffer to remain any piece of paper or other refuse, except in the receptacles designated therefor.

RULE 4. No person shall solicit the acquaintance of or annoy another person; or utter any profane, threatening, abusive or indecent language or loud outcry; or solicit any subscription or contribution; or have possession of or drink any intoxicating liquor; or play any game of chance; or have possession of any instrument of gambling; or do any obscene or indecent act; or preach; or pray aloud; or make an oration or harangue, or any political or other canvass; or move in a military or civic parade, drill or procession; or lie down upon a bench or go to sleep thereon; or play any musical instrument except by written authority from said Metropolitan Park Commission.

RULE 5. No person shall bathe except in a proper costume and at places designated therefor, or loiter or run about or lie upon the beach or shore in bathing costume.

RULE 6. No person shall cross the driveways in bathing costume except residents of Revere holding permits issued by the Commission.

RULE 7. No person in charge of any animal, other than a dog, shall allow it to go upon the Reservation unless such animal be used for pleasure travel on a way or place provided therefor.

RULE 8. No person shall ride or drive an animal not well broken and under proper control; or ride or drive an animal or vehicle faster than ten miles an hour, or coast with a cycle or sled down any hill.

RULE 9. No person shall ride or drive an animal or vehicle except upon the driveways, or on portions of the beach where such travel is not prohibited, or upon other than the right hand side of the road except when passing another animal or vehicle, or past an animal or vehicle except to the left thereof, or across a road unless the right of way is given to all other animals or vehicles, or by the side of more than one vehicle; or ride a cycle past an animal or vehicle going in the same direction without sounding a bell; or hitch a horse or other animal to a fence, tree, bush or shrub.

RULE 10. No person shall stop an animal or vehicle so as to obstruct a parkway, boundary road or driveway, or a sidewalk or crossing thereof, or so as to prevent the passing of other vehicles, or otherwise than lengthwise with a parkway, boundary road or driveway and close to the sidewalk thereof.

RULE 11. No person having charge of an animal or vehicle shall neglect or refuse to stop, place, change the position of or move said animal or vehicle as directed by a police officer.

RULE 12. No person having charge of an animal shall allow the same to stand without some proper person to take charge of the same, except that an animal hitched to a place provided therefor or to a weight of not less than twenty pounds, may be allowed to stand unattended for not more than five minutes.

RULE 13. No person shall have or allow a vehicle for carrying merchandise, or a vehicle in use for carrying merchandise or articles other than the equipments proper for a pleasure vehicle, or a hearse, or any vehicle in a funeral procession, except upon a traffic road, or to gain access by the shortest way from the nearest street to the front entrance of a house facing on the Reservation.

RULE 14. No person shall saunter or loiter within the Reservation after being directed by a police officer to move on.

RULE 15. No person shall refuse or neglect to obey any reasonable direction of a police officer.

Any person violating any one of the above rules is liable to a fine of twenty dollars for each offence.

The reservations, parkways and roads under the control of the Metropolitan Park Commission are public property and it is the duty of every person to see that the above rules are observed, and to call the attention of the police to any violation thereof.

Noted amendments riddle the margins of this form detailing Metropolitan Park Commission rules and regulations passed on June 10, 1903. These regulations attest to the heightened morality and stringent decorum that governed proper society during the early years of the 20th century. The rules were clearly posted in or about Metropolitan Park Commission facilities and were strictly enforced by reservation police officers, whose presence on the beach was well noted. Concerning the government and use of Revere Beach Reservation, rules and regulations existed concerning employment of designated entrances and exits, the safety and comfort of both visitors and denizens, proper bathing attire and acceptable behavior in such clothing, animal conduct, transport of goods, and vehicular navigation. Those in violation of any of the posted rules were subject to a minimum fine of $20. Contemporary readers may perceive the rules and regulations to be excessively prohibitive, amusing, or even ridiculous—especially those pertaining to the conduct of bathing-costumed individuals. (Courtesy MDC Archives, Boston.)

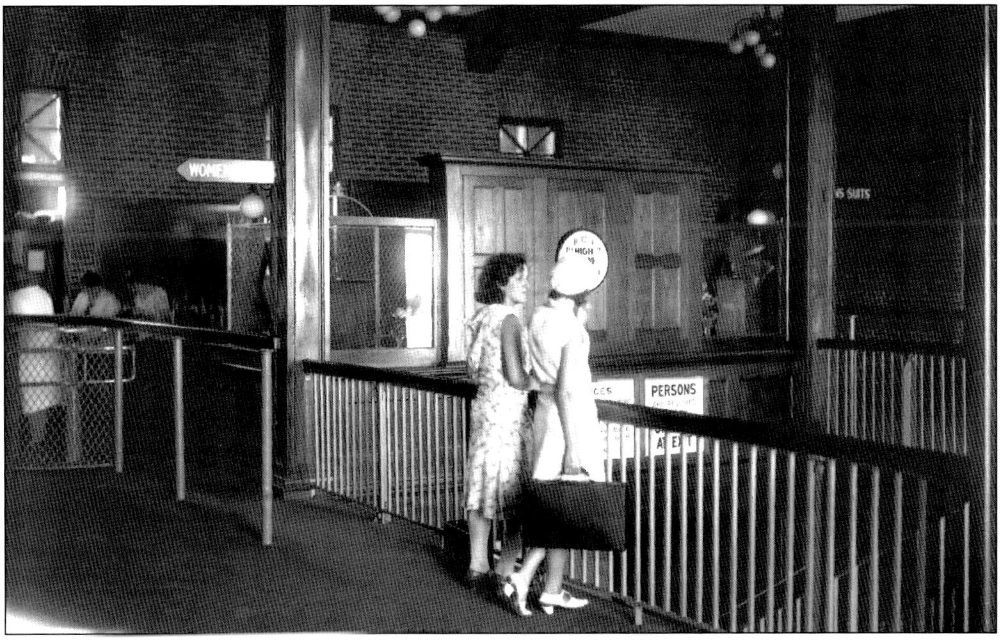

The ornate wood-and-brick interior of the State Bath House featured noble yet functional construction. Pictured here in 1930, two young women in warm-weather attire gaze down the broad central staircase, above which are posted public notices detailing MDC policies and related rental requirements. Elaborate chandeliers strategically sited near the gender-segregated bathing suit rental gates provided the ample interior with warm and graceful illumination. (Courtesy MDC Archives, Boston.)

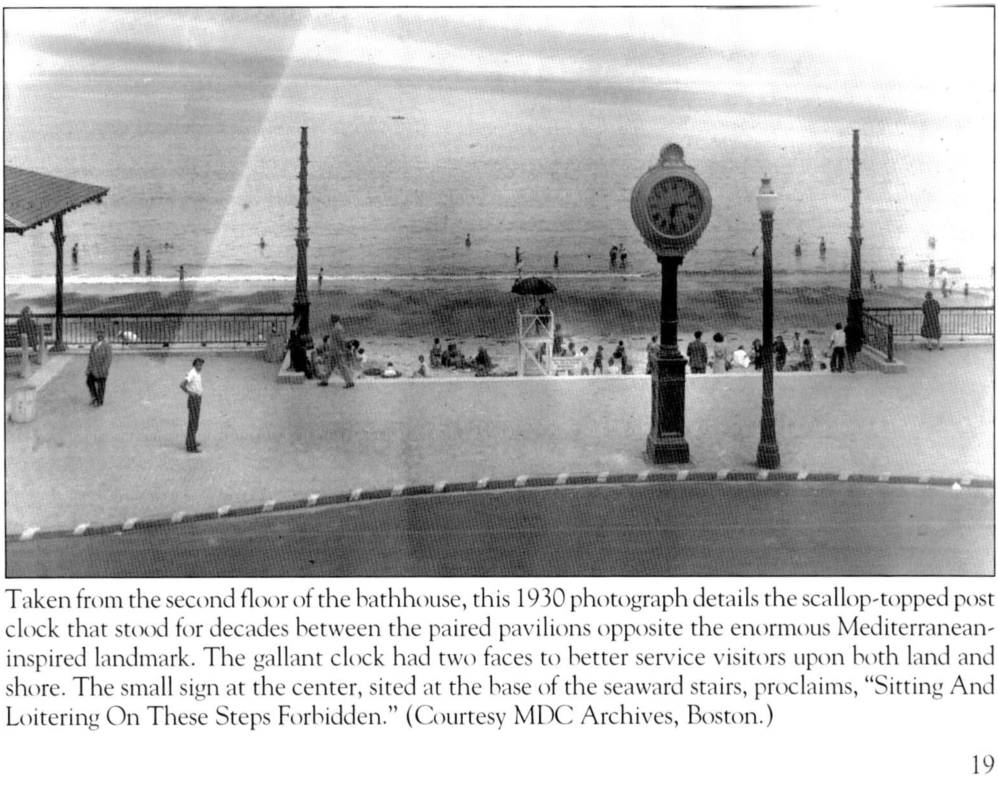

Taken from the second floor of the bathhouse, this 1930 photograph details the scallop-topped post clock that stood for decades between the paired pavilions opposite the enormous Mediterranean-inspired landmark. The gallant clock had two faces to better service visitors upon both land and shore. The small sign at the center, sited at the base of the seaward stairs, proclaims, "Sitting And Loitering On These Steps Forbidden." (Courtesy MDC Archives, Boston.)

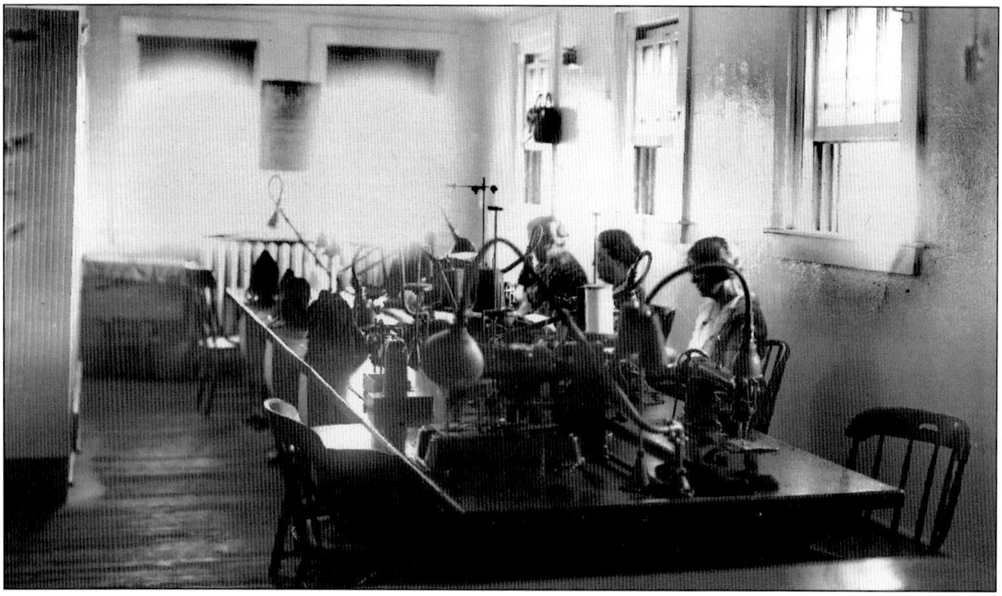

The imposing Metropolitan District Commission Police Station contained a block-shaped wing that extended behind the main building. This unassuming structure housed sewing and laundry facilities, which operated year-round. During the reservation's early years, bathers were required to rent suits at the State Bath House. The garments were later transferred next door to be laundered and repaired on-site. This 1930 photograph depicts seamstresses at work in the sun-diffused facility. (Courtesy MDC Archives, Boston.)

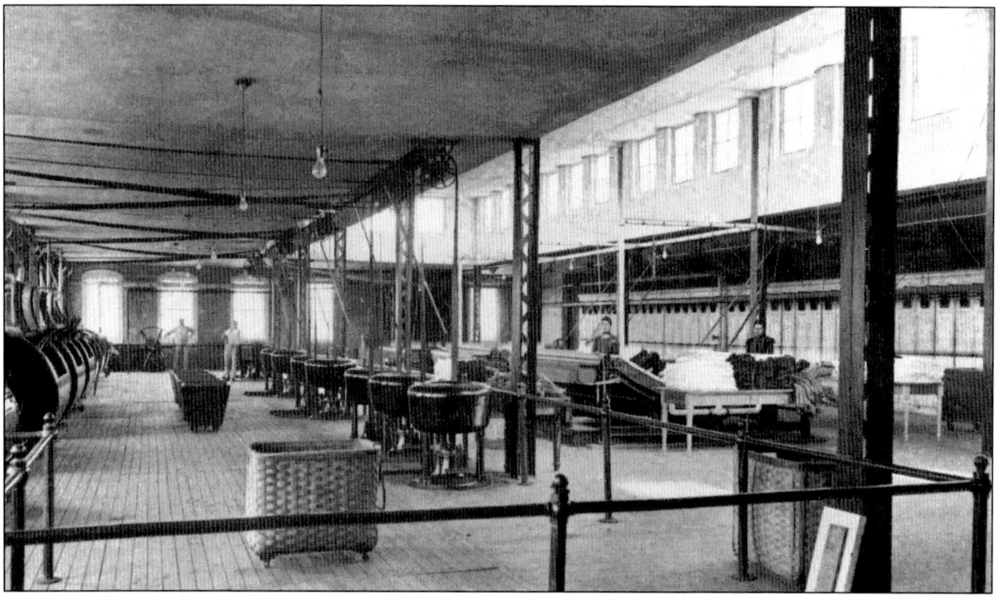

Nathaniel L. Stebbins captured on film the modern building, which was located behind the Italian Renaissance police station's main building, shortly after its completion at the end of the 19th century. The extensive laundry employed year-round personnel, who toiled faithfully to provide patrons with meticulously laundered towels and bathing suits. Here, staff members pause to be photographed within the vast facility containing large wicker baskets, iron railings, and cauldron-like machinery. (Courtesy MDC Archives, Boston.)

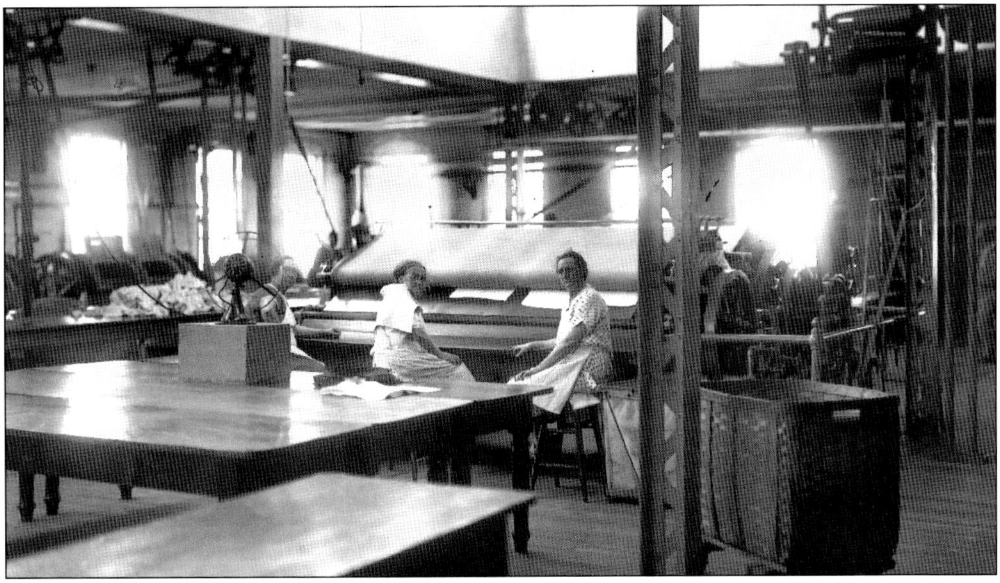

In this 1930 photograph, three hardworking laundresses turn and cast weary glances at the unnamed photographer who has interrupted their toil. The spacious facility, located one-quarter mile from Revere Street, provided its employees with large wooden tables, advanced machinery, and multiple windows, through which streamed ample amounts of illuminating sunlight. On overcast days, the enormous room was lighted by single-bulbed, overhead electric light fixtures. (Courtesy MDC Archives, Boston.)

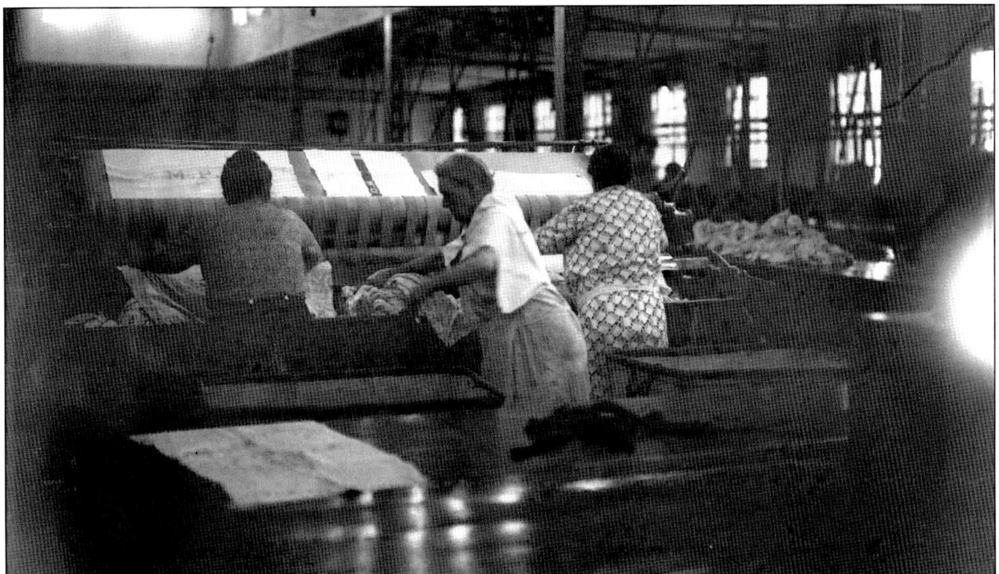

This 1930 photograph reveals three laundresses operating a large press within the state facility located along Revere Beach Boulevard. The towel at the left that is stretched across the wide machine bears the initials MPC and is a well-preserved relic predating 1919, when the Metropolitan Park Commission merged with the Metropolitan Water and Sewerage Board to form the Metropolitan District Commission. Above, natural light pours through numerous windows to lighten the laundry. (Courtesy MDC Archives, Boston.)

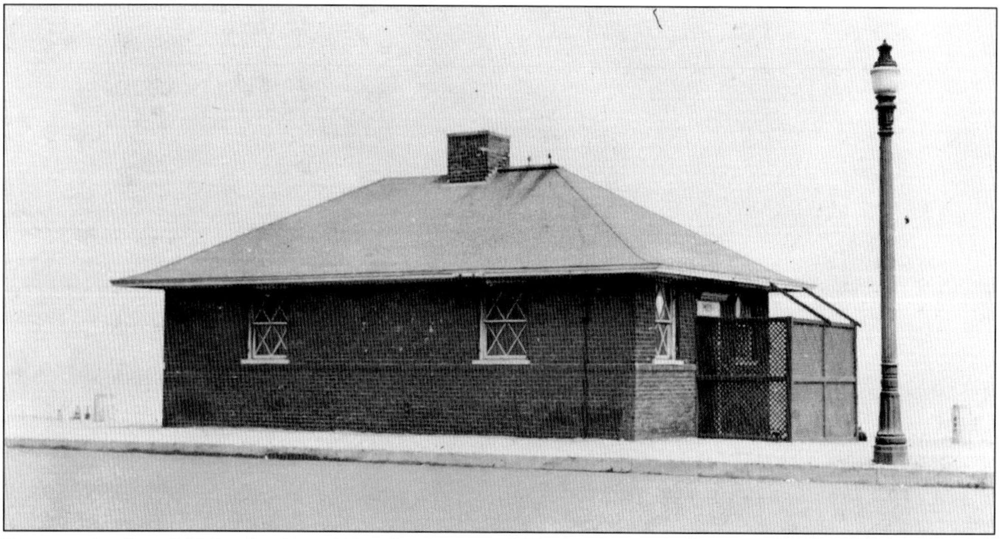

During the late 1920s, the Bond Brothers received a construction contract to erect a rest room facility south of Shirley Avenue along the roadway's seaward side. The building was constructed during the summer months and cost approximately $30,000. The facility was replaced in 1939 by a Colonial Revival–style brick sanitary, constructed to match a similar facility that had been built north of Oak Island Street in 1938. (Courtesy MDC Archives, Boston.)

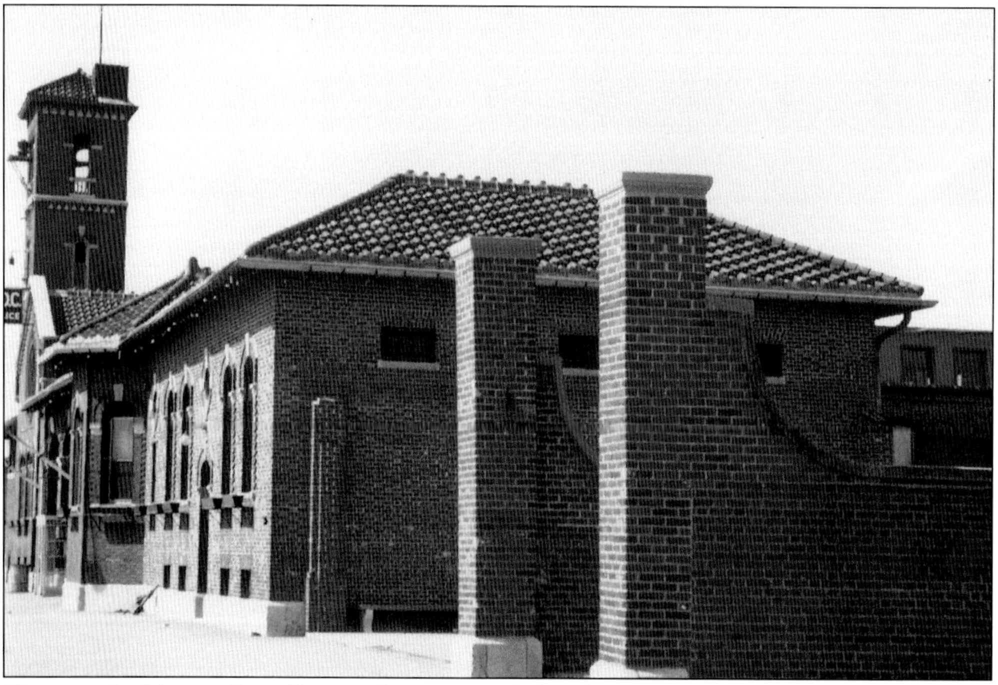

Shown is the Metropolitan District Commission Police Station as it appeared in 1974. In 1920, William Austin designed an addition that used matching tapestry brick and extended the original facade by six bays. Photographed more than 50 years later, the core building remains easily recognizable and intact, but the extensive brick walls that extended north and south of the original structure are absent. Dominant brick pillars mark the driveway that curves behind the facility. (Courtesy Jack Cook.)

Two

The Boston, Revere Beach & Lynn Railroad

BOSTON AND LYNN.

Ten Miles of Harbor and Ocean Scenery. Four Miles on the Crest of Revere Beach.

HOURLY TRAINS.

DEPOT IN BOSTON — No. 350 Atlantic Avenue, foot of High Street; within three minutes' walk of Summer, Congress, and Pearl Streets.

DEPOT IN LYNN—on Market Street, in the immediate neighborhood of the Shoe Manufacturing Interest of that city.

Metropolitan "Atlantic Avenue" Horse Cars connect with EVERY TRAIN to and from all parts of the City of Boston.

Connection with B. W. and P. S. R. R. at Winthrop Junction for Winthrop, Ocean Spray, and Point Shirley.

OFFICERS

EDWIN WALDEN, President. **JOHN G. WEBSTER. Treas.** **EDW. H WHORF, Supt.** **JOHN A. FENNO, Gen. Ticket Agt.**

GENERAL OFFICES

No. 350 ATLANTIC AVENUE, over the Boston Station.

An early advertisement for the Boston, Revere Beach & Lynn Railroad (also known as the Narrow Gauge Railroad) extols the virtues of the line's fine service, including convenience of station locations and ample connections to outlining areas. Careful phrasing proclaiming hourly train service and extensive scenic seashore trackage, including four miles on the crest of Revere Beach, implies that this antiquated piece appeared prior to 1897, when the railroad was relocated to provide unobstructed beach access to the public. (Courtesy Lynn Public Library.)

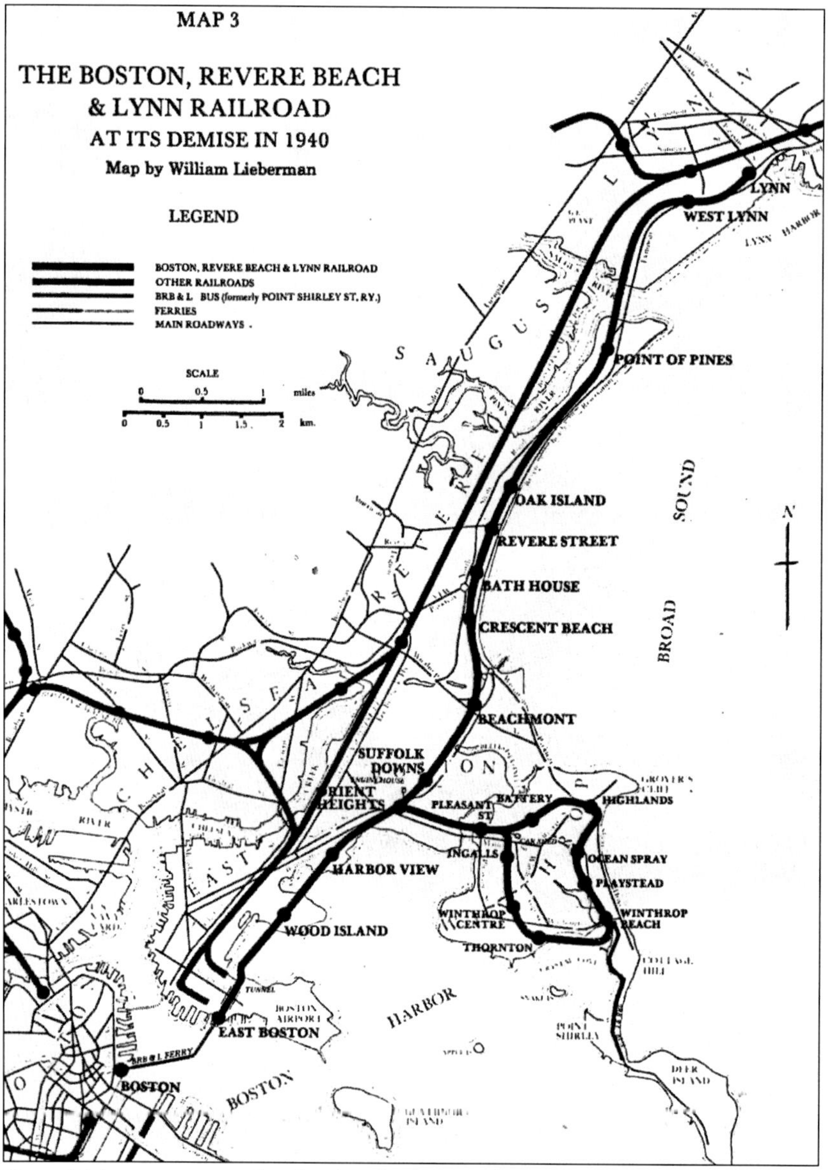

This William Lieberman map clearly details the trackage and stations maintained by the Boston, Revere Beach & Lynn Railroad. The popular railroad, which was chartered in 1874, ran along eight and a half miles of track from Lynn to East Boston and connected to Boston via passenger ferry service. For many years, much of its trackage ran directly along the crest of Revere Beach. In 1897, the Metropolitan Park Commission reportedly expended $100,000 to relocate the track, which was impeding the progress of the redevelopment project along Revere Beach. The newly relocated track was sited a short distance to the west. At this time, the fare decreased from 20¢ to 10¢ from terminal to terminal, and from 10¢ to 5¢ from either terminal to Revere Beach. When service began on July 29, 1875, the line operated three locomotives, 11 train cars and two ferry boats; by 1915, the railroad possessed 26 locomotives, dozens of train cars, and four ferry boats. The railroad maintained at least four stations along Revere Beach during its 65 years in operation. Service ended in January 1940. (Courtesy Winthrop Public Library.)

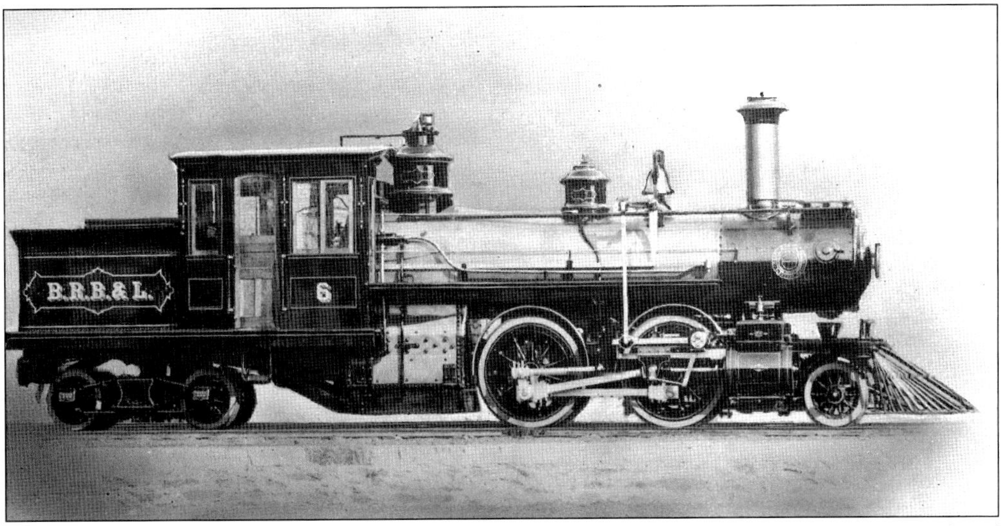

J.R. Sullivan, superintendent of operations on the Boston, Revere Beach & Lynn Railroad during the second decade of the 20th century, originally loaned this photograph of Engine No. 6 for reproduction to Edward Wells of Dumont, New Jersey. Records indicate that this stately locomotive was built by Mason Machine Works in 1876 for $5,300 and that it was scrapped in 1885. An enlarged framed print hangs proudly in the Winthrop Public Library. (Courtesy Winthrop Public Library.)

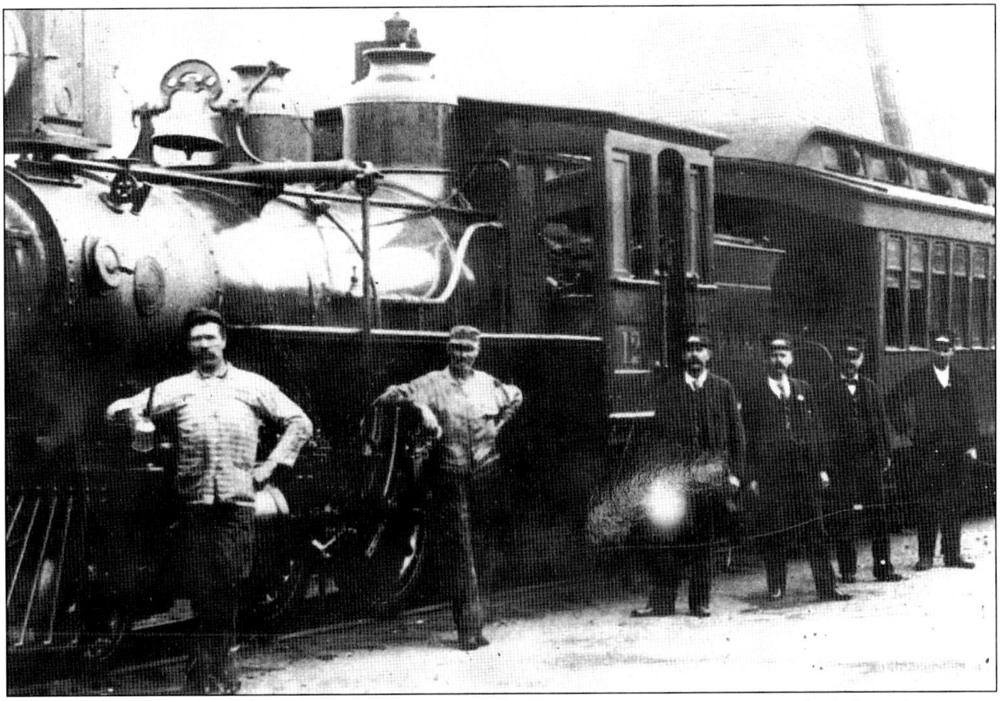

Locomotive No. 12 is shown with six unidentified crewmen on an unspecified date during its illustrious 39-year career with the Boston, Revere Beach & Lynn Railroad. The steam engine was built in 1890 by Taunton Locomotive Manufacturing for approximately $10,000 and was rebuilt by Manchester Locomotive Works in 1920. The regal engine served the line faithfully for nine additional years before it was scrapped in 1929. (Courtesy Winthrop Public Library.)

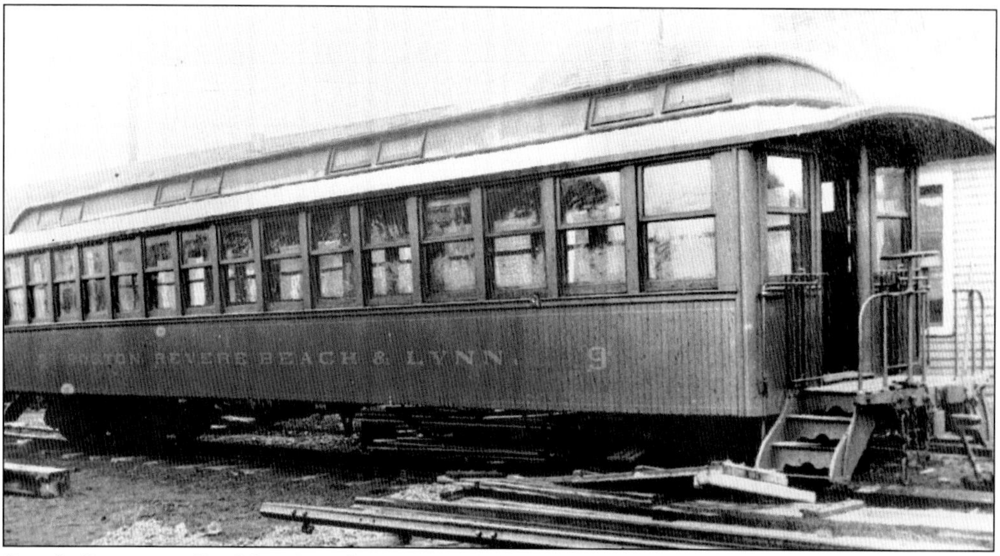

Stately Passenger Car Nos. 9 and 66 serviced the Boston, Revere Beach & Lynn Railroad for nearly four decades. These beautifully crafted cars featured 15 rows of divided seating able to comfortably accommodate 60 passengers and weighed a staggering 52,000 pounds each. While both were built by Laconia for the Boston, Revere Beach & Lynn Railroad, No. 9 (above) was reportedly built prior to 1905 while No. 66 (below) was produced at an unspecified later date. Indeed, No. 66 boasts a more streamlined and less ornamental exterior than its older counterpart. Both former steam coaches were converted to electric service in 1928. Sadly, records indicate that the gracious conveyances were burned for scrap once the line ceased operation in 1940. (Courtesy Lynn Museum.)

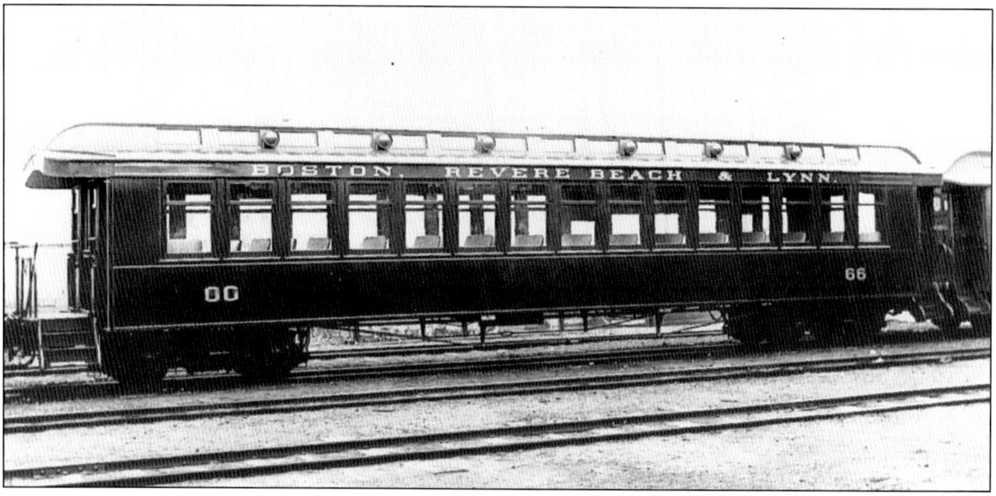

The gracious interior of Car No. 25 is shown on June 10, 1920. Attractive and ornate overhead lamps, spaced at appropriate intervals, illuminate the roomy passenger compartment. The stylish interior is further enhanced by tasteful trim and ample usage of warm, dark-grained wood. As in contemporary commuter trains, elevated advertisements adorn each side of the car. (Courtesy Winthrop Public Library.)

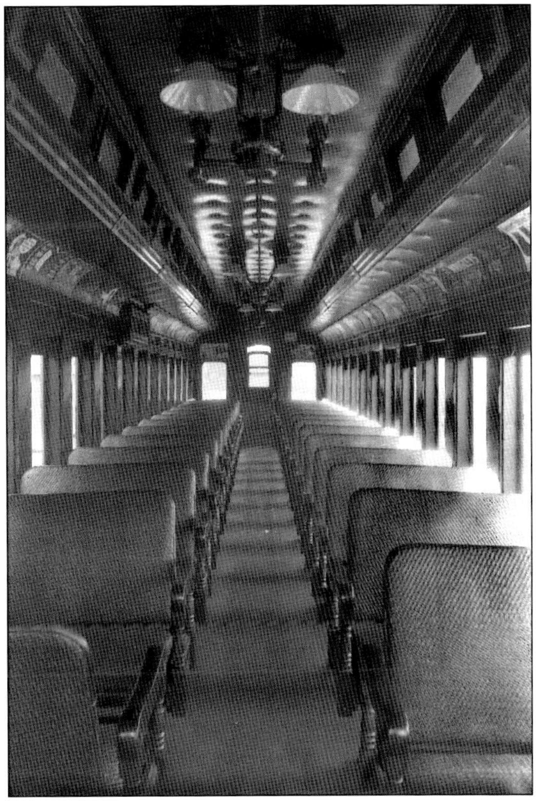

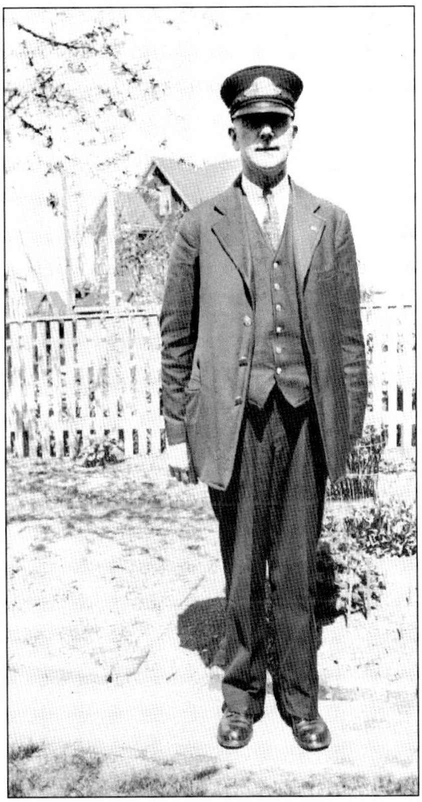

Baggage master Jesse B. Witham poses in uniform near his residence in this c. 1925 photograph. Witham enjoyed a successful career with the Boston, Revere Beach & Lynn Railroad and, in 1928, he and three other crewmen were photographed with the last steam train to travel the tracks of the esteemed railroad. Emily W. May donated this picture to her local library on May 12, 1935. (Courtesy Winthrop Public Library.)

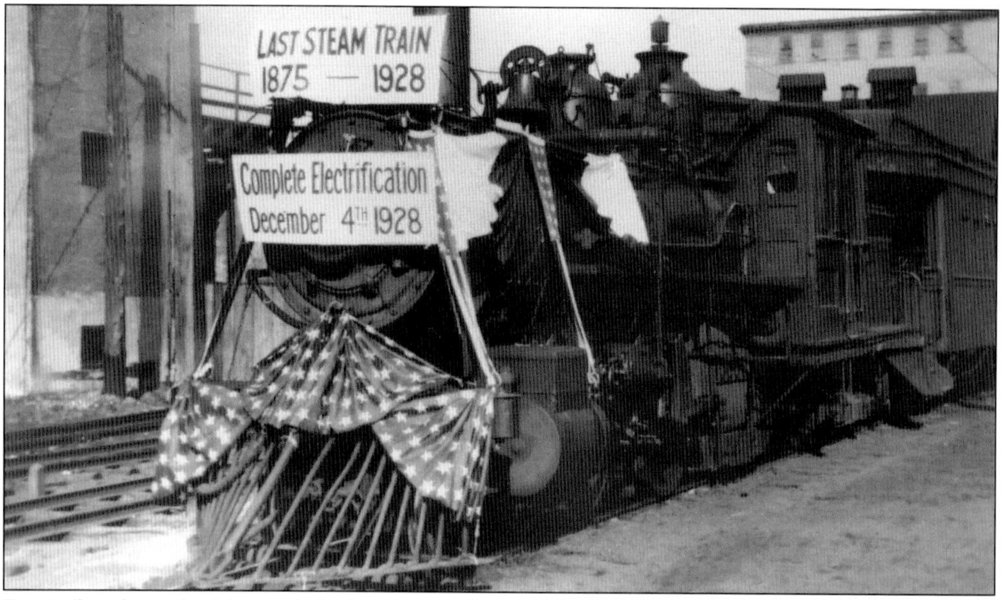

Festively adorned with patriotic bunting and signs, the last steam train to run on the Boston, Revere Beach & Lynn Railroad is photographed for posterity both alone (above) and with its devoted crew (below) prior to departing Lynn Station for East Boston at 1:45 p.m. on December 4, 1928. Pictured from left to right are Edward Shaw, fireman; William Lemmers, conductor; Jesse B. Witham, baggage master; and Archie McCarthy, engineer. Locomotive No. 5 was built by Hinkley Locomotive Company in 1874 and was later sold to Brown Company in Florida. During the early years of the Boston, Revere Beach & Lynn Railroad, locomotives sported stately names such as *Leo, Orion*, *Pegasus*, *Draco,* and *Jupiter* rather than mere numeric designations. The handsome engine pictured here was originally known as *Leo*. (Above courtesy Lynn Museum; below courtesy Winthrop Public Library.)

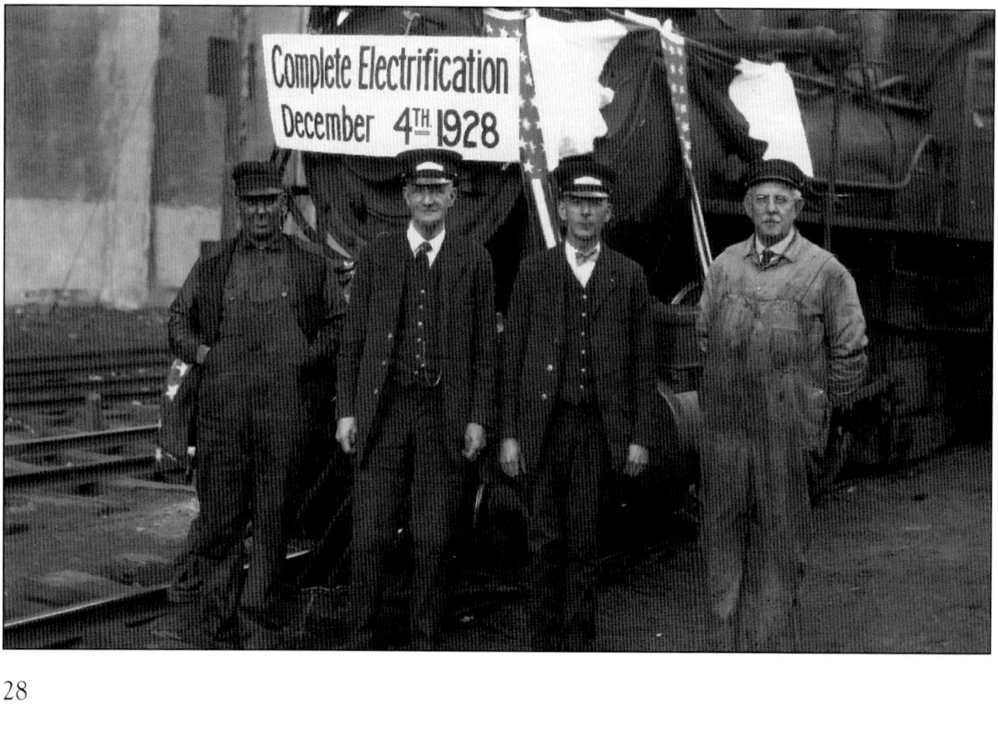

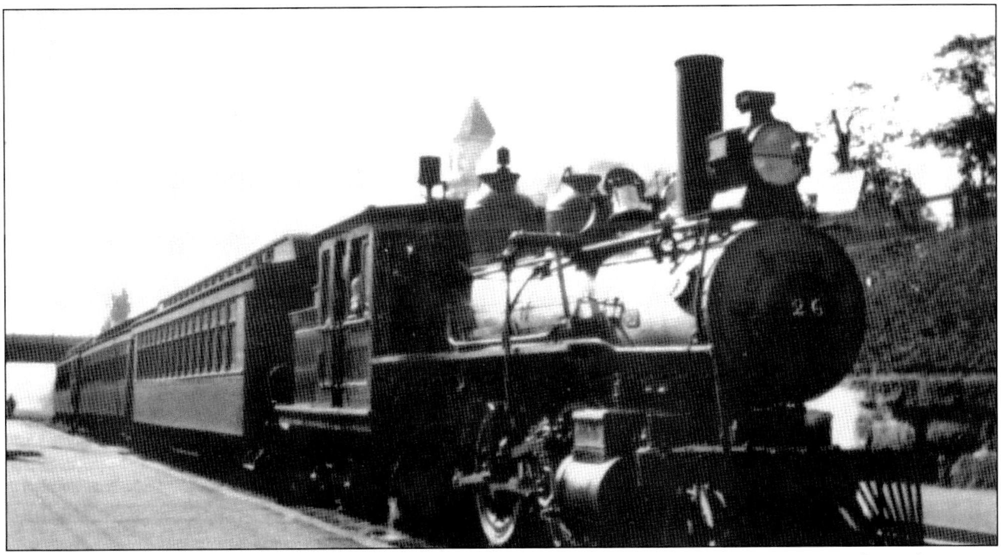

The majestic Locomotive No. 26, shown in 1916 at Crescent Beach Station, must have been an impressive sight indeed as it steamed into the various stations along the Boston, Revere Beach & Lynn Railroad line during its 15 years of service. Built in 1914 by Schenectady Locomotive Works at an approximate cost of $10,000, this trusty engine dutifully plied the tracks north of Boston until it was scrapped in 1929. (Courtesy Lynn Museum.)

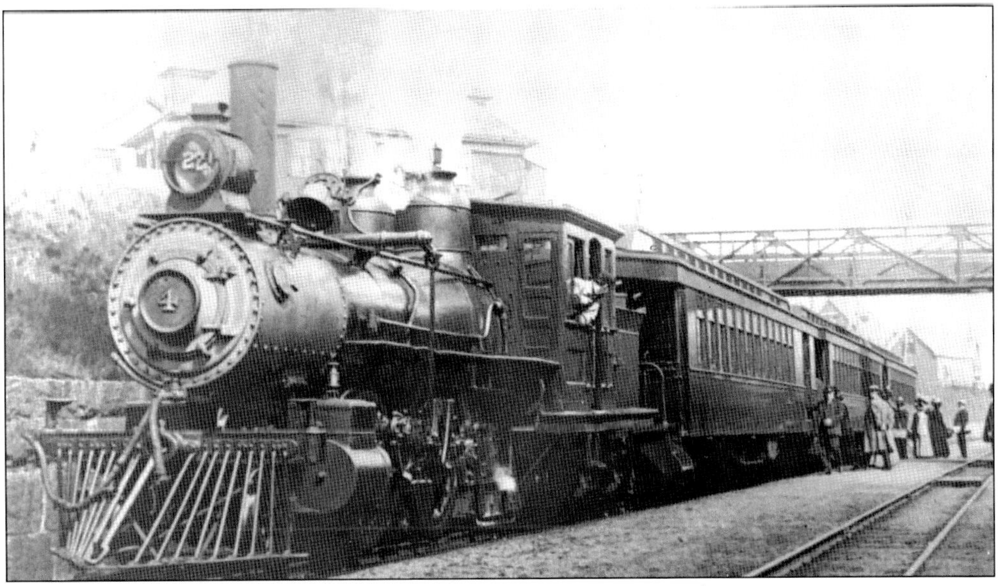

Boston, Revere Beach & Lynn Railroad Locomotive No. 4 and passenger cars are waiting to depart Revere Beach Station, arguably the most popular and centrally located of the four narrow-gauge stations located along the beach. Built in 1904 by Manchester Locomotive Works, this mighty engine named *Mercury* was in service until 1929, when it was scrapped. (Courtesy Lynn Museum.)

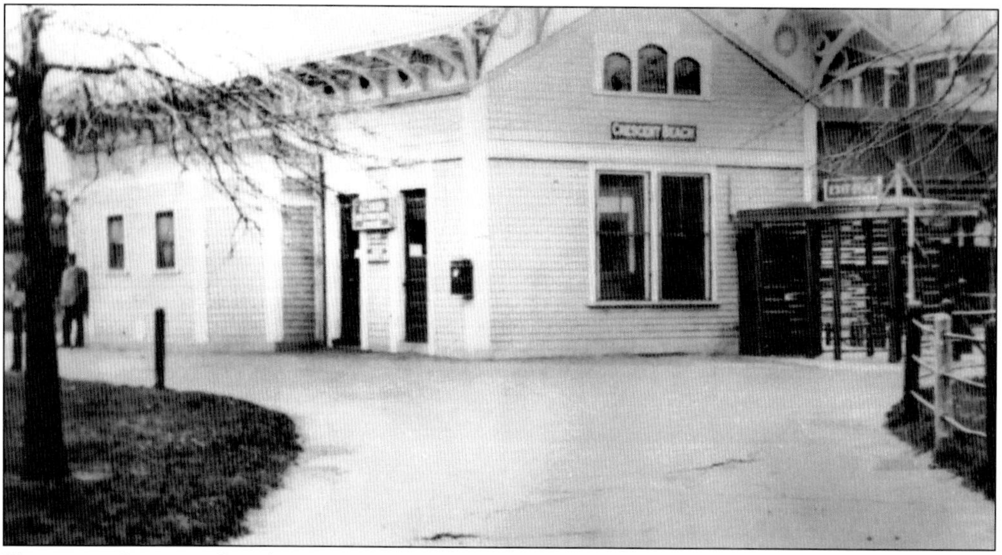

Shown is Crescent Beach Station as it appeared in the 1930s. One of four stops near the delicate crest of Revere Beach, the station was located between the Beachmont and Bath House stops and was among the most utilized stations operated by the Boston, Revere Beach & Lynn Railroad. Once located in the immediate vicinity of Revere Beach Boulevard, the restructuring project initiated by the Metropolitan Park Commission resulted in the relocation of all line operations in 1897. (Courtesy Lynn Museum.)

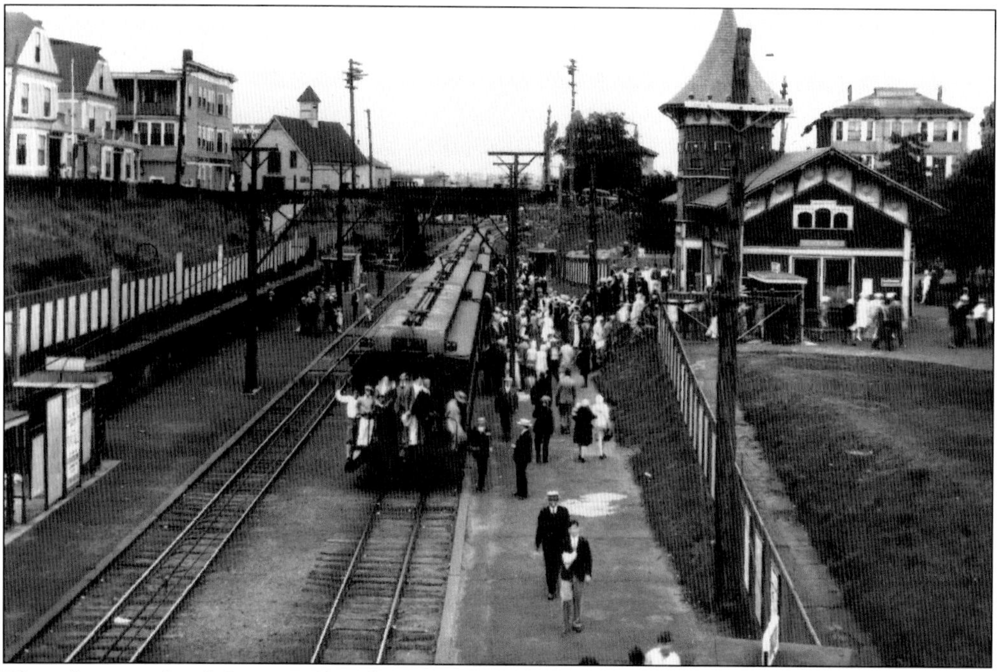

This photograph of Crescent Beach Station was taken during the early decades of the 20th century. The popular station was located west of Ocean Avenue, and the bridge at the center spans Beach Street. For years, the Victorian Eclectic station house at the right gracefully presided over the mechanical activity on the tracks, as well as over the hordes of passengers who surged through the station daily. (Courtesy Lynn Museum.)

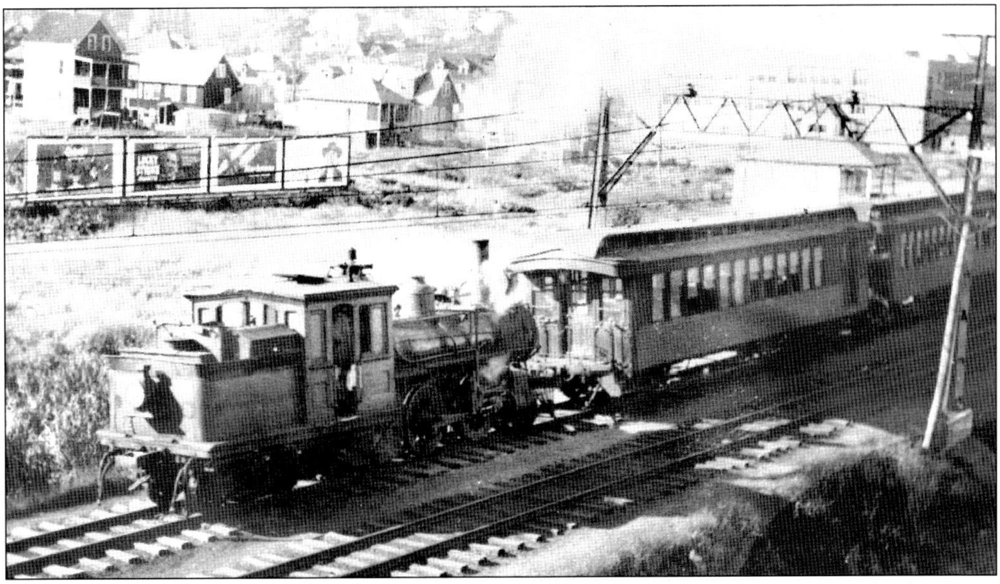

Locomotive No. 26 is shown leaving Revere Beach Station on October 14, 1928. At the upper right is the Garfield Elementary School. At the left are billboards advertising various products including cigarettes and cereal. This fine engine was built in 1914 at an approximate cost of $10,000 by American Locomotive Company, Schenectady Works. It was scrapped one year after this photograph was taken. (Courtesy Winthrop Public Library.)

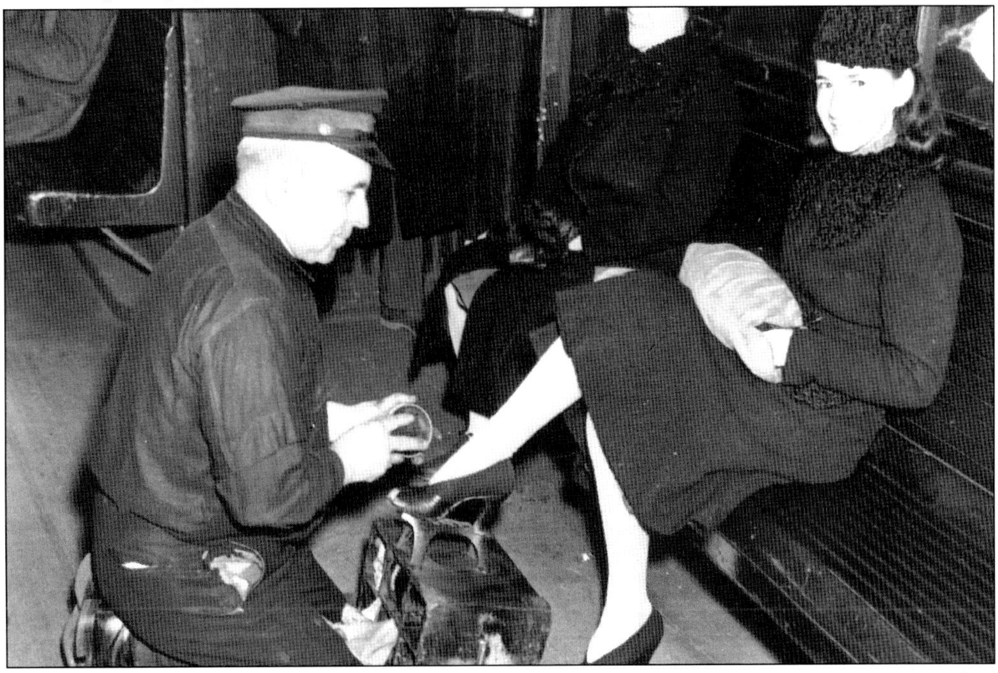

A fashionably attired young woman smiles charmingly for the camera while an unidentified bootblack shines her shoes aboard an unspecified Boston, Revere Beach & Lynn passenger ferry. Information inscribed on the reverse of this photograph states that the older man in the picture had held his position for many years and that he enjoyed a steady customer base. Each patron paid 10¢ to have his or her shoes buffed to perfection. (Courtesy Winthrop Public Library.)

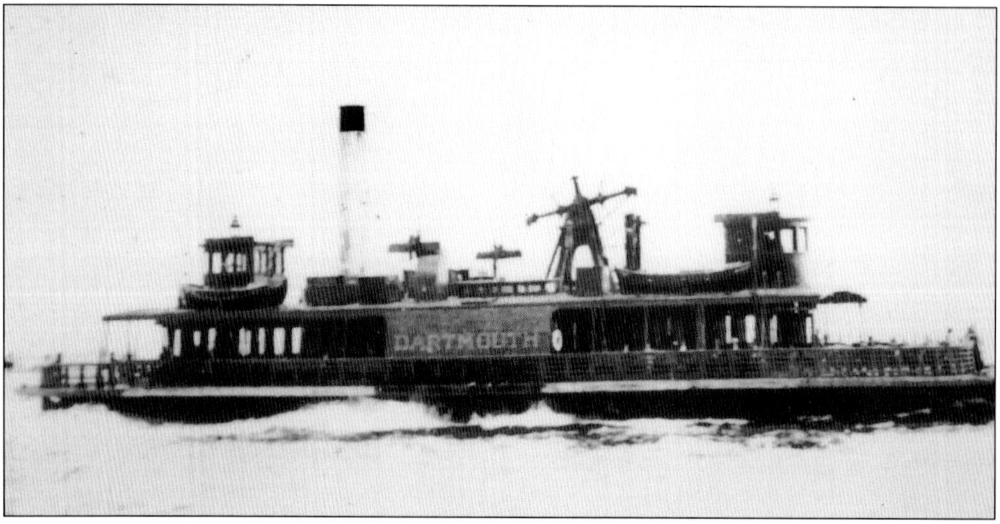

Built at East Boston for the Boston, Revere Beach & Lynn Railroad, the *Dartmouth* was launched on April 22, 1899. Introduced during the final year of the 19th century, this admirable vessel was the oldest and enjoyed the longest career of the four boats that serviced the line through the 1930s. It was removed from service in March 1939 after four solid decades of employment. (Courtesy Lynn Museum.)

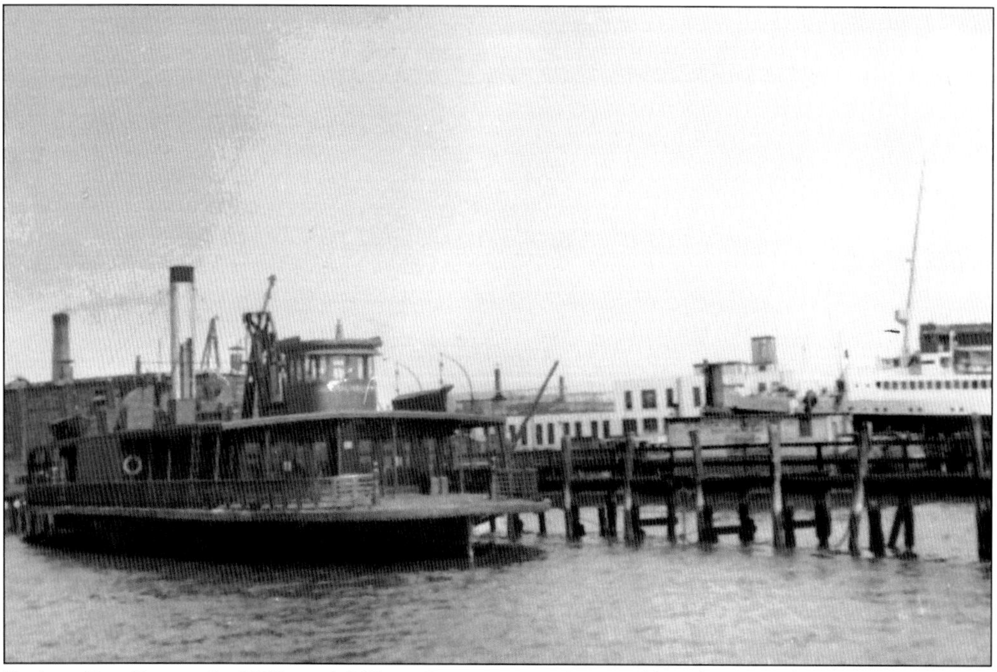

Built at East Boston by William McKee, the passenger ferry *Ashburnham* was launched on March 18, 1905. In early January 1918, the vessel became icebound while crossing Boston Harbor. After two hours, Captain Nelson managed to free the boat by first reversing its engines before forging ahead. In November 1939, the *Ashburnham* was removed from service and, in June 1940, it was purchased by ship broker William S. Nolan for $1,500. (Courtesy Lynn Museum.)

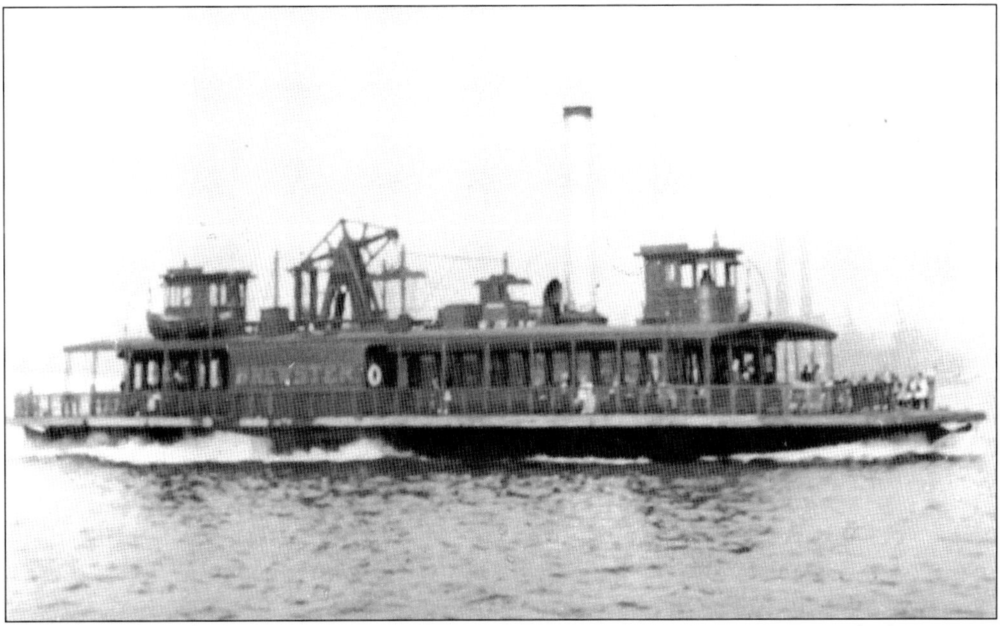

The *Brewster* was built in Boston in 1906 and enjoyed an extraordinary career with the Boston, Revere Beach & Lynn Railroad. On February 24, 1933, a snapped strap caused the vessel to drift out into the harbor with 50 passengers aboard. A tugboat successfully rescued the hapless craft. The *Brewster* plied the waters on the line's final night in operation and, in June 1940, it was sold at auction for $1,500 to William S. Nolan. (Courtesy Lynn Museum.)

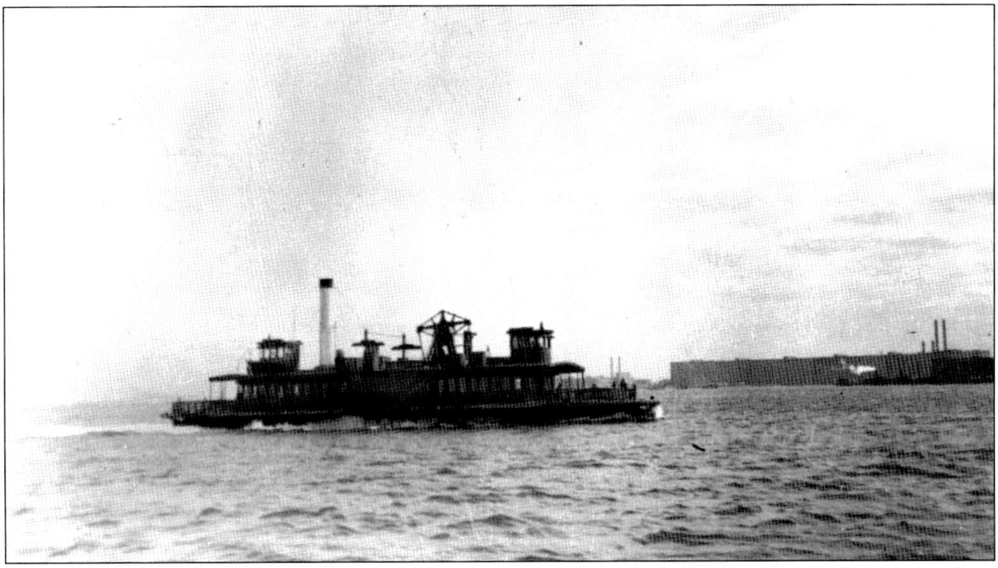

Put into service on April 26, 1909, the *Newtown* was the last ferryboat built for the Boston, Revere Beach & Lynn Railroad and enjoyed a rather uneventful career. However, on September 15, 1924, Captain Bloomquist suffered a fatal heart attack aboard *Newtown* immediately following a collision between his vessel and the *Ashburnham*. The boat remained in service to the line for an additional 16 years before it was decommissioned and towed to Portland, Maine. (Courtesy Lynn Museum.)

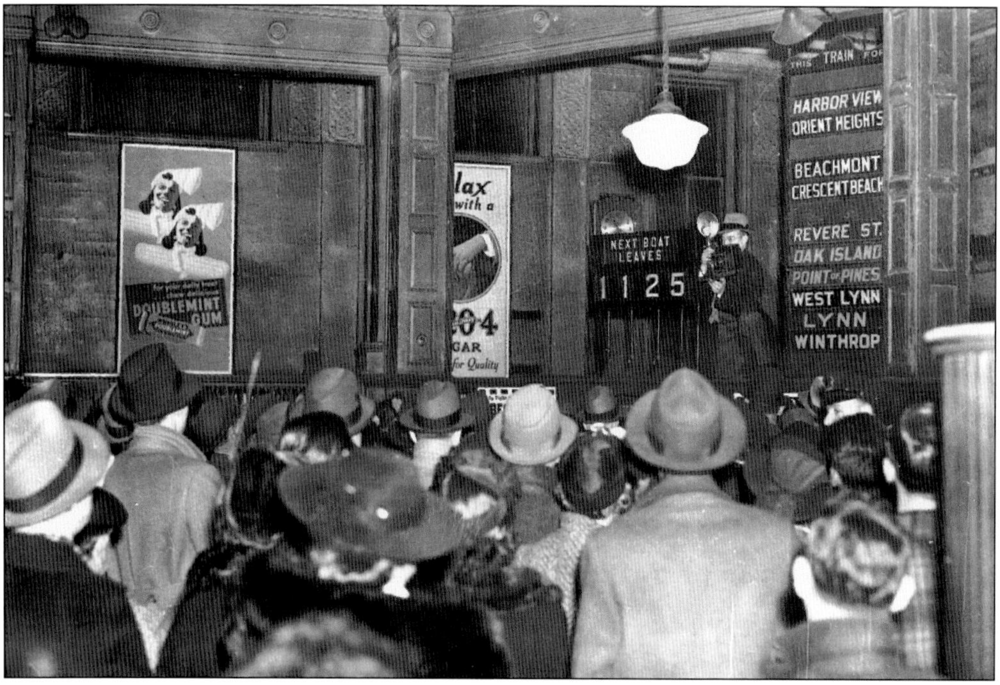

The *American* newspaper ran this picture detailing the crowd gathered inside the Atlantic Avenue ferry terminal in Boston prior to the departure of the 11:25 p.m. boat on January 27, 1940, the final day of operation for the Boston, Revere Beach & Lynn Railroad. A photographer perches above the gathering to better capture the moment for posterity. Intricately engraved wooden pillars enhance the terminal, and large posters advertising familiar products bedeck the walls. (Courtesy Winthrop Public Library.)

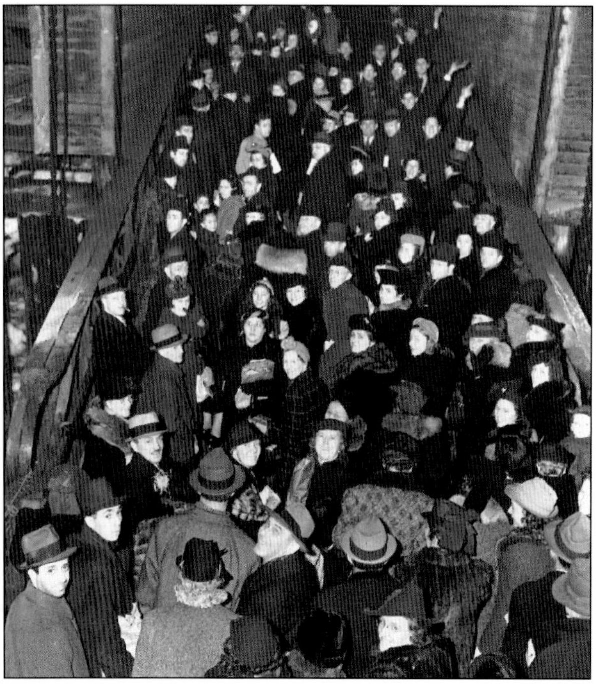

The *Boston Post* published this photograph of passengers crowding the East Boston train shed gangway as they disembarked the final ferry operated by the Boston, Revere Beach & Lynn Railroad. Visible on either side are the enormous chains that raised and lowered the 15- by 60-foot gangway from train shed to boat deck. The photograph ran on January 28, 1940. (Courtesy Winthrop Public Library.)

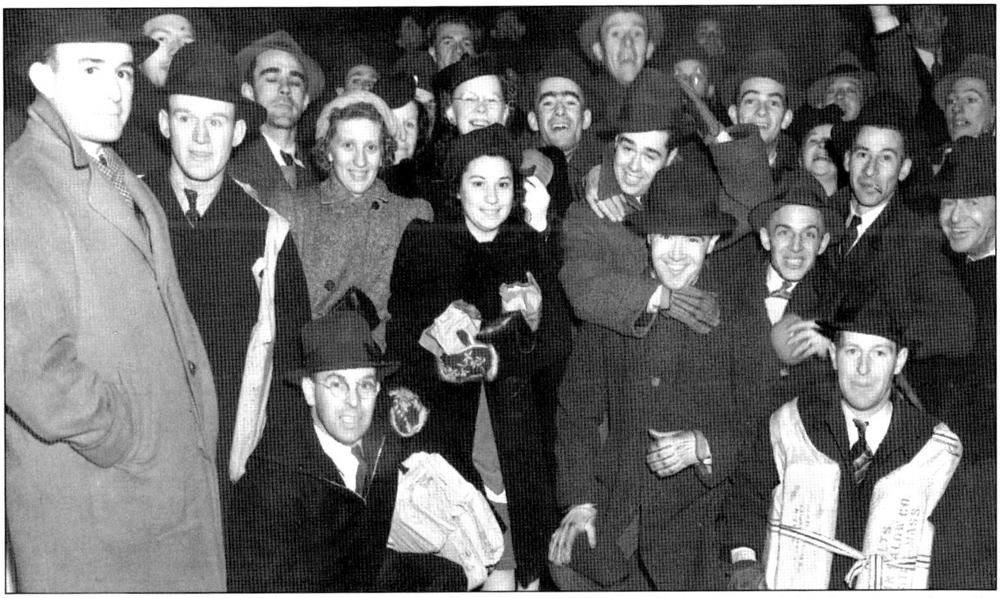

Handsomely attired men and women, who had lately endured the mercifully brief yet frigidly cold passage aboard the *Brewster*, strike a joyful pose for the *Boston Post*. Photographed within the East Boston train shed, many of the passengers clutch souvenirs taken from the passenger vessel. One fellow (lower right) has donned his prized keepsake, a large life vest. (Courtesy Winthrop Public Library.)

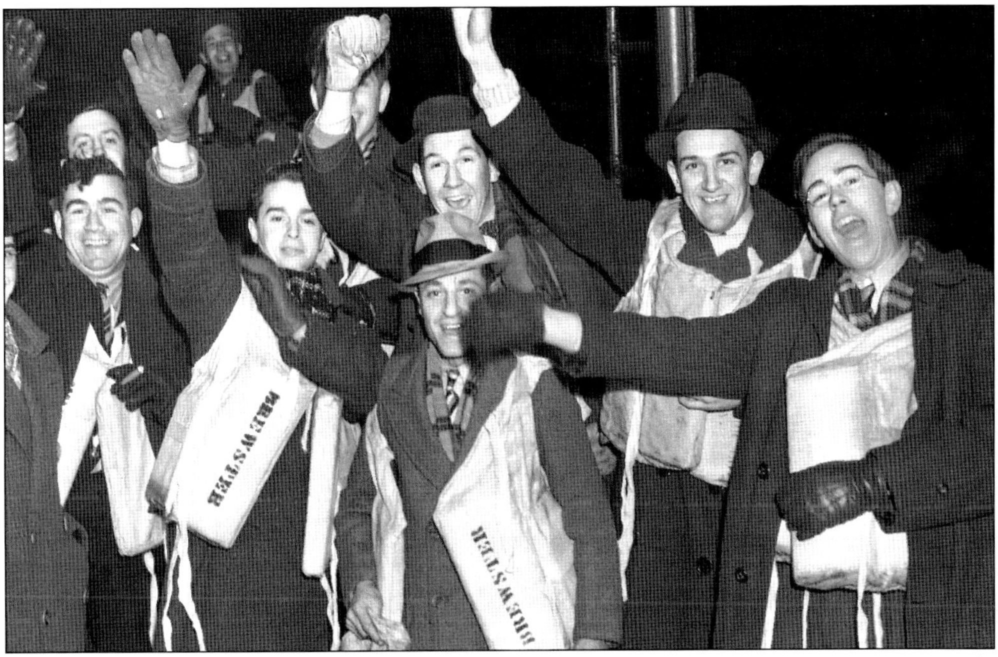

Despite the low temperature and late hour, merrymakers aboard the *Brewster* wave enthusiastically for a *Boston Post* photographer on the line's final night in operation. The dapper young men pictured here, clad in long coats to ward off the January cold, sport life vests bearing the name of the vessel that reliably serviced the line for more than 30 years. (Courtesy Winthrop Public Library.)

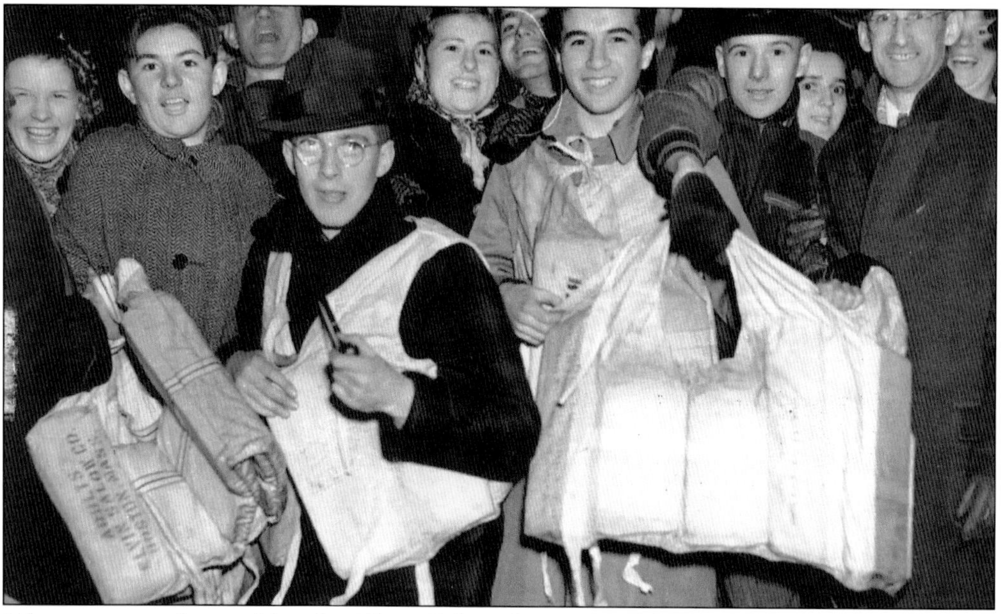

Life vests manufactured by the Elvin Salow Company of Boston, boat hooks, and other equipment from the line's ferryboat are claimed by passengers to commemorate the Boston, Revere Beach & Lynn Railroad's passage into history. In this view, some jovial souvenir seekers pause briefly to be photographed by the *Boston Sunday Herald* before rushing off to catch the last northbound train. (Courtesy Winthrop Public Library.)

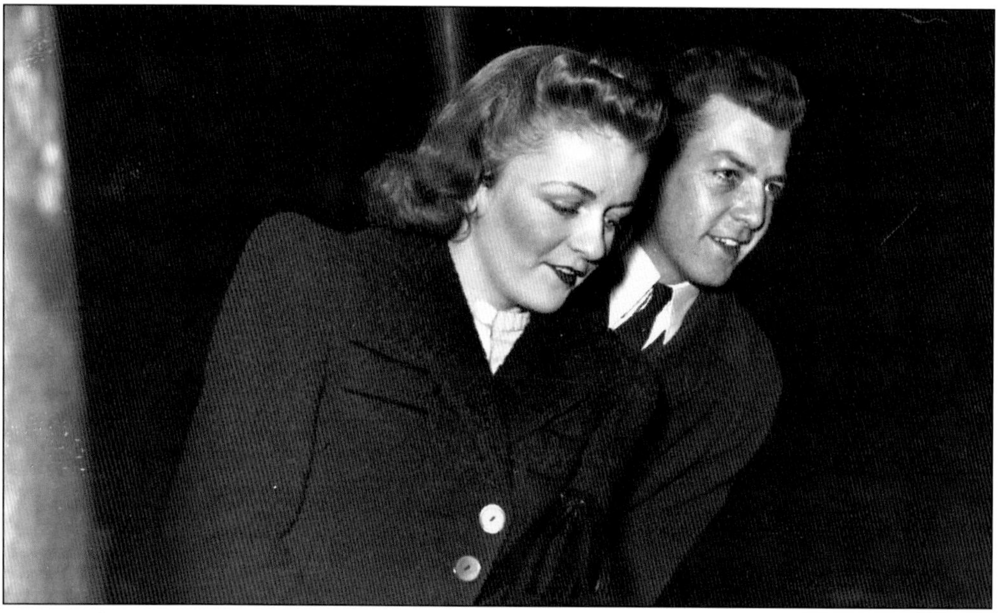

Betty and "Ace" McNeil are shown in a *Boston Globe* photograph taken at an unspecified point during their passage aboard the Boston, Revere Beach & Lynn Railroad on the evening of January 27, 1940. The pleasant couple were among the vast numbers of people who personally witnessed the final journey of the railroad, which had provided reliable passenger service for 65 years between Market Square in Lynn and Atlantic Avenue in Boston. (Courtesy Winthrop Public Library.)

An unidentified couple takes a moment while aboard *Brewster* to pose within the vessel's large life preserver. While the man, wearing a life vest bearing the ferryboat's name, appears quite calm and at ease, his companion seems considerably less comfortable evidenced by the tentative positioning of her left hand and her distracted gaze. (Courtesy Winthrop Public Library.)

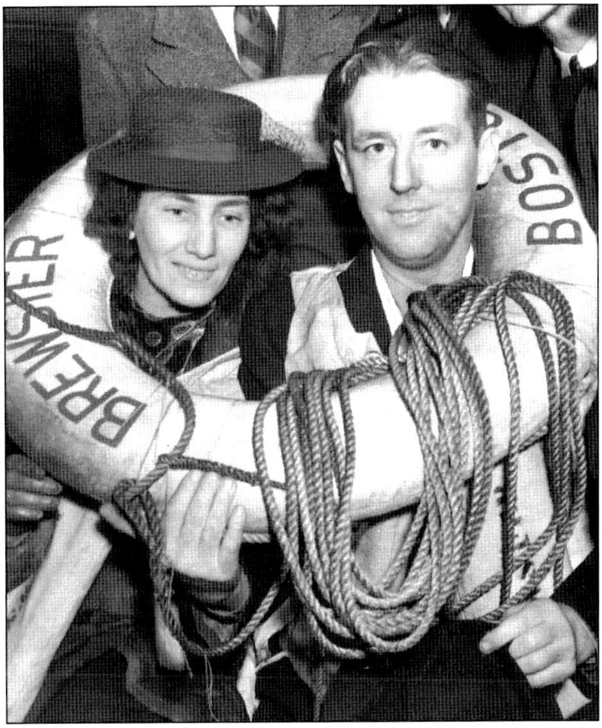

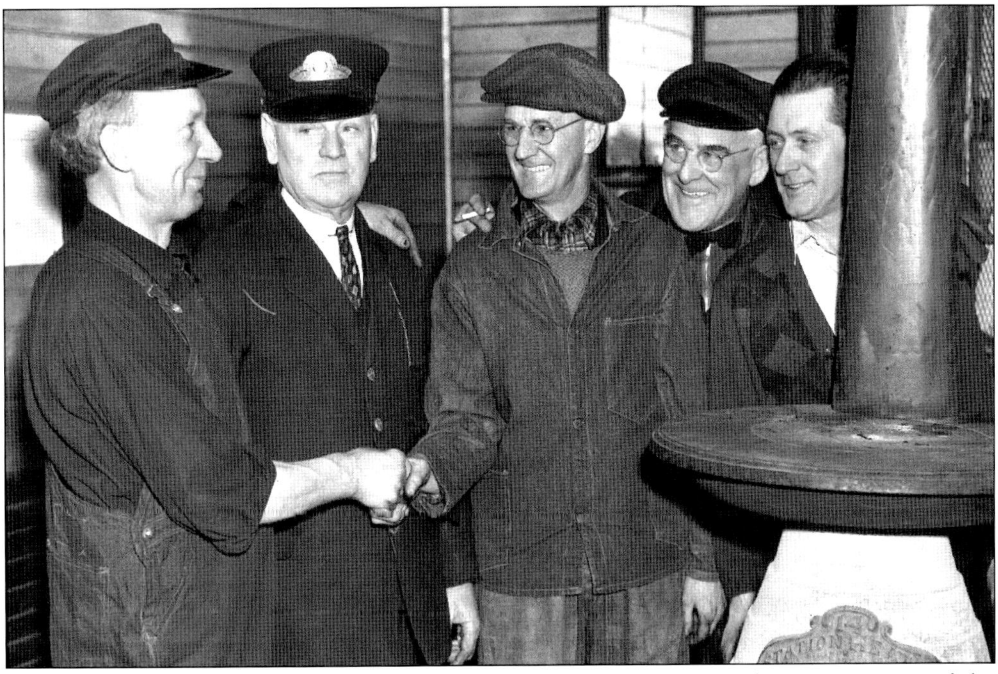

This animated *Boston Post* photograph shows unidentified station and train crewmen of the Boston, Revere Beach & Lynn Railroad. Smiling faces and amicable stances abound despite the fact that the impending demise of the railroad was soon to result in unemployment or forced early retirement for many. At the lower right stands a potbelly stove, a familiar and necessary fixture in every early train station and shed. (Courtesy Winthrop Public Library.)

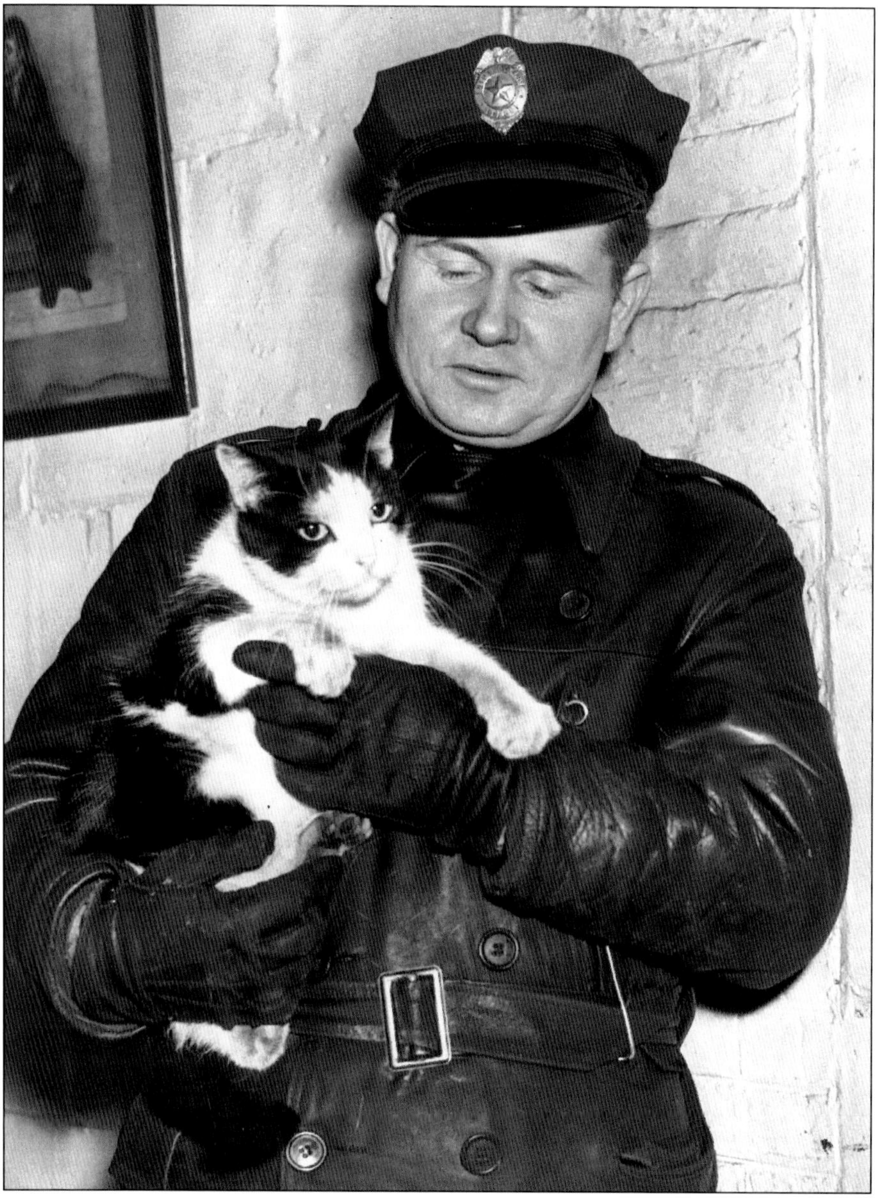

A *Boston Post* photographer snapped this heartwarming photograph of an unidentified crewman gingerly holding Bingo the cat on the Boston, Revere Beach & Lynn Railroad's last day of service. The closing of the respected line displaced the adorable feline, who had been station cat of the Rowe's Wharf terminal since 1933. Rather reluctantly, the train staff relinquished Bingo to the Animal Rescue League of Boston on January 27, 1940. The following day, more than 300 employees were out of work. In May of that year, the line's physical assets were sold to Chelsea scrap dealers S. Gordon & Sons for approximately $119,000. In addition, an auction was held the following month in East Boston, where 605 narrow-gauge railroad items were offered for sale to more than 200 eager bidders. The successful auction brought in more than $15,000. In November 1940, the East Boston terminal and ferry slip were razed. Today, little remains of the historic railroad that reliably serviced local passengers for over six decades. (Courtesy Winthrop Public Library.)

Three

Wonderland Amusement Park

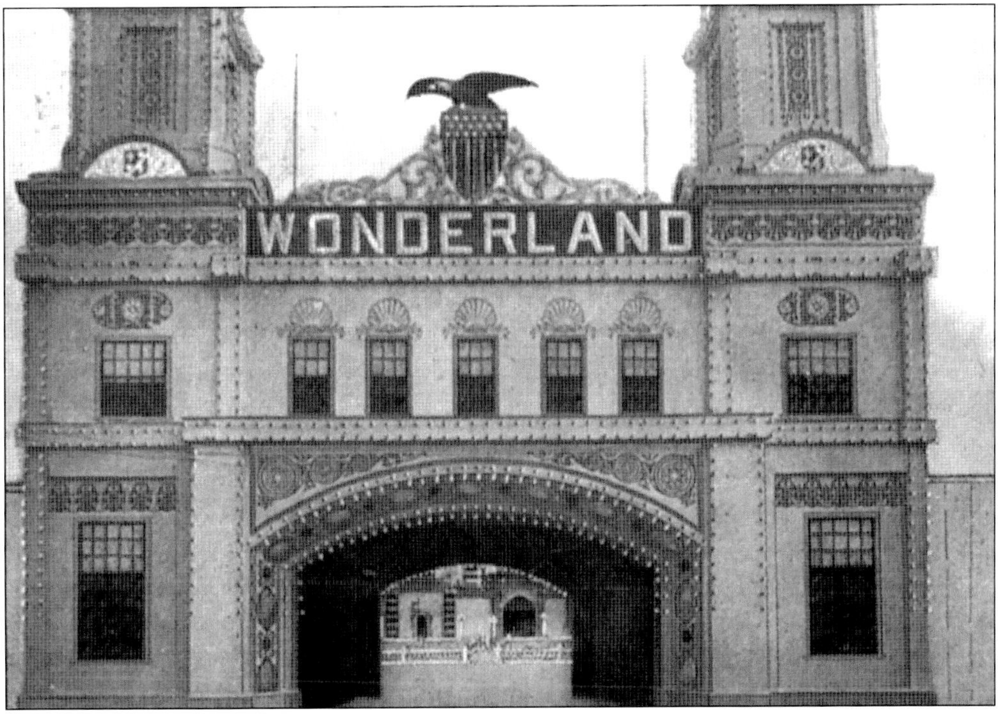

This postcard depicting an artist's rendition of Wonderland Park's main entrance and administration building circulated for years. A graceful eagle presides over the entranceway from its patriotic perch at the center between two imposing domed towers. Thousands of electric lights embellish the preeminent architectural marvel. The mere sight of the magnificent structure quickened visitor's pulses and evoked awe, as well as speculation as to what wonders existed beyond the elaborate entrance. (Courtesy Jack Cook.)

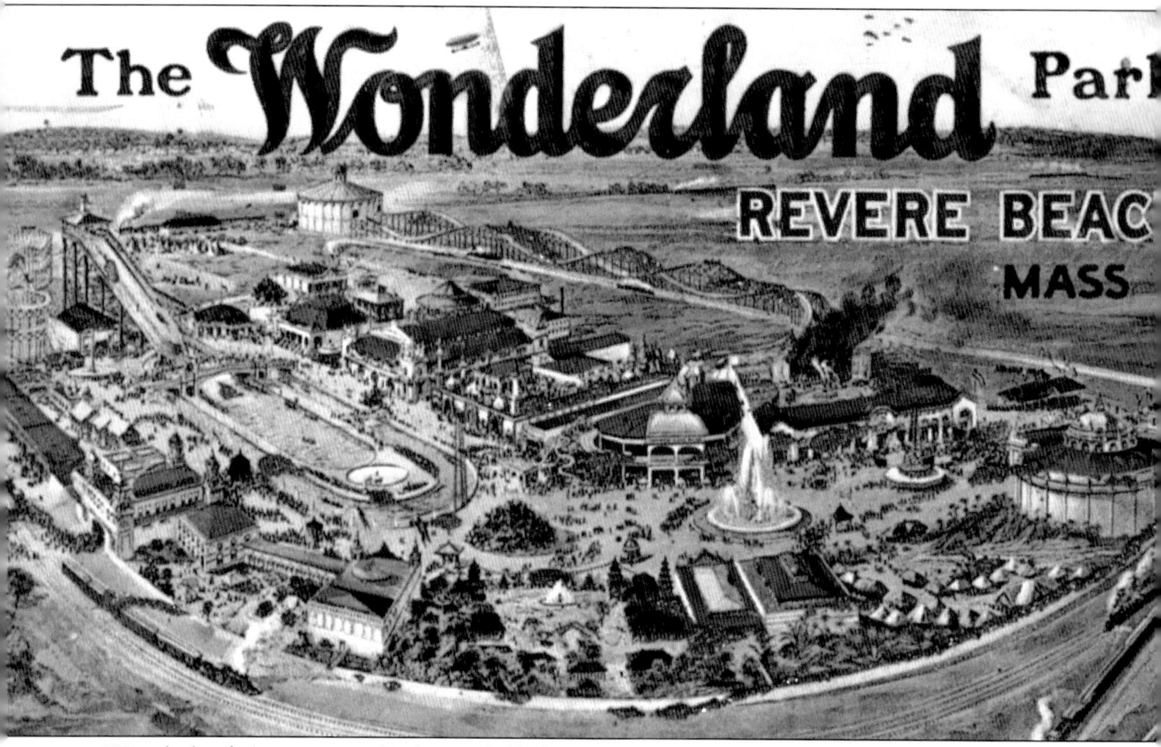

Wonderland Amusement Park was billed as New England's premier amusement destination and was quite arguably America's first theme park. A place of imaginative discovery, Wonderland was truly reminiscent of the well-known children's story that inspired the park's creation. Designed by Boston architect John Lavalle and built by the renowned Aldrich and Shea Construction Company, the amusement park cost more than $1 million to complete. It featured innovative and popular attractions including aquatic acts, a central flume ride, a Japanese Village, a Wild West Show, a large roller coaster, a roller-skating rink, a spacious ballroom, and an operative hospital. Opening day, on May 30, 1906, reportedly attracted more than 100,000 visitors. Unfortunately, enormous overhead, including rising construction costs and entertainers' fees, ultimately resulted in the park's closing on Labor Day in 1911. Reichner Brothers, a successful printing company with offices in Boston and in Munich, Germany, produced this aerial postcard in 1906. Embellished with silver glitter, this colorful greeting sold for slightly more than the average postcard due to its distinctive and appealing ornamentation. (Courtesy Jack Cook.)

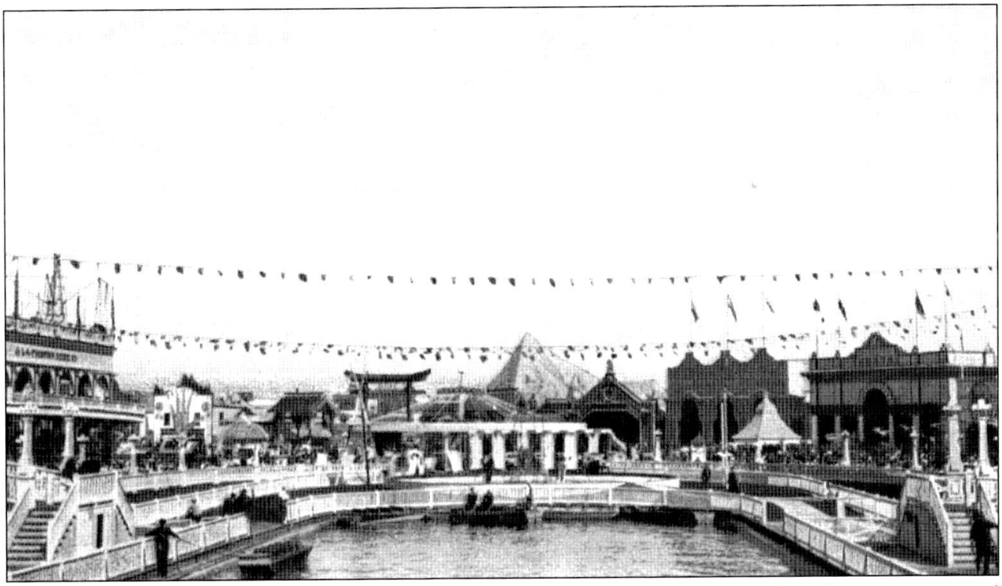

Published in 1913—two years after Wonderland's premature demise—this German postcard depicts multiple strands of multicolored flag garland stretching merrily over the amusement park's Central Lagoon, upon whose placid surface small boats rest. Behind the lagoon, from left to right, are various attractions including Thompson's Scenic Railway, a palmist, the imperial entrance gate to the Japanese Village, Love's Journey, Mount Fujiyama, Fatal Wedding, and Wonderland Theatre. (Courtesy Jack Cook.)

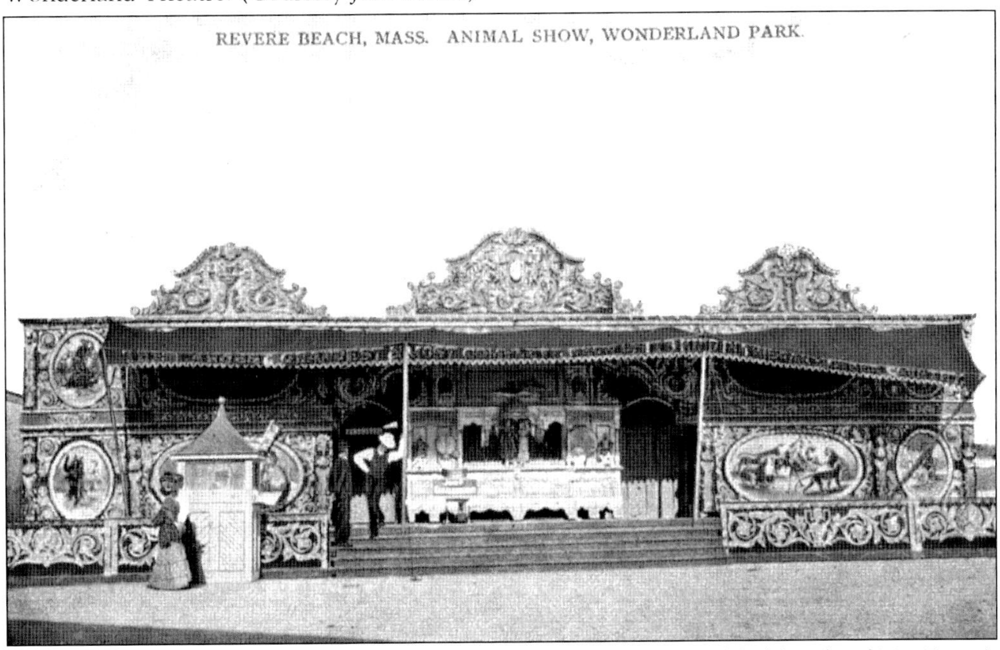

This early-20th-century postcard printed in Germany reveals the gilded facade of Mr. Ferari's Animal Show. The attraction showcased exotic and majestic animals, including leopards, panthers, and tigers of various ages and sizes. The wide awning boasts that visitors passing through the elaborate facade will experience the "Largest, Grandest And Most Complete Show Of Its Kind In This Or Any Other Country." (Courtesy Jack Cook.)

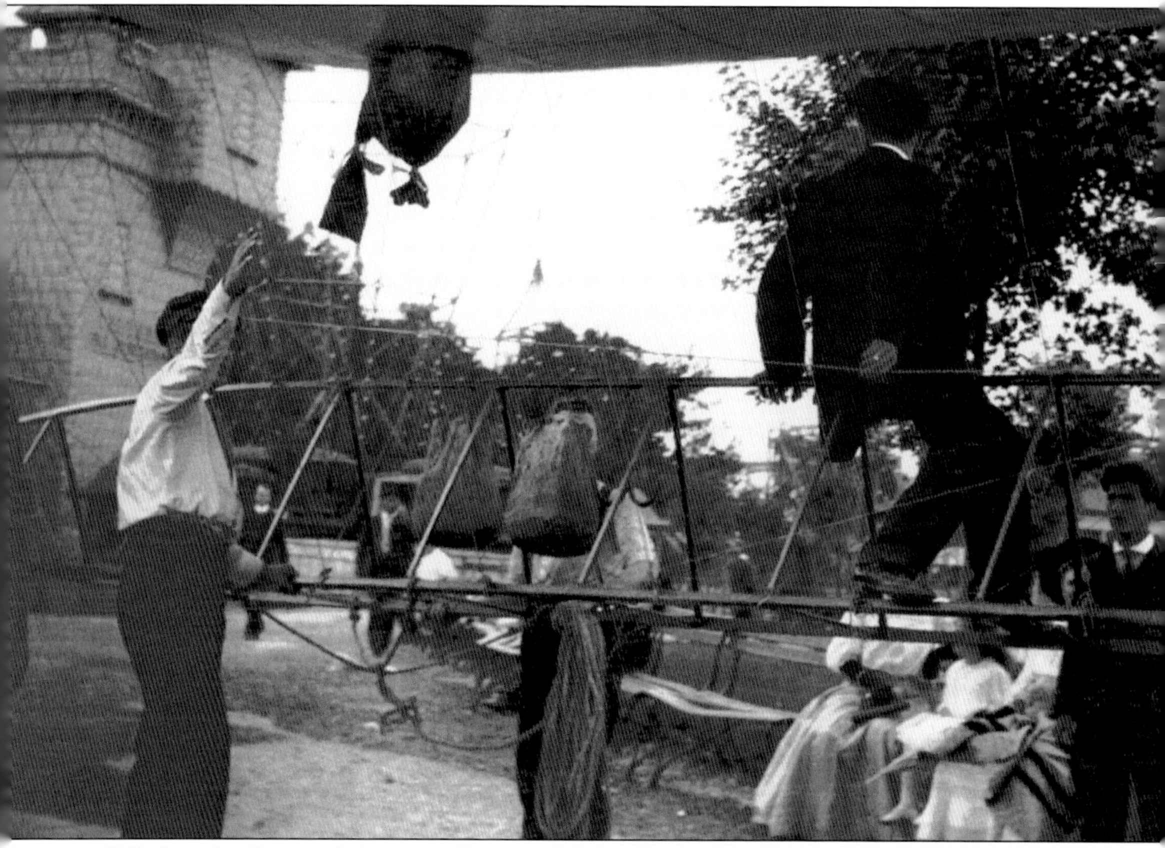

Billed as the "Intrepid Aeronaut," renowned aviation pioneer Lincoln Beachey was engaged for a brief period of time during the 1907 season by the popular Greater Boston amusement park, where he performed daily ascensions in his cleverly crafted airship. This rare photograph was taken by an unidentified individual sometime between May 30 and June 6, 1907. It shows Beachey straddling his airship's skeletal frame on the scenic grounds of Wonderland Park. An early proponent of flight, the 20-year-old aviator hailed from the West Coast, where much of his young adulthood had been invested in flight-related endeavors. By the early years of the 20th century, he had had extensive experience with both airships and gas-propelled balloons. His fine reputation and skilled exhibitions fueled his popularity to the point where his ascensions were in high demand throughout the country. In fact, his Wonderland Park appearances drew record crowds from all over New England, earning both pilot and park further favorable recognition. (Courtesy Carroll F. Gray Aeronautical Collection.)

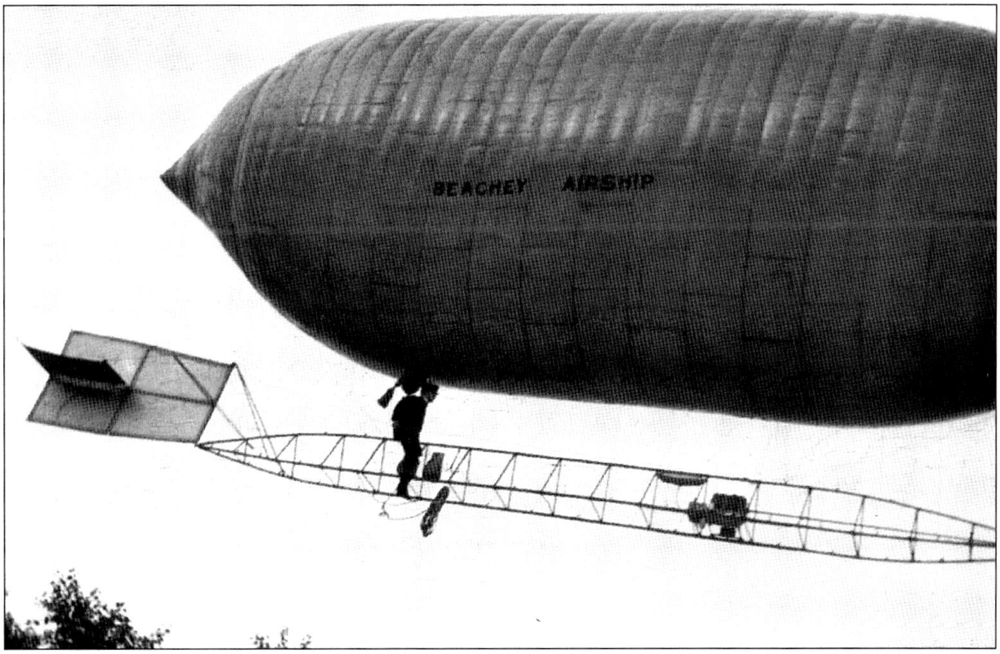

An air-bound Lincoln Beachey is shown above Wonderland Park sometime during late May or early June 1907. An aviation enthusiast who had been captivated by the concept of flight since childhood, the San Francisco, California native designed, constructed, and maintained this remarkable craft, which he piloted daily over Revere Beach's famous amusement park. While engaged here, the respected aviator reportedly commanded $1,000 per ascension. (Courtesy Carroll F. Gray Aeronautical Collection.)

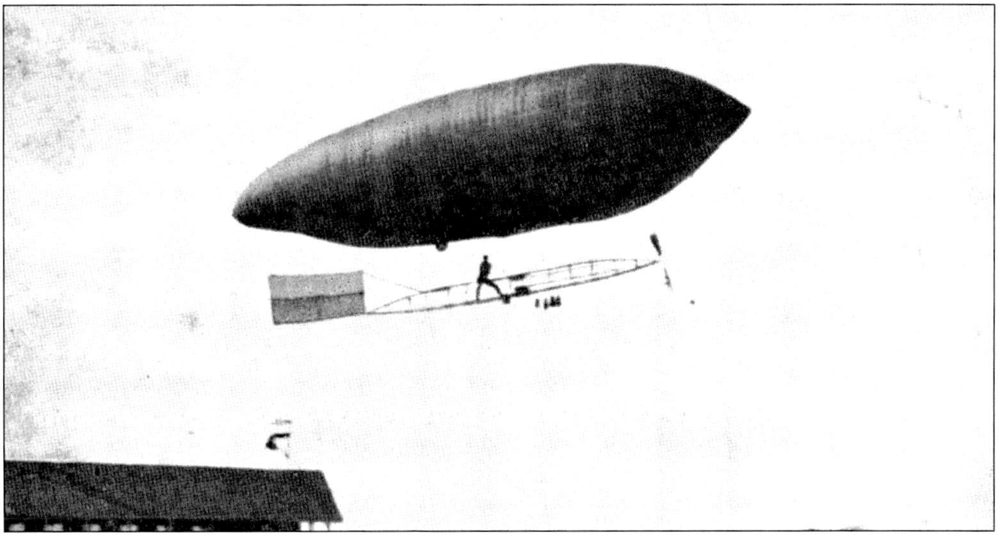

This picture postcard of Lincoln Beachey represented one of many thrilling discoveries existing within Wonderland Amusement Park. Moreso, the dramatic image attested to the aviator's intrepid spirit and further fueled his popularity. Some years after his famous Revere Beach appearances, Beachey turned to piloting aeroplanes. A daring pilot, he consistently strove to achieve new heights. His productive career ended with his untimely death in 1915. (Courtesy Revere Society for Cultural and Historic Preservation.)

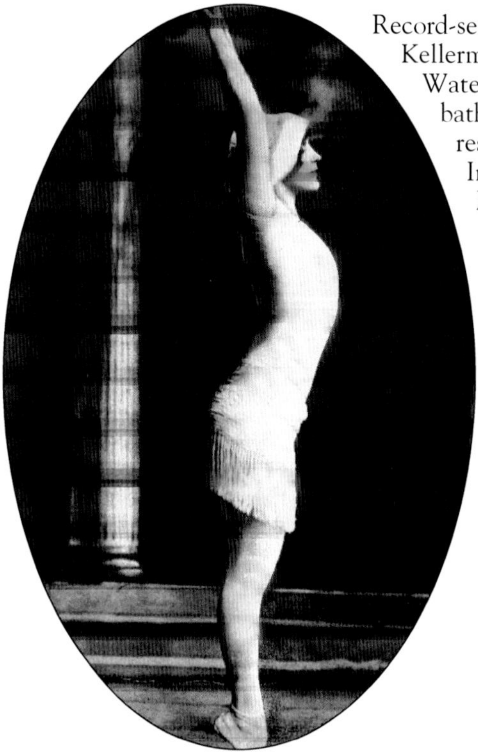

Record-setting Australian swimmer and diver Annette Kellerman was a popular performer in Wonderland's Water Palace in 1908. She also introduced the one-piece bathing suit to America while on Revere Beach, resulting in her immediate arrest for indecent attire. In 1951, Esther Williams portrayed her in MGM's *Million Dollar Mermaid,* in which the scandalous scene was depicted. Scenes from the movie were shot on location on Revere Beach. (Courtesy Boston Public Library, Prints Department.)

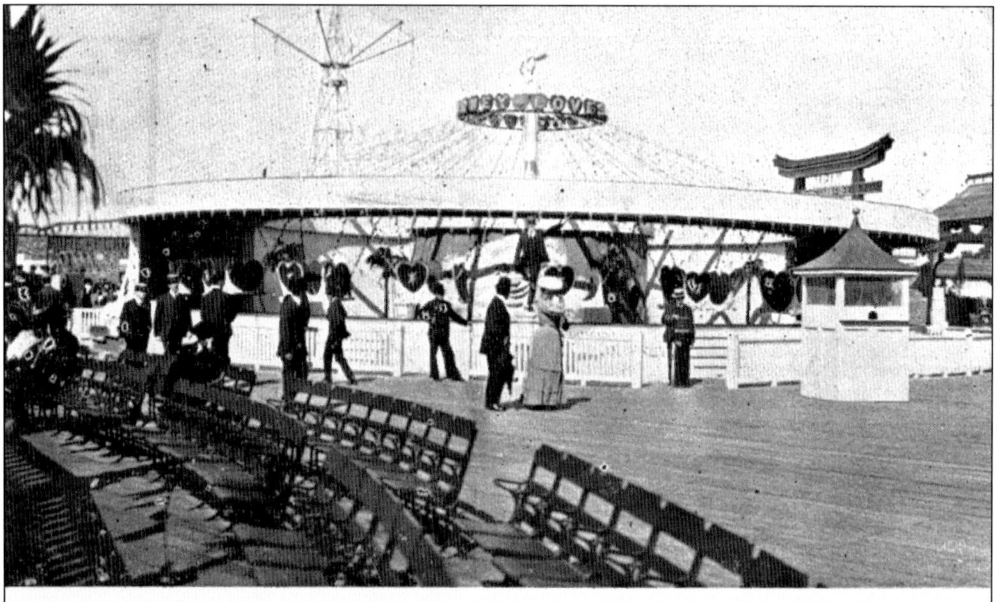

Love's Journey, Wonderland Park, Revere Beach, Mass.

James T. Allen & Company of Revere produced this postcard depicting Love's Journey, a well-attended attraction favored by sweethearts. Located along the broad central promenade in close proximity to the Japanese Village and circle swing ride known as the Airships, the mild-mannered ride was an early incarnation of the tunnel-of-love attraction that enjoyed tremendous popularity among young couples in later decades. (Courtesy Jack Cook.)

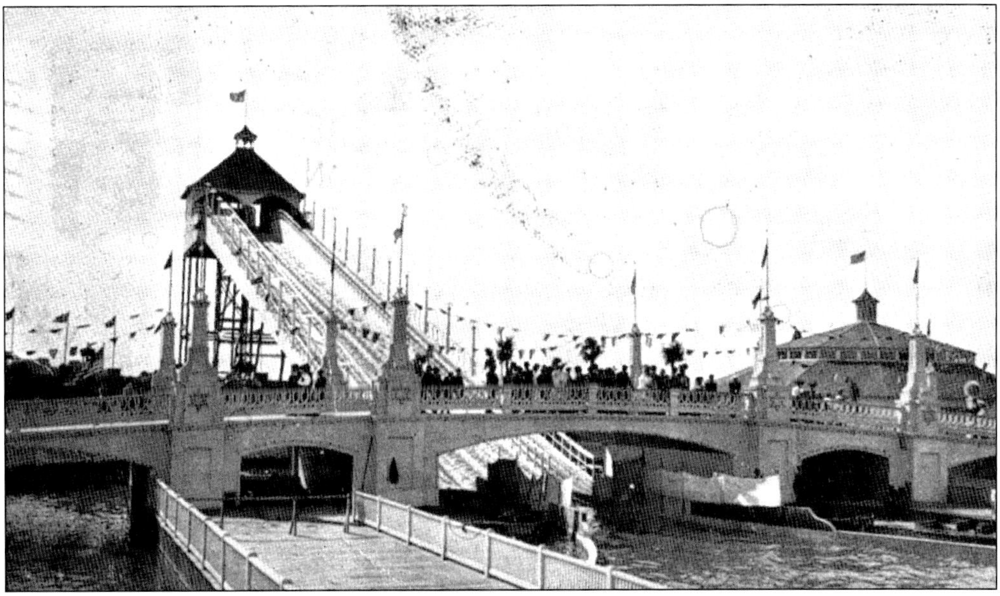

Postmarked on August 2, 1907, this Allen & Company postcard features the Shoot-the-Chutes, the tallest and most recognized of all Wonderland Park attractions. Sturdily constructed gondolas conveyed riders to the roofed apex of the innovative attraction, which afforded a stunning yet short-lived panoramic view of Revere Beach. Moments later came the breath-robbing plunge that hurled the small crafts downward beneath the graceful bridge and into the Central Lagoon. (Courtesy Jack Cook.)

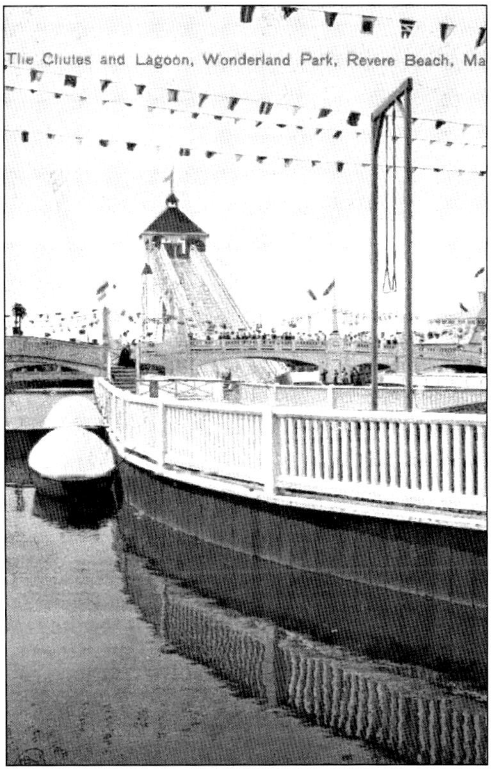

This Robbins Brothers postcard clearly illustrates the moat that encircled the Central Lagoon. At the center, a crowd of visitors has gathered on the expansive bridge to better view the exciting descent of the gondolas on the popular Shoot-the-Chutes, which served as the dominant amusement during the park's five-year reign as Greater Boston's premier pleasure park. At the left, two small canvas-covered boats silently await passengers. (Courtesy Jack Cook.)

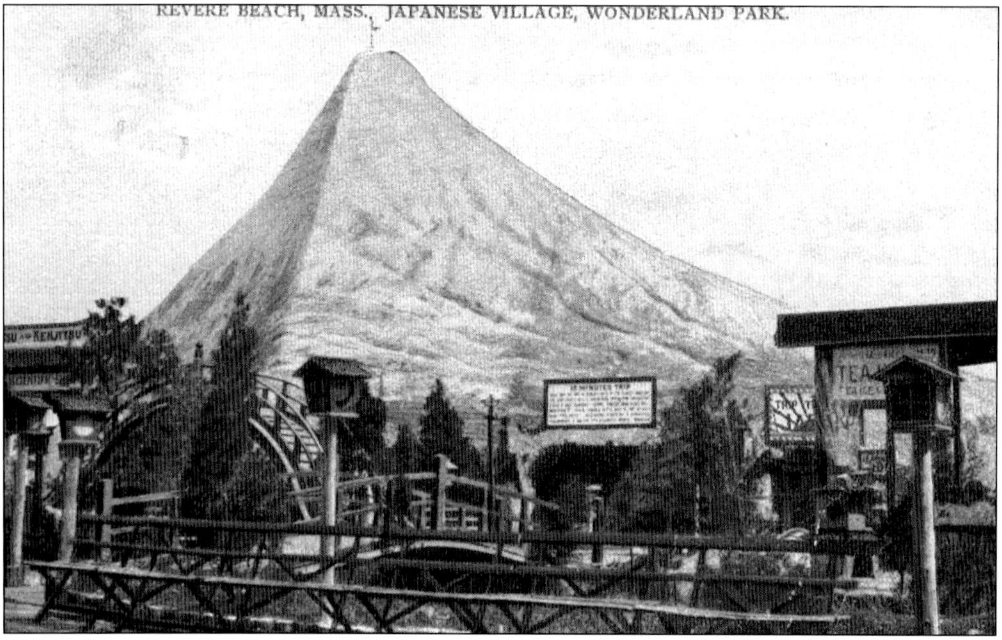

Sited adjacent to the Central Lagoon was the expansive Japanese Village exhibit, complete with a mammoth replica of Mount Fuji crafted from earth excavated during construction of the large lagoon. This marvelous attraction incorporated architectural and cultural aspects of the exotic and distant land. Visitors toured the free attraction at their own pace and often lingered at the pinnacle of the Royal Arch (left), built over a tranquil man-made stream. (Courtesy Jack Cook.)

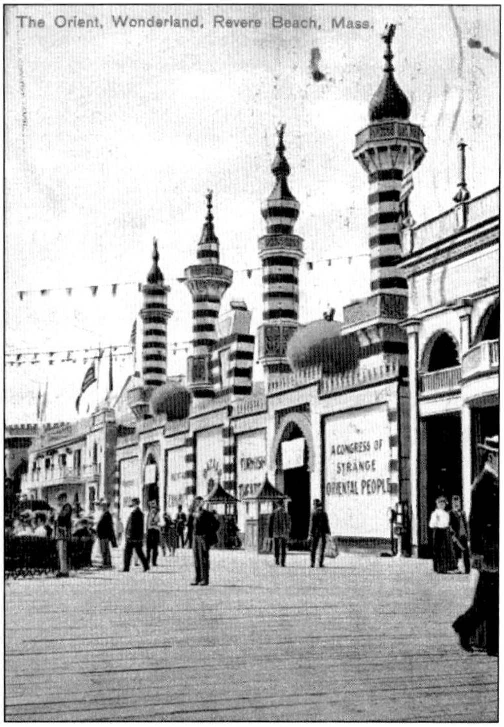

This Robbins Brothers of Boston postcard, postmarked September 17, 1909, portrays the prominent Wonderland attraction known as the Orient. Located near Thompson's Scenic Railway, the multifaceted, exotic-themed exhibit contained a live Turkish theater, a bazaar, and other related delights. The structure's lavish, mosque-like facade featured four distinctive towers. The disturbing proclamation at the center recalls a distant era in America when non–Anglo Saxon ethnicity evoked curiosity and wonder. (Courtesy Jack Cook.)

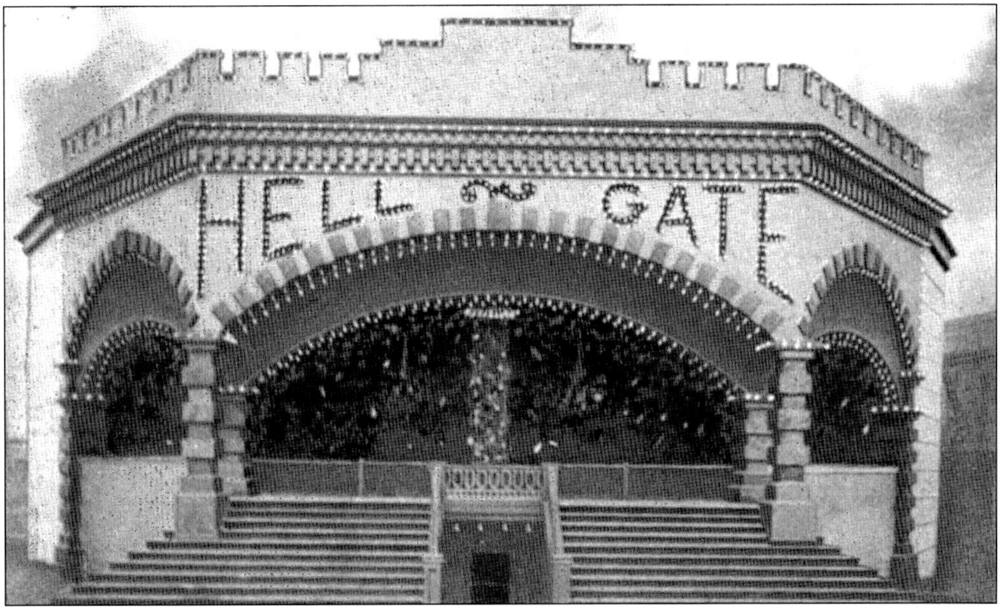

Dated September 16, 1907, the amusing inscription on the side of this postcard reads. "This is where Mrs. L and I were standing when your son tapped us on the shoulder a week ago—we did not try it." Allegedly loosely based on Dante's *Inferno*, Hell Gate was a fright-filled water attraction that conveyed passengers through a simulated underworld replete with sparse lighting, impish minions, and an encounter with Lucifer. (Courtesy Jack Cook.)

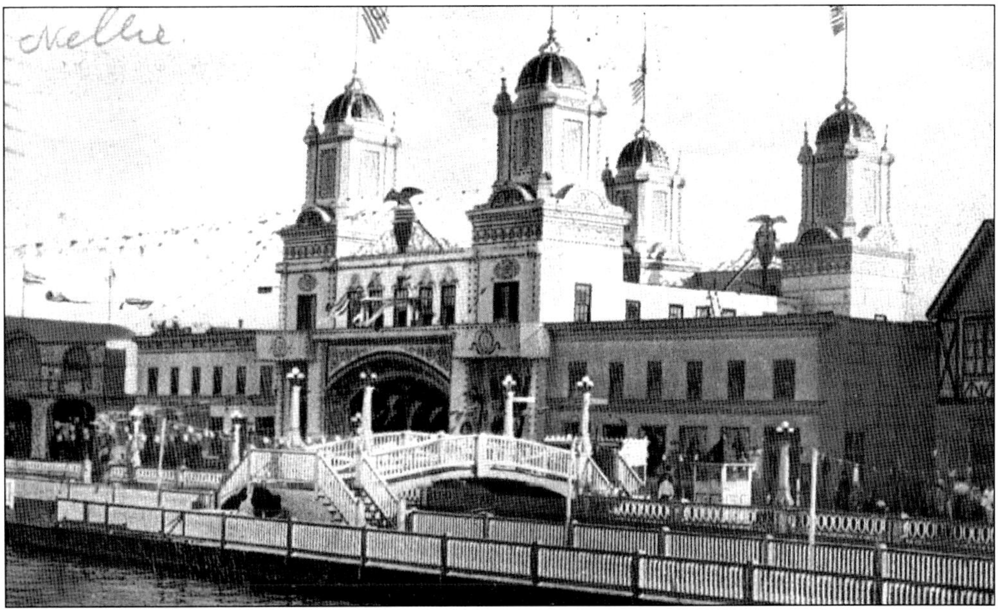

Reichner Brothers, with offices in both America and Germany, produced this postcard exhibiting Wonderland's stately main entrance and administration building. Viewed from the bridge spanning the Central Lagoon, the ornate, flag-surmounted structure proved a memorable passageway through which sated visitors returned to the routine of daily life. At the right stands the park's staffed hospital, which featured an innovative exhibit showcasing live premature infants receiving advanced medical care. (Courtesy Jack Cook.)

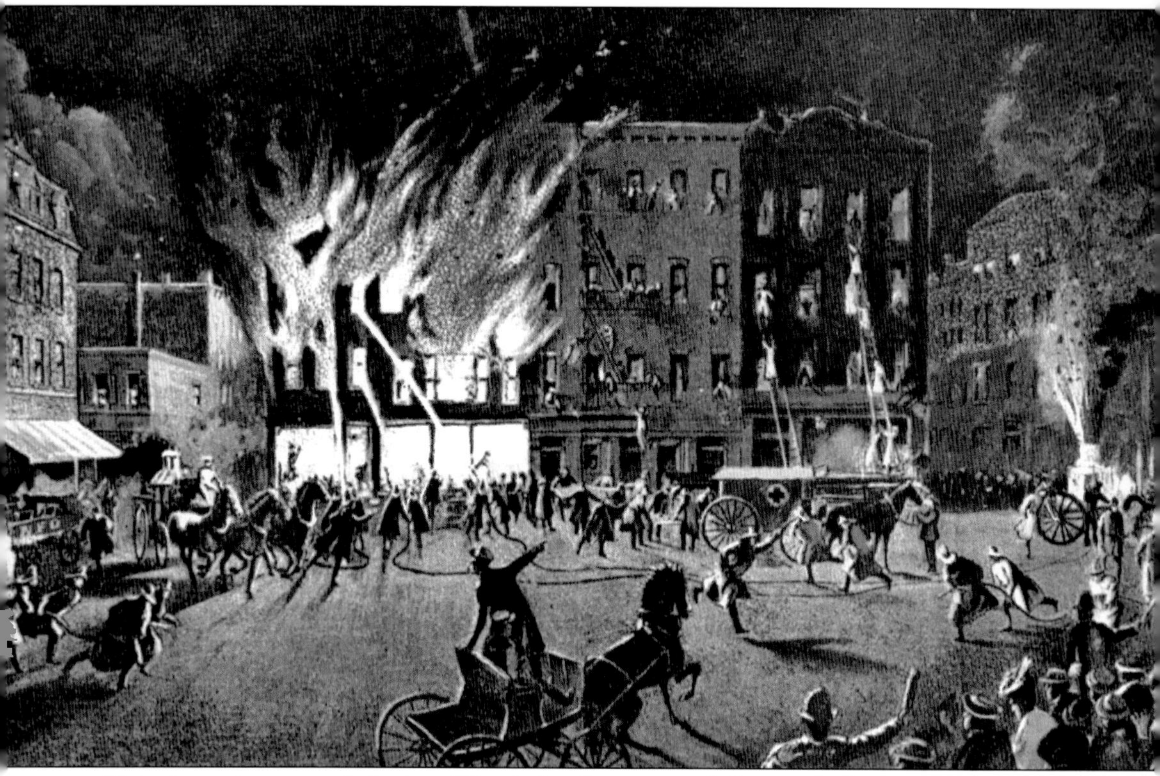

This dramatic postcard depicts Wonderland's renowned Fire and Flames attraction. Long considered the most spectacular theatrical production in Revere Beach history, this remarkable exhibit was produced by W.C. Manning and John J. Armstrong, who had operated a similar auspicious attraction at the 1904 St. Louis Exposition. Located in the park's eastern end, Fire and Flames featured a contrived cityscape constructed of steel and covered with a flammable substance. Twice daily, the set "accidentally" caught fire before an audience often exceeding 3,000, who were safely seated in a nearby grandstand. Hundreds of actors, some posing as unsuspecting victims and others portraying gallant policemen, scrambled about the flaming set as members of Wonderland's own fire department diligently toiled to extinguish the raging fire. The realistic performance was executed to perfection by gifted actors and professional firemen, whose expertise and employment of modern equipment consistently saved the day. By the end of the 1906 season, tremendous overhead costs exceeding $75,000 marked the swift demise of this sensational live exhibit. In 1908, Pawnee Bill's Wild West Show occupied the former site of Wonderland's hottest attraction. (Courtesy Jack Cook.)

Four

Beach Scenes

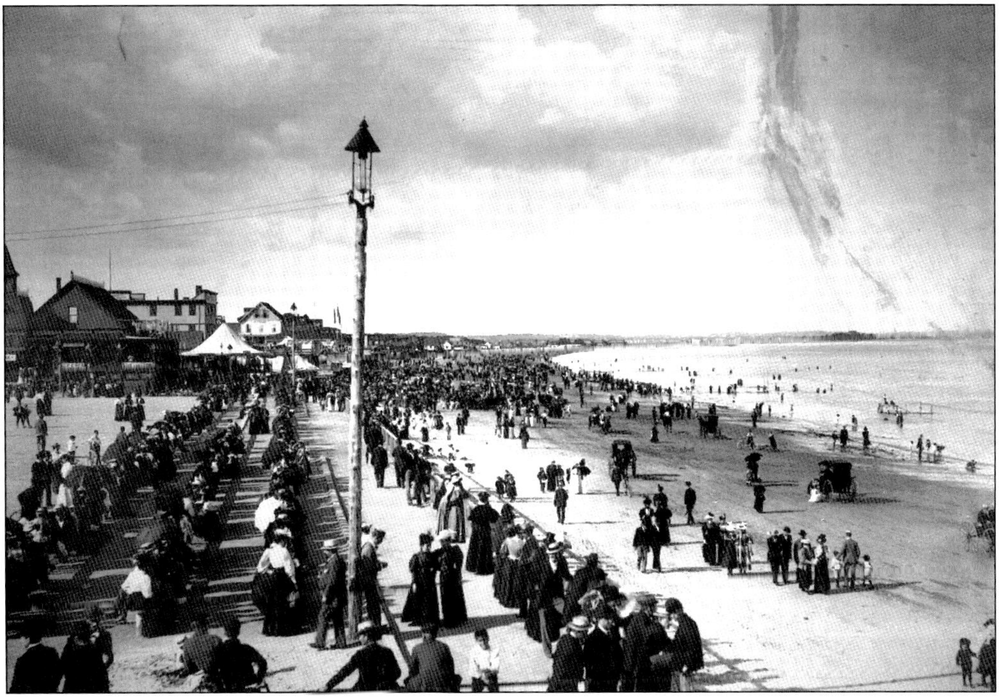

An unidentified photographer took this *c.* 1896 picture detailing typical warm-weather activity on Revere Beach toward the end of the 19th century. Shot from the foot of Beach Street, the photograph reveals a simplistic, wooden-railed promenade stretching toward a densely developed commercial district. At the center, a crude pole providing electric lighting heralds the dawning of a new age, as does the curiosity-provoking horseless carriage upon the beach at the right. (Courtesy Boston Public Library, Prints Department.)

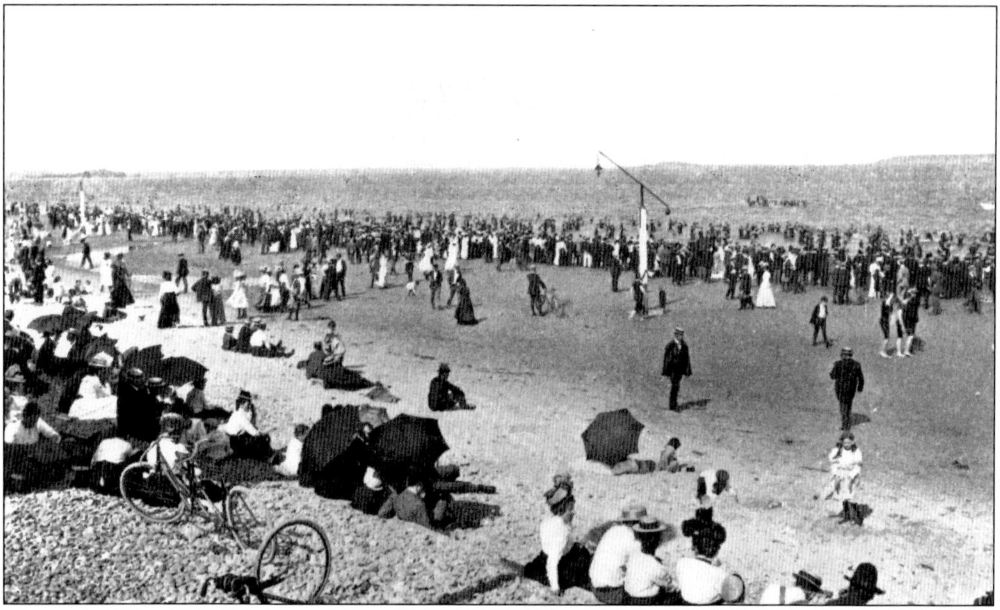

Unable to remain standing given the unstable nature of the terrain, a collapsed bicycle (foreground) rests abandoned on the rocks above the high-water mark in this 1901 photograph. Numerous seated visitors resourcefully employ broad parasols to ward off the sun's glare, while innumerable bathers in rented bathing costumes from the State Bath House crowd the shallow surf. (Courtesy MDC Archives, Boston.)

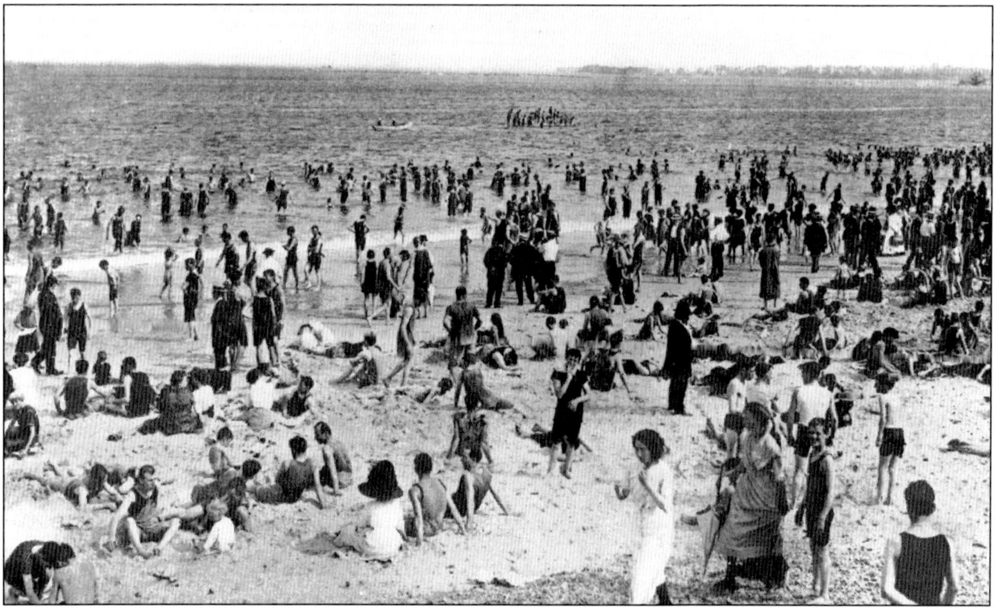

Bathers sporting rented black bathing suits from the State Bath House leisurely enjoy a summer afternoon in 1911 on Greater Boston's most popular ocean beach. Frequently, long-term bathing suit rentals on beautiful weekend days resulted in shortages of both suits and changing rooms, which, in turn, created long lines—and occasionally short tempers—at the popular Metropolitan Park Commission facility. (Courtesy Boston Public Library, Prints Department.)

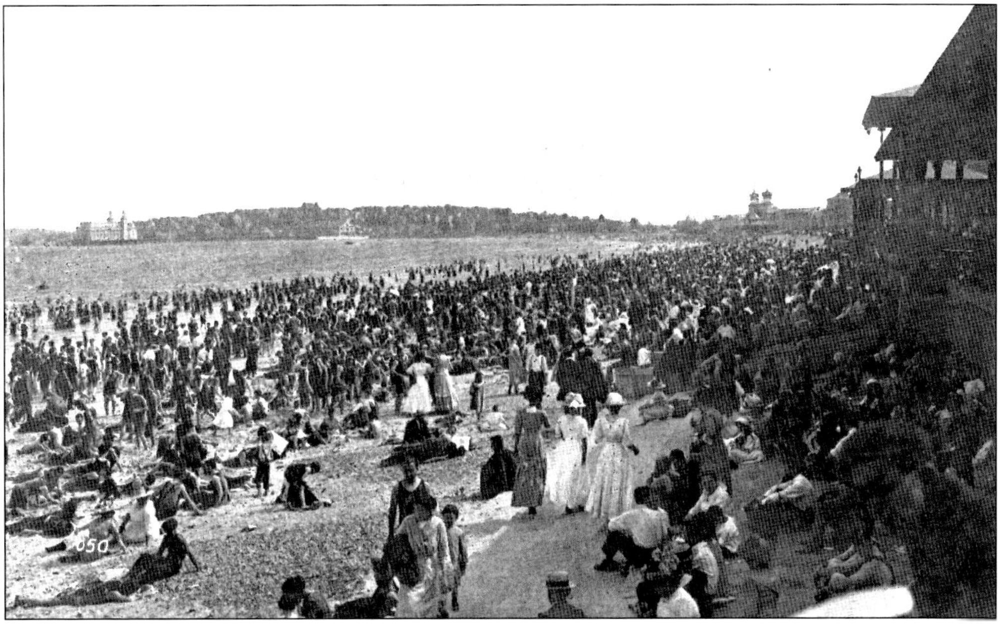

This photograph appeared in the *1913 Metropolitan Park Commission Annual Report* to illustrate the large summer crowds in attendance at Revere Beach Reservation. Visitors clad in white and dark clothes sit in the cooling shadow of the concrete-based pavilions while others dally upon the sand or wade in the gentle surf. At the far left center is the majestic hall located at Ocean Pier's seaward end followed by Ocean Pier Baths at the right. (Courtesy MDC Archives, Boston.)

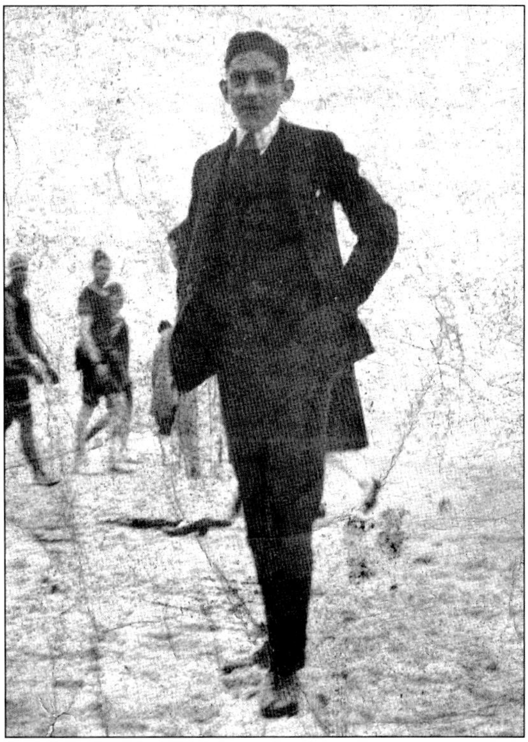

Dapper 16-year-old Moses Resnek poses on the sand near Shirley Avenue for an unidentified photographer during an outing to Revere Beach in 1917. Clad in a three-piece woolen suit and wearing handsome leather shoes, the young Chelsea resident enjoyed passing time with friends at Punk's Corner, a favorite scenic hangout for generations of respectable youth, located by the gracious bandstand and accompanying pavilions. (Courtesy Joshua Resnek.)

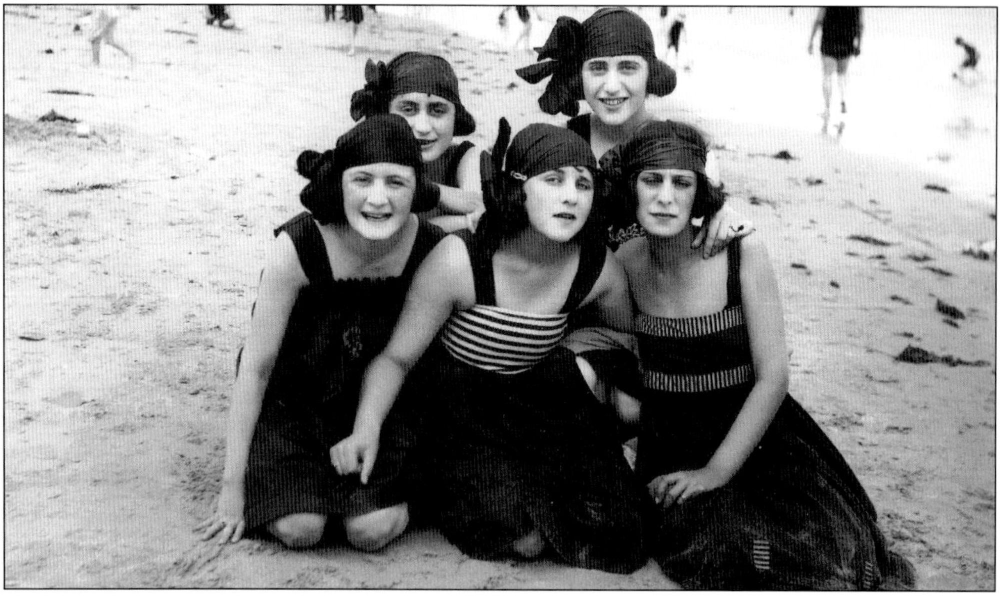

This 1919 photograph by Leslie Jones captures five darkly yet fashionably attired young women kneeling upon the sparsely packed sand. The unidentified girls wear long, sleeveless bathing costumes, whose hems bear abundant traces of seashore terrain. In contrast, their meticulously styled hair is carefully secured by attractive bathing kerchiefs. Around the small cluster of chums, the disturbed sand suggests that the beach has been well attended during the day. (Courtesy Boston Public Library, Prints Department.)

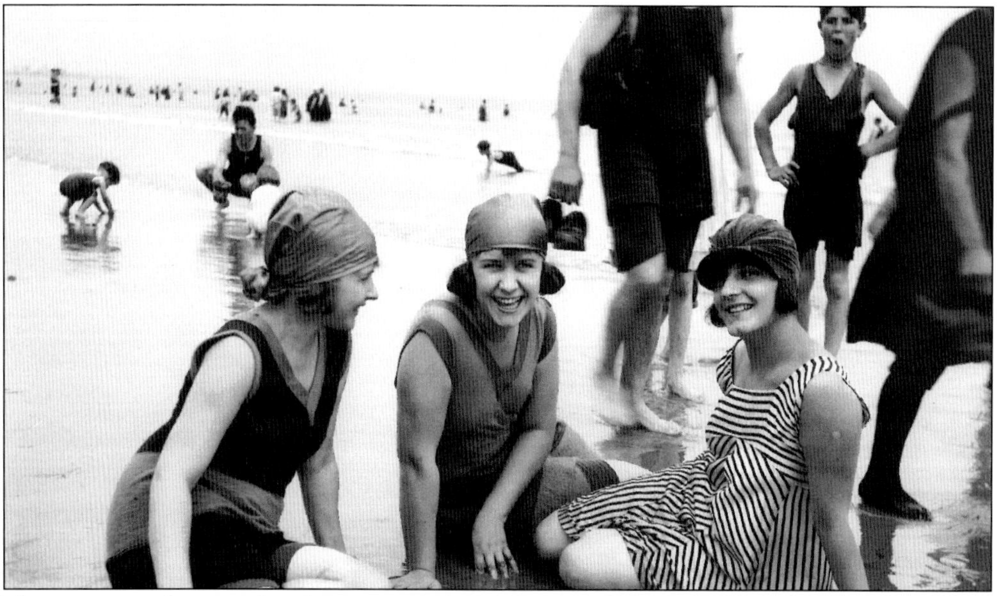

This amusing photograph taken in 1919 by *Boston Herald-Traveler* staff photographer Leslie Jones immortalizes the spirited verve of youth. In the foreground, three captivating young women laugh as they recline in the shallow surf at water's edge. Behind them, an animated adolescent boy contemplates the camera with a confounded expression as if he wishes to convey doubt concerning the photographic merit of the subjects before him. (Courtesy Boston Public Library, Prints Department.)

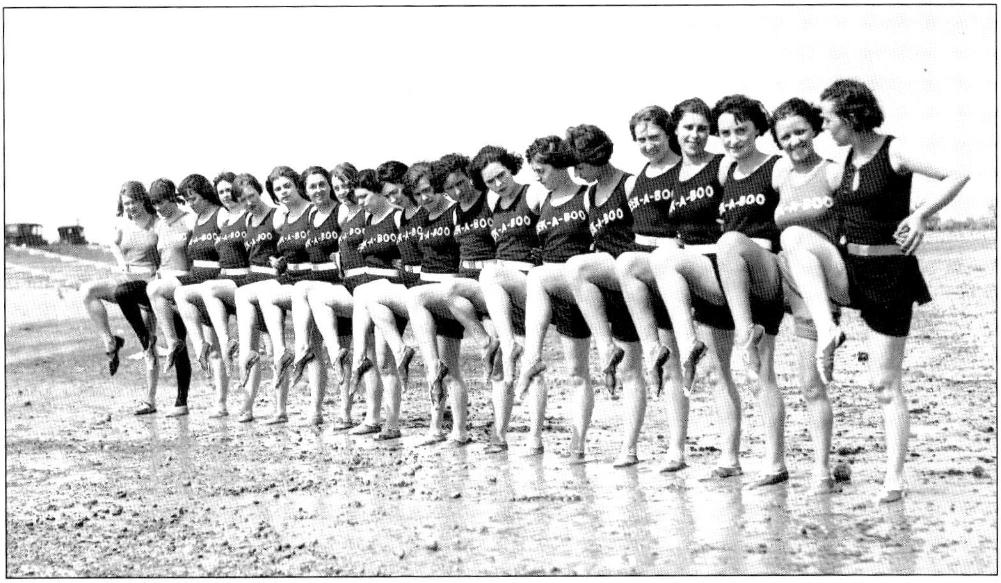

These 20 young women, most wearing sleeveless costumes with "peek-a-boo" emblazoned across the front, pose in classic chorus-line fashion for professional photographer Leslie Jones on Revere Beach in 1919. The faces of the unidentified performers betray a range of expressions including intent concentration, mild confusion, and abject confidence. At the left, two automobiles are parked alongside the concrete-stepped shore protection, which extends northward. (Courtesy Boston Public Library, Prints Department.)

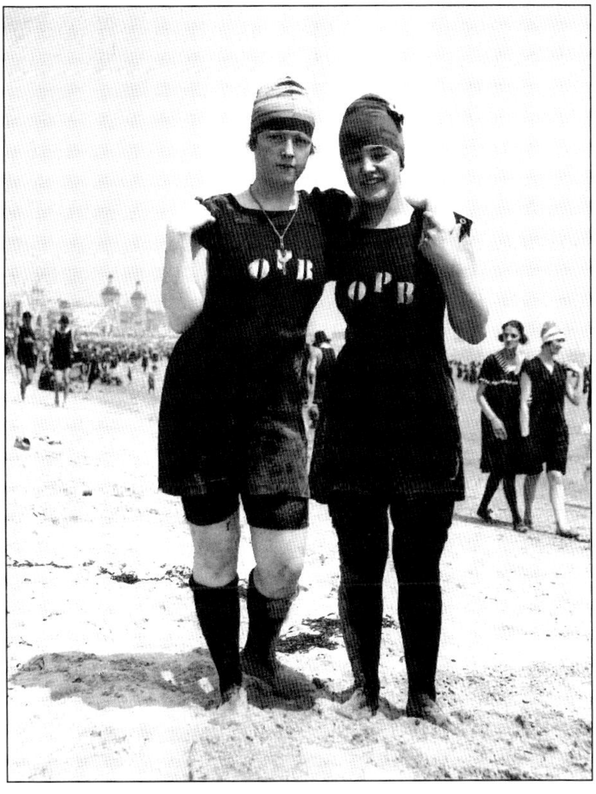

These two compliant chums, clad in rented suits from Ocean Pier Baths, smile demurely for photographer Leslie Jones during a 1919 visit to Revere Beach. A locker key dangles around the neck of the young woman at the left. During this period, one could rent a suit, locker, and towel from the popular facility for a nominal fee. In the background, the two spires of the Nautical Garden are readily apparent. (Courtesy Boston Public Library, Prints Department.)

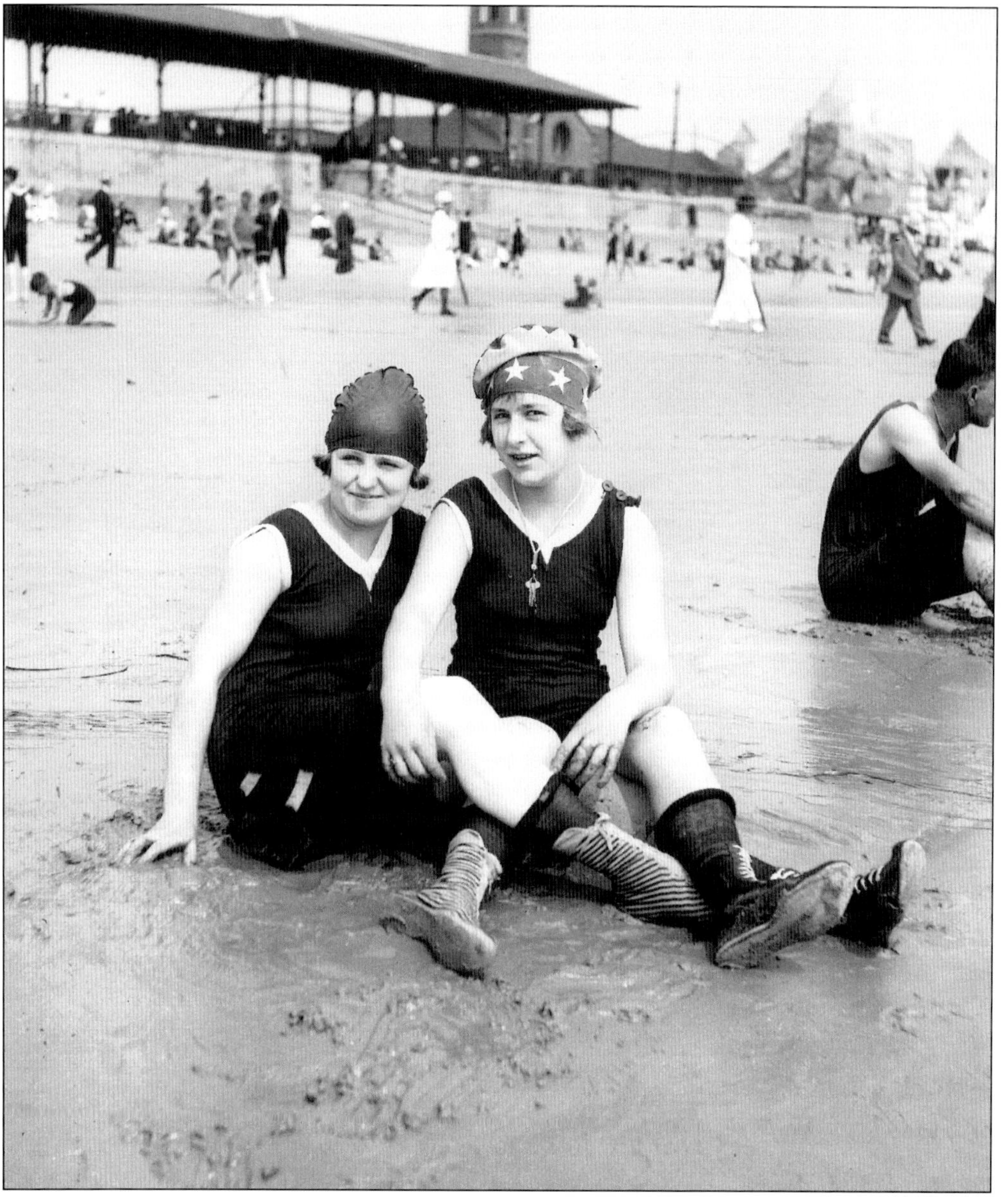

Captured on film by prolific photographer Leslie Jones in 1919, two close friends sit on the damp sand opposite the State Bath House Pavilions and flash tentative smiles for the camera. The young woman at the right sports a decorative starred bathing cap and wears around her neck a silver key, which may open a rented locker in the nearby State Bath House. Behind the subjects, a pedestrian tunnel entrance leading to the Metropolitan District Commission facility is clearly visible. At the upper center stands the stately police station, with its tower divided into three distinct sections, each separated by a granite beltcourse. The top section contains an observation deck. In this photograph, double-arched, open-air windows look eastward out to sea and southward toward Boston. These openings, separated by granite columns and featuring low granite balustrades, were later protectively enclosed with plate glass. The large ocular window visibly gracing the building's gabled central section has been protectively preserved as well. (Courtesy Boston Public Library, Prints Department.)

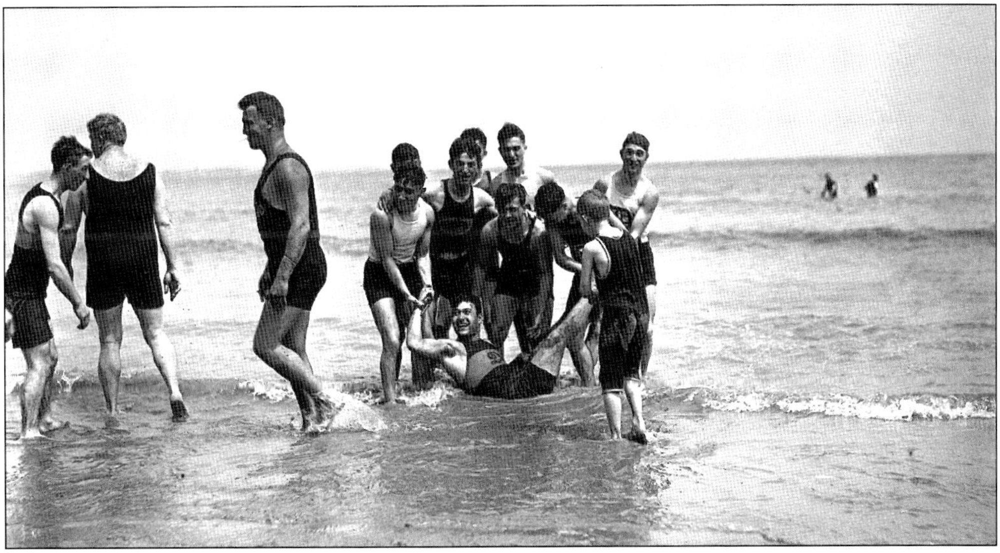

Their roguish antics recorded on film, unidentified members of the Dummy Associates grin blatantly before the camera in this spirited 1921 photograph. The mischievous young men have apparently soaked the good-natured fellow at the center. However, the bemused expression of the cigarette-sporting man sloshing through the surf at the left suggests that he might have had an initial stake in the impish behavior transpiring behind him. (Courtesy Boston Public Library, Prints Department.)

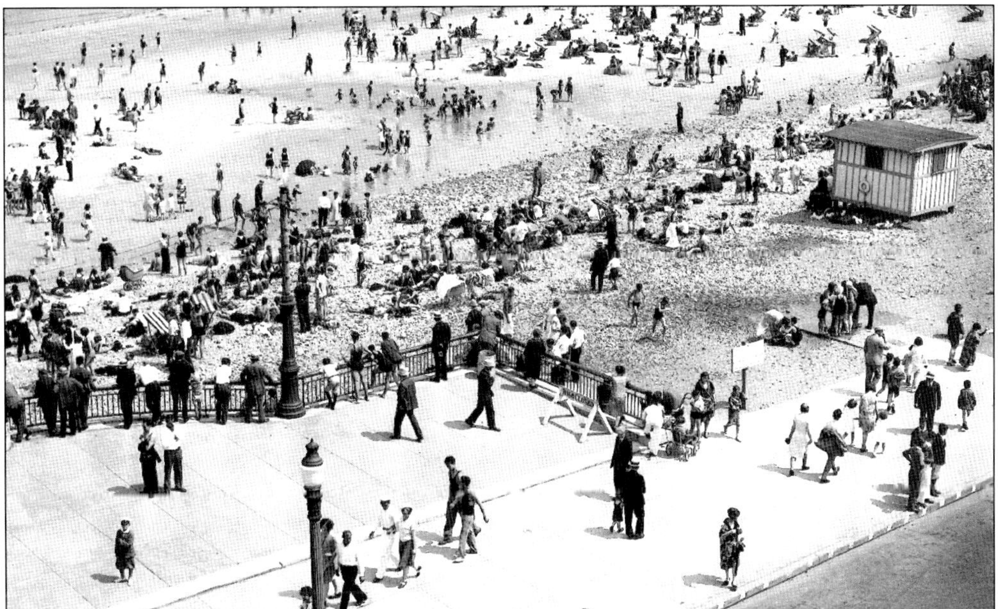

In this 1920s-era beach scene photographed by Leslie Jones, people of all ages and in various attire enjoy themselves on an undisclosed southerly stretch of sand. Prominently featured in this picture is a broad promenade with ample iron-railed observation area. To left of center stands an isolated electrical pole topped by an unprotected light bulb. A gaily striped wooden cabana stands on the sand at the right. (Courtesy Boston Public Library, Prints Department.)

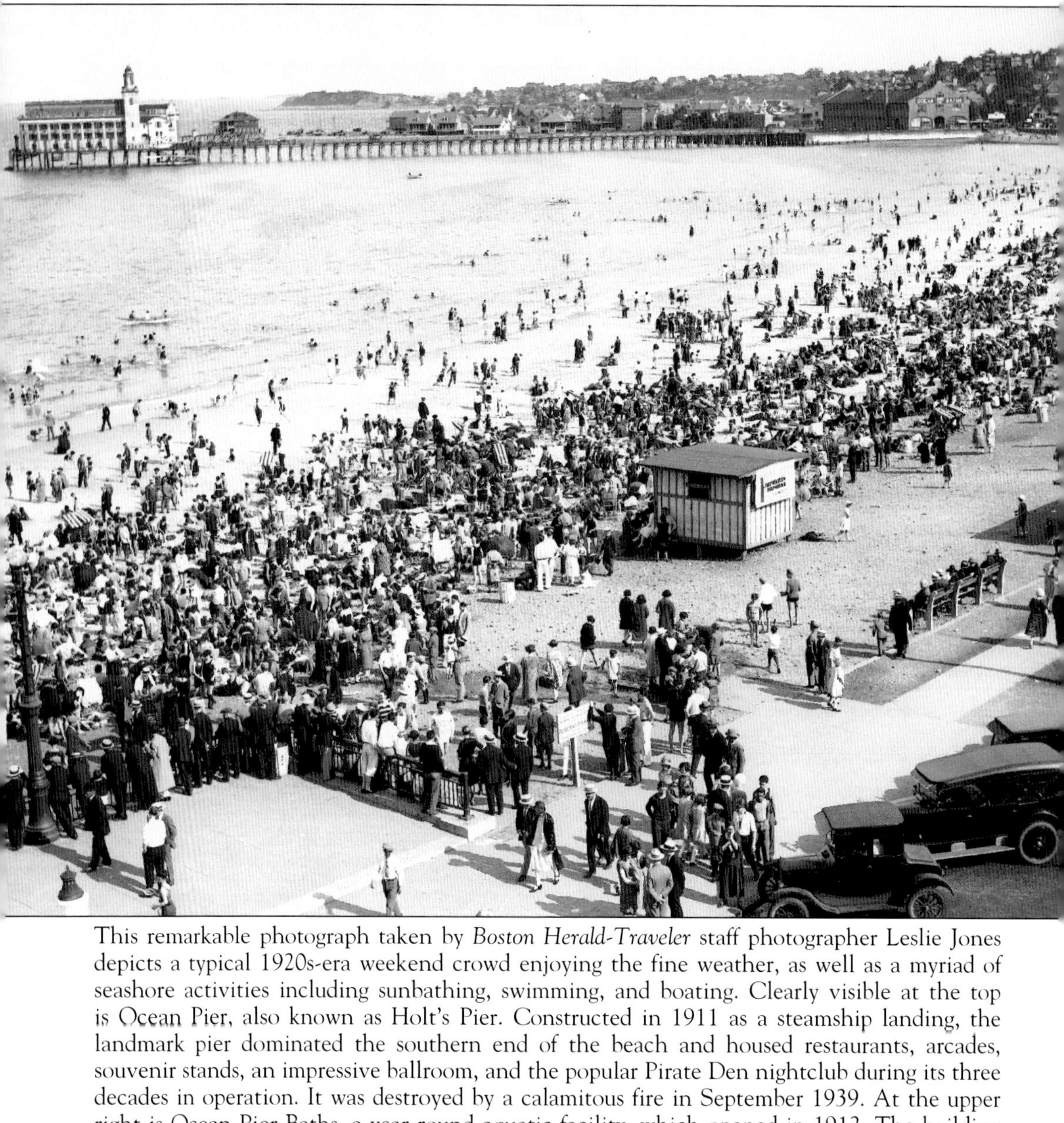

This remarkable photograph taken by *Boston Herald-Traveler* staff photographer Leslie Jones depicts a typical 1920s-era weekend crowd enjoying the fine weather, as well as a myriad of seashore activities including sunbathing, swimming, and boating. Clearly visible at the top is Ocean Pier, also known as Holt's Pier. Constructed in 1911 as a steamship landing, the landmark pier dominated the southern end of the beach and housed restaurants, arcades, souvenir stands, an impressive ballroom, and the popular Pirate Den nightclub during its three decades in operation. It was destroyed by a calamitous fire in September 1939. At the upper right is Ocean Pier Baths, a year-round aquatic facility, which opened in 1912. The building contained two heated saltwater swimming pools and offered bathing suit rentals as well as swimming lessons. During its later years, Ocean Pier Baths advertised the medicinal benefits of soaking in its hot saltwater tubs. The enormous wood-and-stucco structure was itself consumed by flames on April 19, 1945. (Courtesy Boston Public Library, Prints Department.)

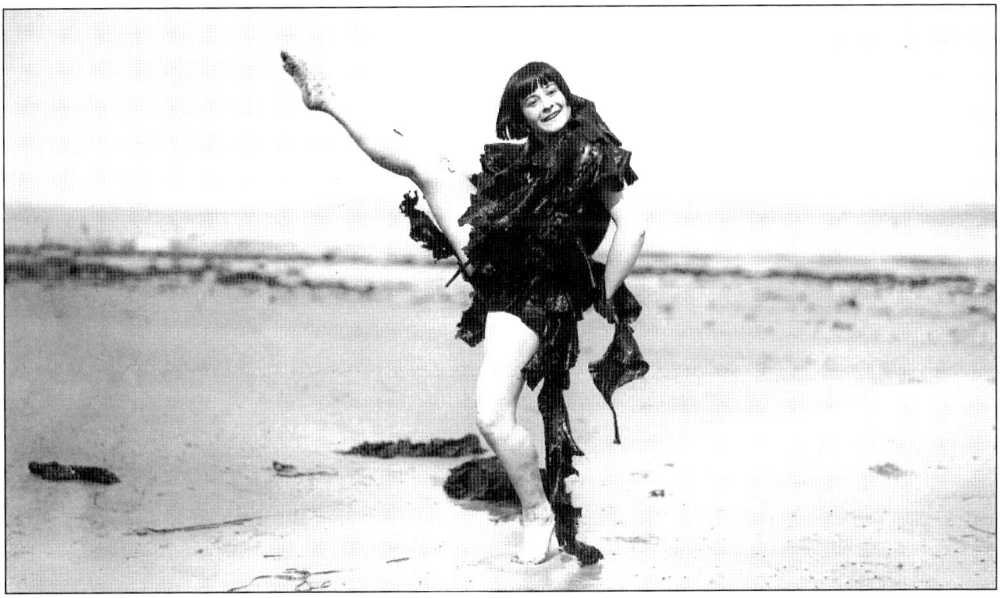

Gertrude Fuller extends a sandy foot toward the sky in this playful 1930 photograph snapped by Leslie Jones. Clad in black aquatic attire typical of the period, she has draped her animated frame with an ample garland plucked off the seaweed-strewn shore. Her clever costume is further enhanced by the broad smile adorning her youthful face. (Courtesy Boston Public Library, Prints Department.)

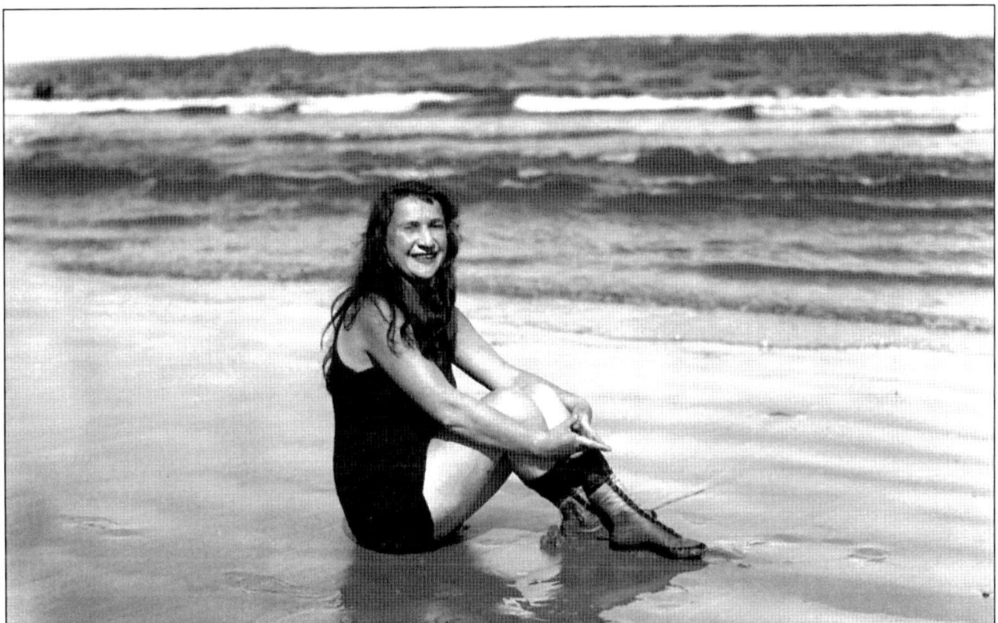

Sitting placidly in the wave-etched shoals at the ocean's edge, local shore enthusiast Eileen Geller of 49 Dix Street strikes a modest pose before the camera of Leslie Jones. Wearing laced aquatic footwear extending well above the ankle, she smiles reticently as her dark tresses cascade unbound to chastely conceal her shoulders. (Courtesy Boston Public Library, Prints Department.)

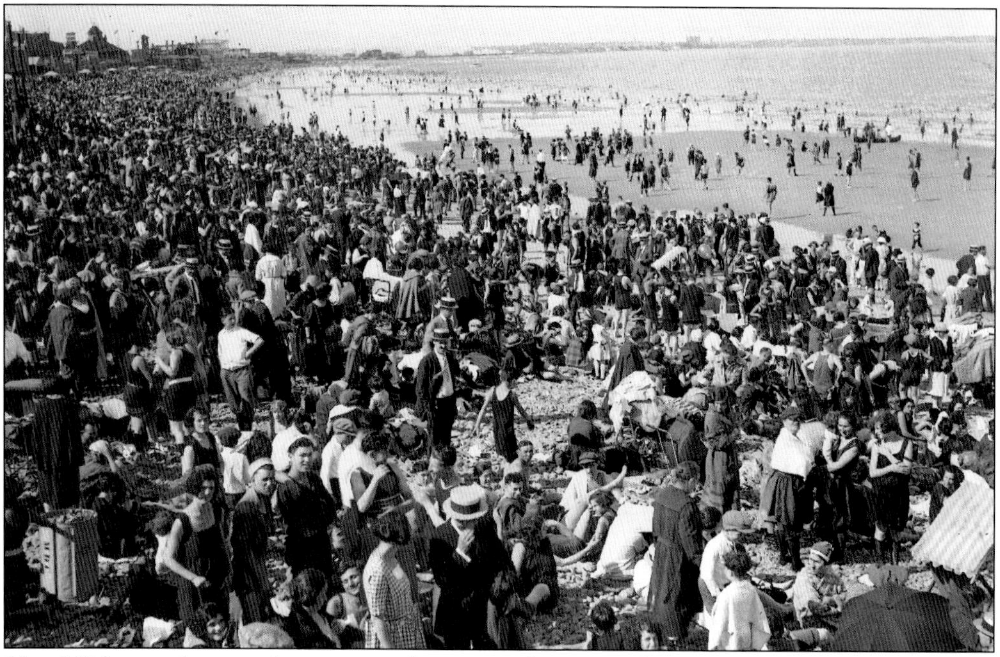

This 1930s-era photograph attests to the tremendous appeal Revere Beach had generated by the third decade of the 20th century. Battalions of bathers crowd the beach and clamor to stake claim to tiny parcels of sand so that they might enjoy the many delights of a populated seashore resort. Women exhibiting bobbed hair and lengthy, sleeveless bathing suits comfortably coexist with men sporting cropped cuts and chest-concealing aquatic attire. (Courtesy Boston Public Library, Prints Department.)

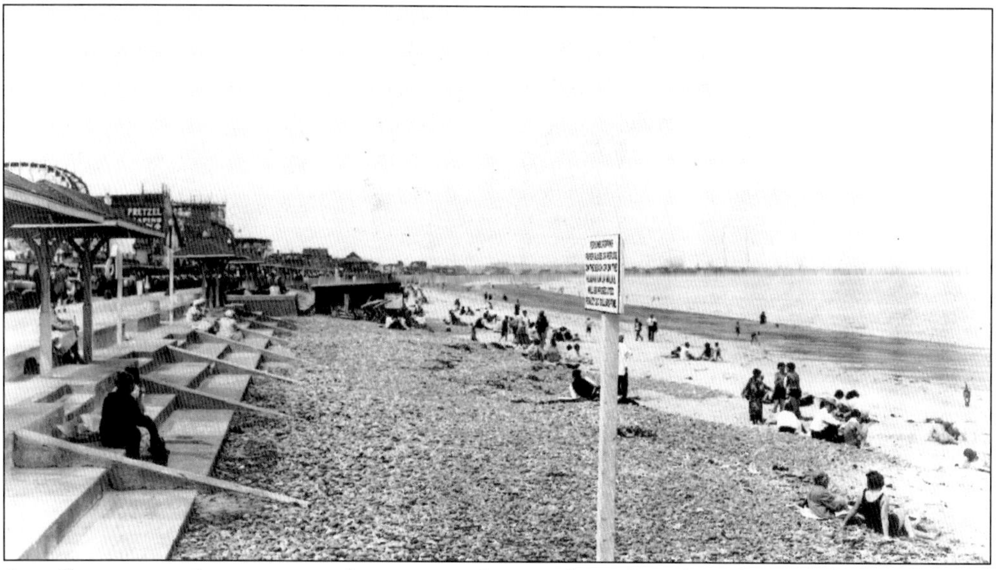

A well-represented amusement district stretches northward in this photograph taken during the 1930s. Wide, gently sloping concrete steps complete with several sun shelters, provide easy passage from the beach onto a broad promenade lined with automobiles. By 1936, parking lines for 1,111 vehicles had been painted between Eliot and Northern Circles. The sign at the center warns of a $20 fine imposed for littering. (Courtesy Massachusetts Archives.)

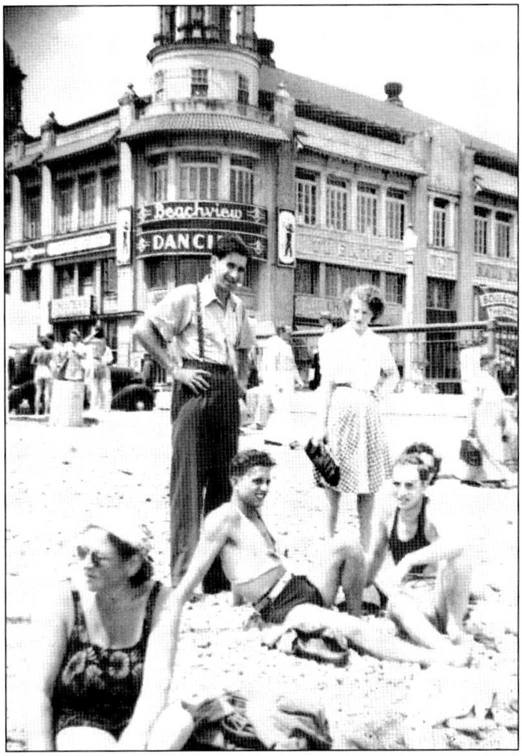

The magnificent Crescent Gardens proves an impressive backdrop to those reclining on the sand in this 1941 photograph. From left to right are the following: (front row) unidentified; (middle row) "Squeakie" ? and Ralph Fritz; (back row) Nathan Abrams and Honey Cutler. When this snapshot was taken, the looming landmark had been a familiar site along Revere Beach Boulevard for approximately 40 years and housed the Beachview Ballroom and the Boulevard Theatre. (Courtesy Jack Cook.)

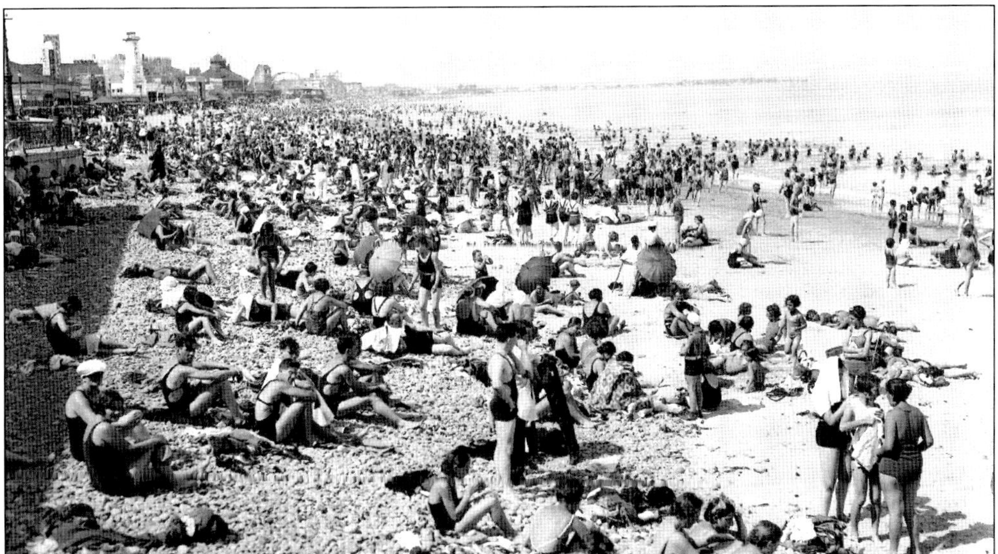

This c. 1950 photograph depicts a well-populated central section of shore replete with sun and conventional saltwater bathers. Sited along the Revere Beach Boulevard at the left are amusements and attractions that appear to extend northward into infinity, including the State Ballroom, the lighthouse-towered Nautical Amusement Center, State Bath House, and the Metropolitan District Commission Police Station. Behind the Italian Renaissance building curve the graceful elevated contours of the Cyclone and Thunderbolt. (Boston Public Library, Prints Department.)

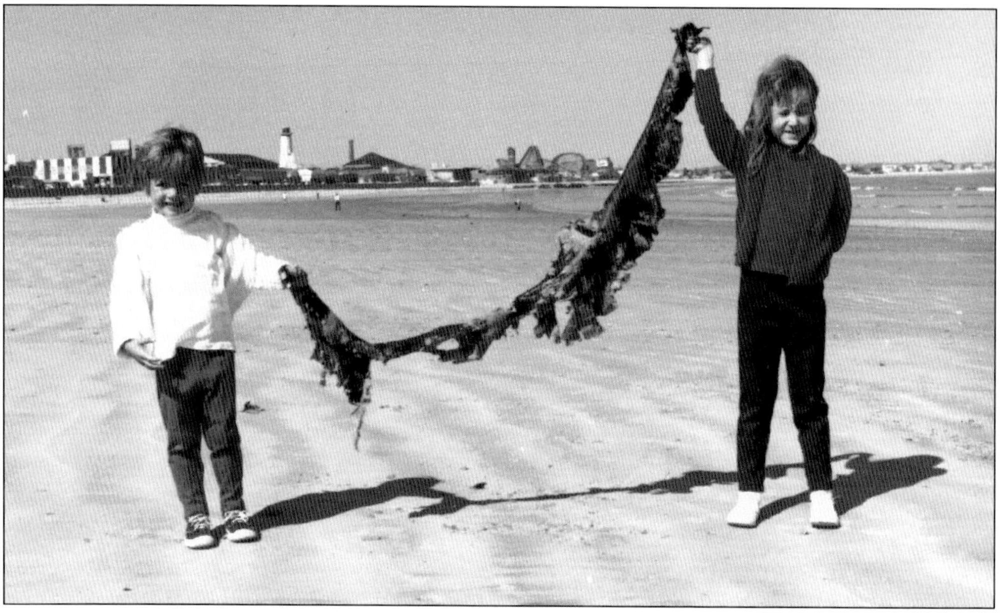

Sisters Judy (left) and Tammy Moscaritolo swing a large ribbon of seaweed between them during a September jaunt to Revere Beach in 1969. Behind them, the remaining attractions located along Revere Beach Boulevard extend toward Revere Street. From left to right stand the red-and-white-striped Bazaar, contemporary bathhouse, Nautical Bowling Alley, and Cyclone coaster. (Courtesy Jack Cook.)

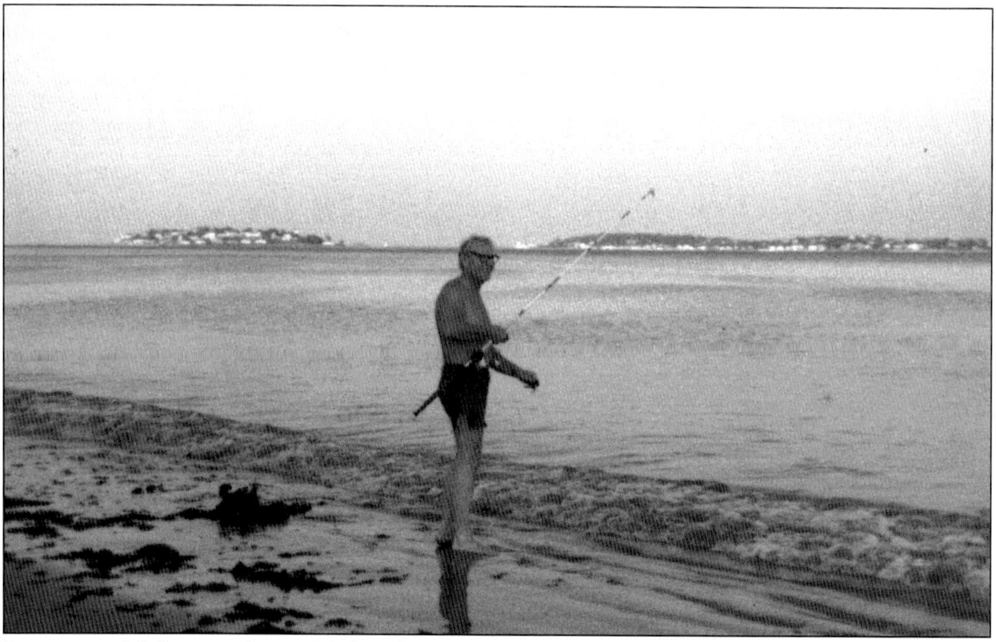

Recreational fisherman Samuel Schmidt gingerly approaches the seaweed-laden edge of the calm Atlantic with baited rod in hand during a 1970s-era August afternoon. Hailing from the Midwest, the water sports-minded anesthesiologist (and father of the author) enjoyed fishing for bluefish and sailing off the coast of Greater Boston's crescent-shaped beach, despite the fact that he had never learned to swim. Behind him, Nahant is clearly visible. (Courtesy Leah Schmidt.)

Five

RIDES AND ATTRACTIONS

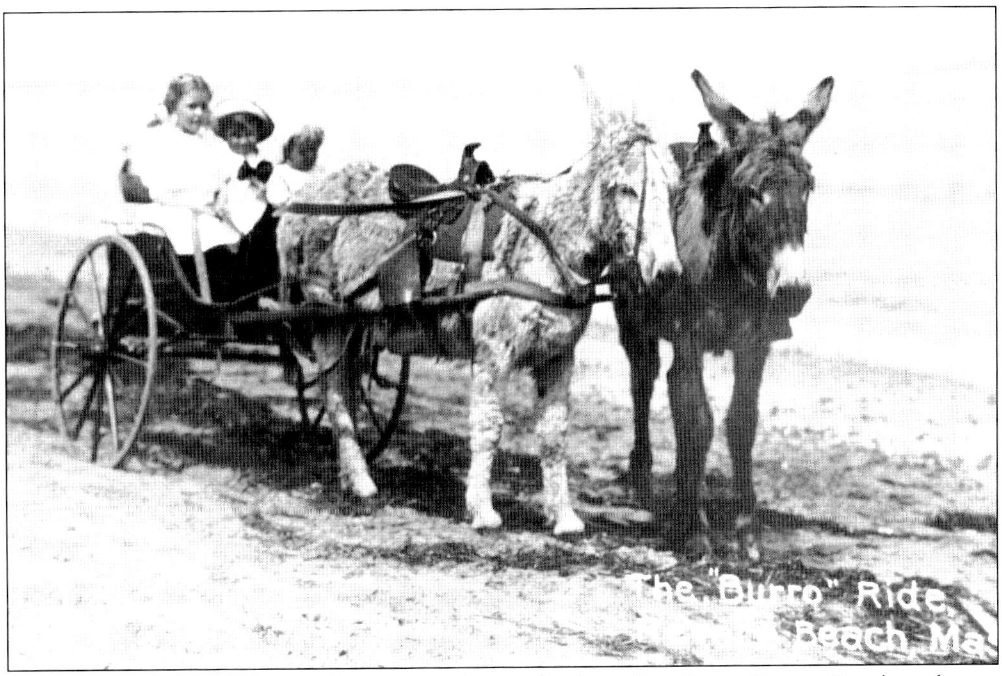

The donkey rides were a popular activity that took place directly on Revere Beach and were first noted in print locally during the late 19th century. This photograph depicts two gentle burros drawing a modest two-wheeled carriage bearing three children along an unidentified stretch of soft sand. A nominal nickel fee entitled the payee to an approximate half-mile round-trip excursion. (Courtesy City of Revere.)

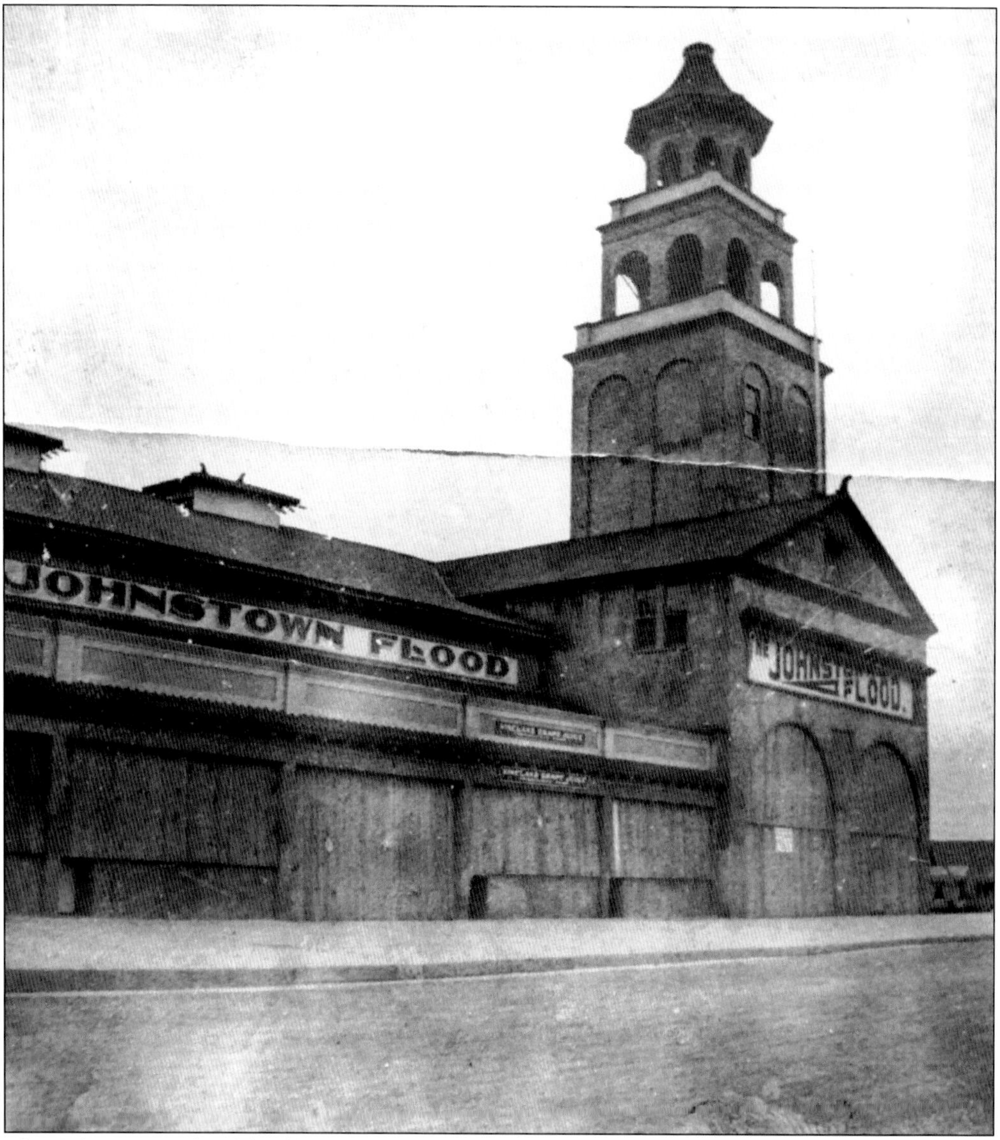

The Johnstown Flood building was located north of the State Bath House toward Revere Street. Boasting possession of the largest stage in Greater Boston, the early-20th-century attraction seated more than 1,000 people and realistically replicated the destruction of the great dam whose unrestrained waters flooded Johnstown, Pennsylvania, in 1889. Opened in June 1903, the engaging theatrical experience was reenacted hourly and covered the fateful period from 10 hours before the damaging waters arrived to five hours after the dam broke and effectively drowned the western Pennsylvanian town. The structure's tiered tower, capped by a small-windowed cupola, was reported to be the tallest of any contemporary construction then located along the beachfront roadway. The structure included flame-retardant metallic shingling concealed beneath external paneling, which helped to arrest the progression of a destructive neighboring fire in 1904. The facility further featured open-air construction, which enabled refreshing Atlantic Ocean breezes to flow freely throughout the building and cool its inhabitants. Two years after it debuted, the $40,000 attraction was destroyed by fire, which, ironically, no amount of water could extinguish. (Courtesy Jack Cook.)

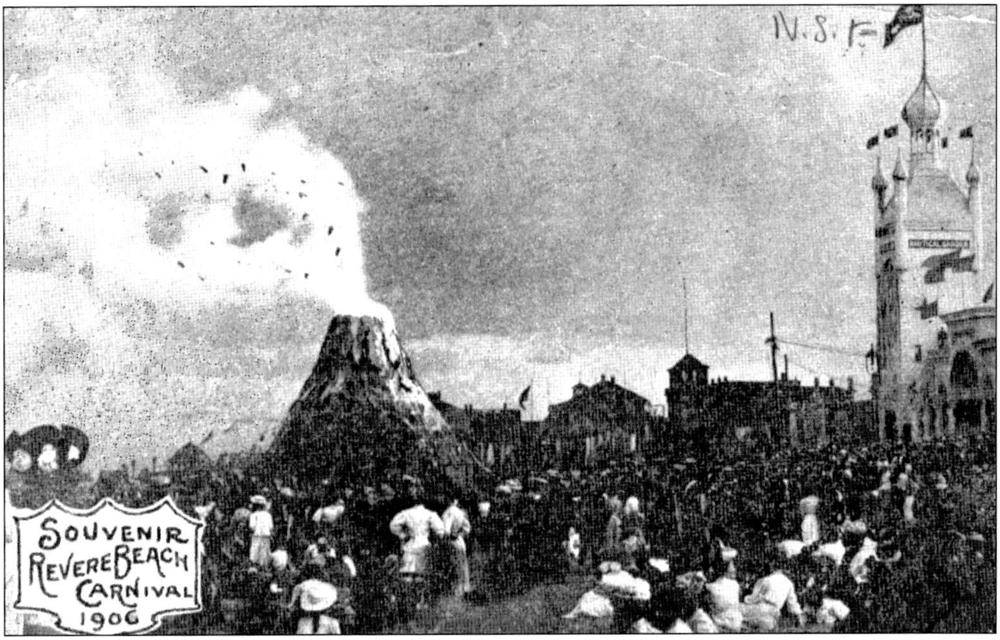

This cleverly crafted wire-and-papier-maché attraction, named for the notorious Italian volcano Mount Vesuvious, was created by noted local businessman Herbert Ridgeway. Sited directly on the sand in front of the Nautical Garden, this splendid simulated volcano erected for Carnival Week of 1906 remained standing for two weeks. The illuminated marvel erupted on cue, ejecting into the air souvenir postcards accompanied by thick smoke and thunderous noise. (Courtesy Jack Cook.)

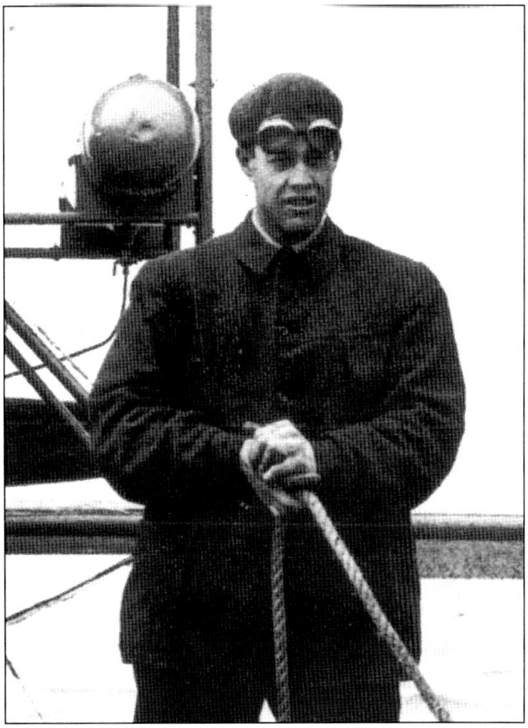

One Sunday in July 1914, Clifford L. Webster participated in a flying exhibition on Revere Beach arranged by the *Boston American*. Webster was the company aviator for the Marblehead-based Burgess Company & Curtis. An enormous crowd witnessed his impressive climbs and other thrilling feats executed in the company's Burgess-Dunne hydroaeroplane. This rare 1915 photograph captures the boyishly handsome young pilot with an accompanying aircraft. (Courtesy Carroll F. Gray Aeronautical Collection.)

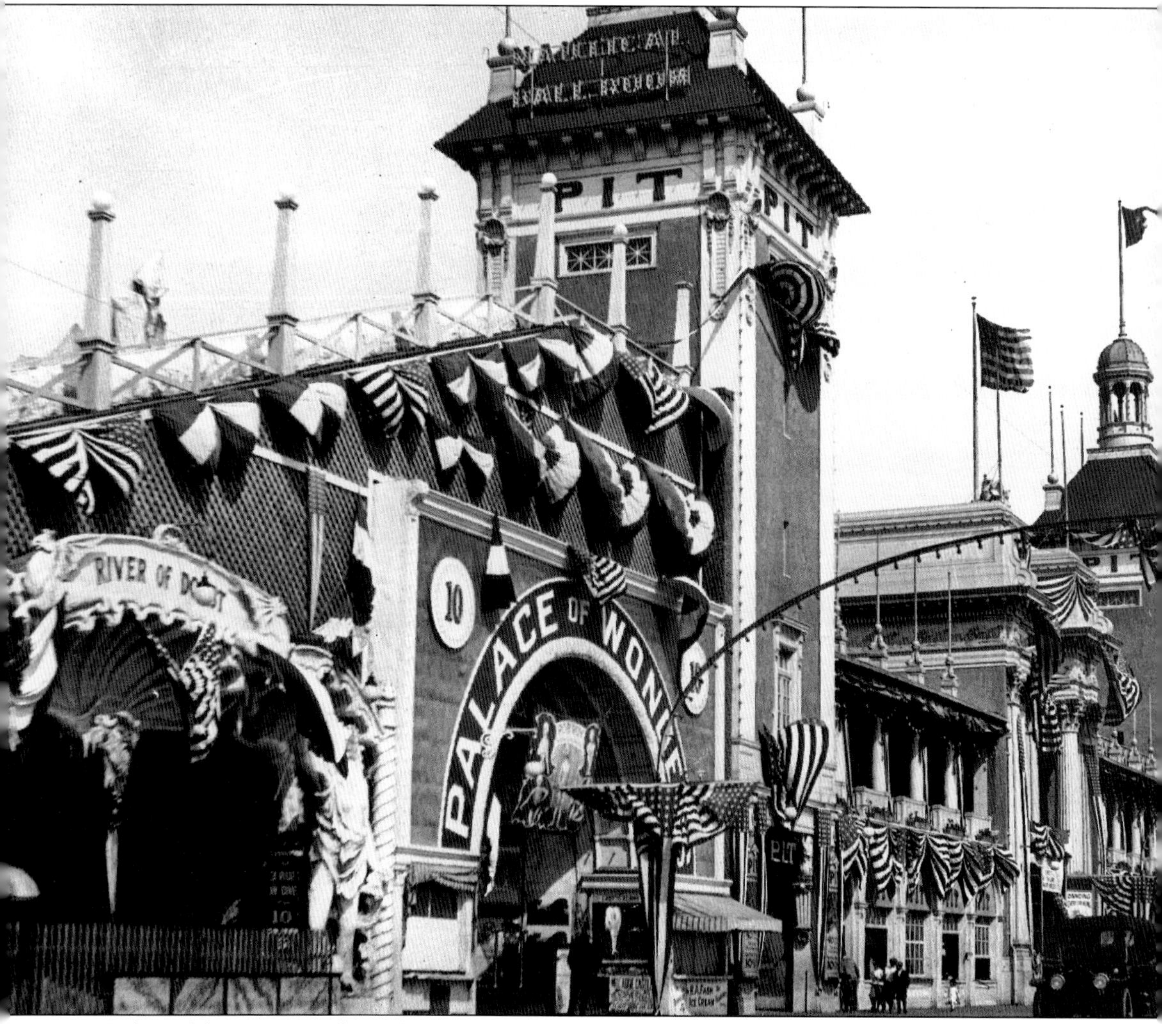

Believed by many to have been the most elaborate structure on the beach, the impressive Nautical Garden, complete with two massive 140-foot towers, presided over Revere Beach Boulevard for decades. The facility evolved from a modest structure in 1902 that housed a submarine ride to an ornate, palatial landmark in 1908 containing a ballroom accessible by grand staircase and central lobby. The Nautical Garden is perhaps best known for its popular fun house called the Pit, which was created by owner Herbert Ridgeway and incorporated many of his patented creations. The building also housed the Palace of Wonders, an attraction that showcased oddities. In 1918 and 1928, the Garden suffered two ravenous fires, only to be determinedly rebuilt again. Following the second fire, the Nautical Garden contained an enormous saltwater swimming pool, which hosted the Olympic sectional tryouts in 1932. The building later housed Scoota-boats and an amusement center with bowling alleys. The facility was destroyed by the Blizzard of 1978. (Courtesy Jack Cook.)

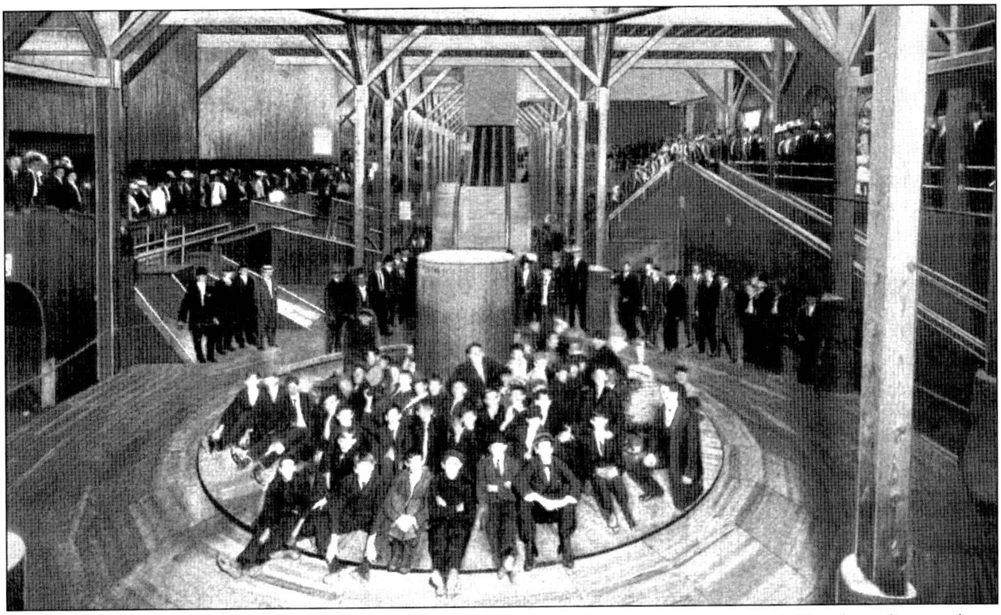

Occupying the sublevel and part of the first floor of the stately Nautical Garden, located on the corner of Beaver Street, was the Pit fun house. The product of owner Herbert Ridgeway's admirable ingenuity, the improved amusement facility opened in 1908. This 1915 postcard details the spacious wooden interior, which provided multiple levels of unexpected thrills. Popular attractions housed within included the Wheel of Fortune (pictured here) and the Avalanche. (Courtesy Boston Public Library, Prints Department.)

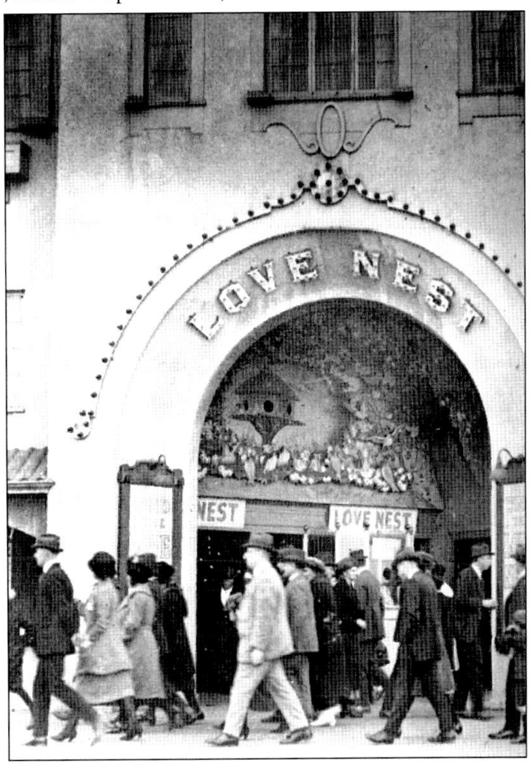

Following the devastating fire that consumed the palatial Nautical Garden in 1918, the facility was rebuilt and reopened the following year. The grand structure, featuring a central domed tower, stood for approximately 10 years before another conflagration necessitated an additional architectural resurrection. During the 1920s, the landmark housed a spacious ballroom, a noted fun house, and a variety of lesser amusements including the avian attraction known as Love Nest. (Courtesy City of Revere.)

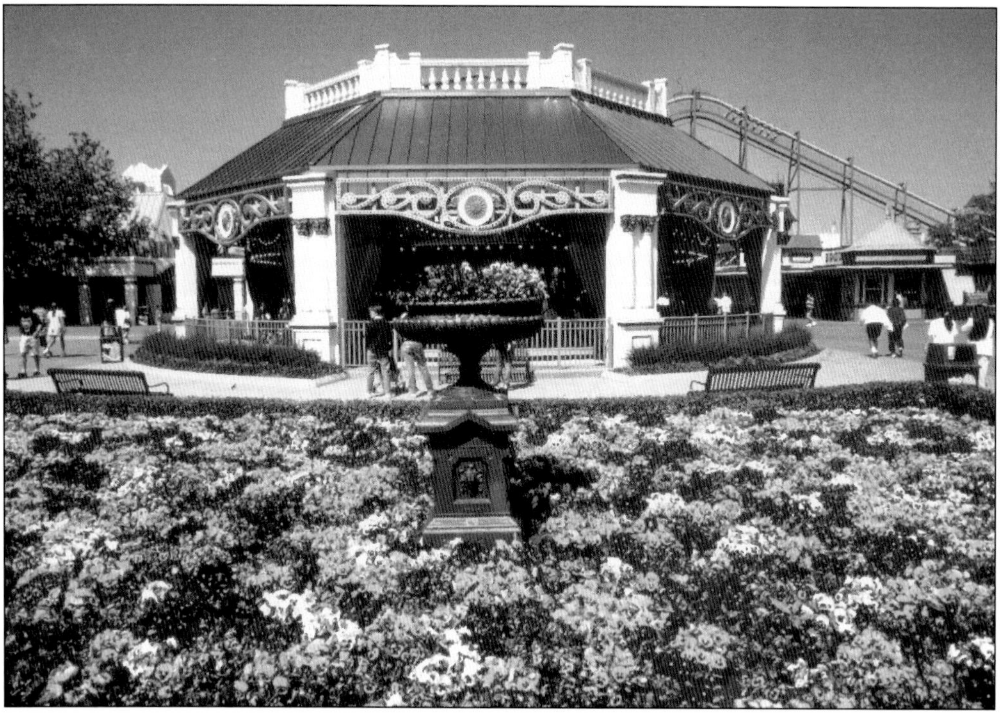

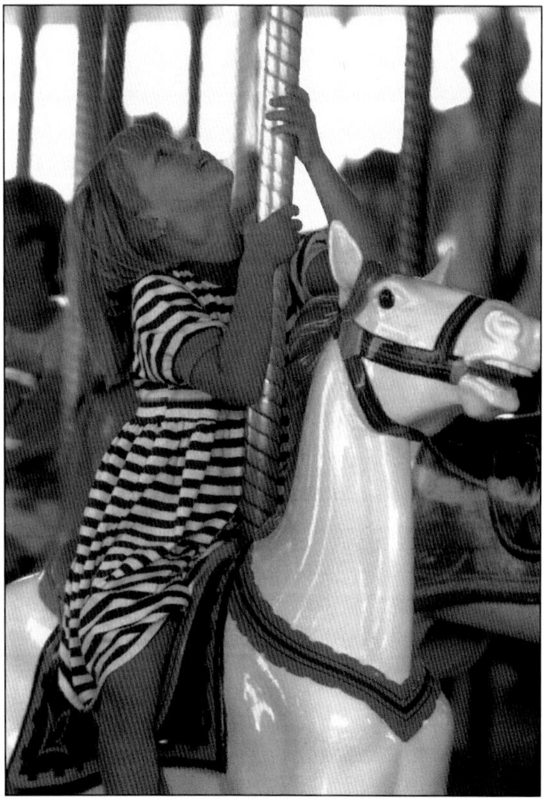

Currently in operation as the Midway Carousel at Cedar Point in Sandusky, Ohio, this historic amusement machine was created in 1912 for John J. Hurley of Revere Beach. Hurley's Hurdlers operated successfully for many years and proved to be one of the grandest and most popular amusements on Revere Beach Boulevard. Ornately hand-carved by master craftsman Daniel Muller, this was originally a five-abreast carousel featuring jumping horses and gracious chariots atop the 57-foot turntable. The carousel was later purchased by the Holzapfel family of Sandusky, Ohio, who operated the amusement at Cedar Point from 1946 until the park bought it in 1963. Made during the 15 years (1903–1918) when brothers Daniel and Alfred Muller were in business together for themselves, this exceptional and nostalgic carousel enjoys ongoing restoration efforts and continues to entertain and enthrall visitors of all ages, who marvel at its extraordinary craftsmanship. (Courtesy Cedar Point.)

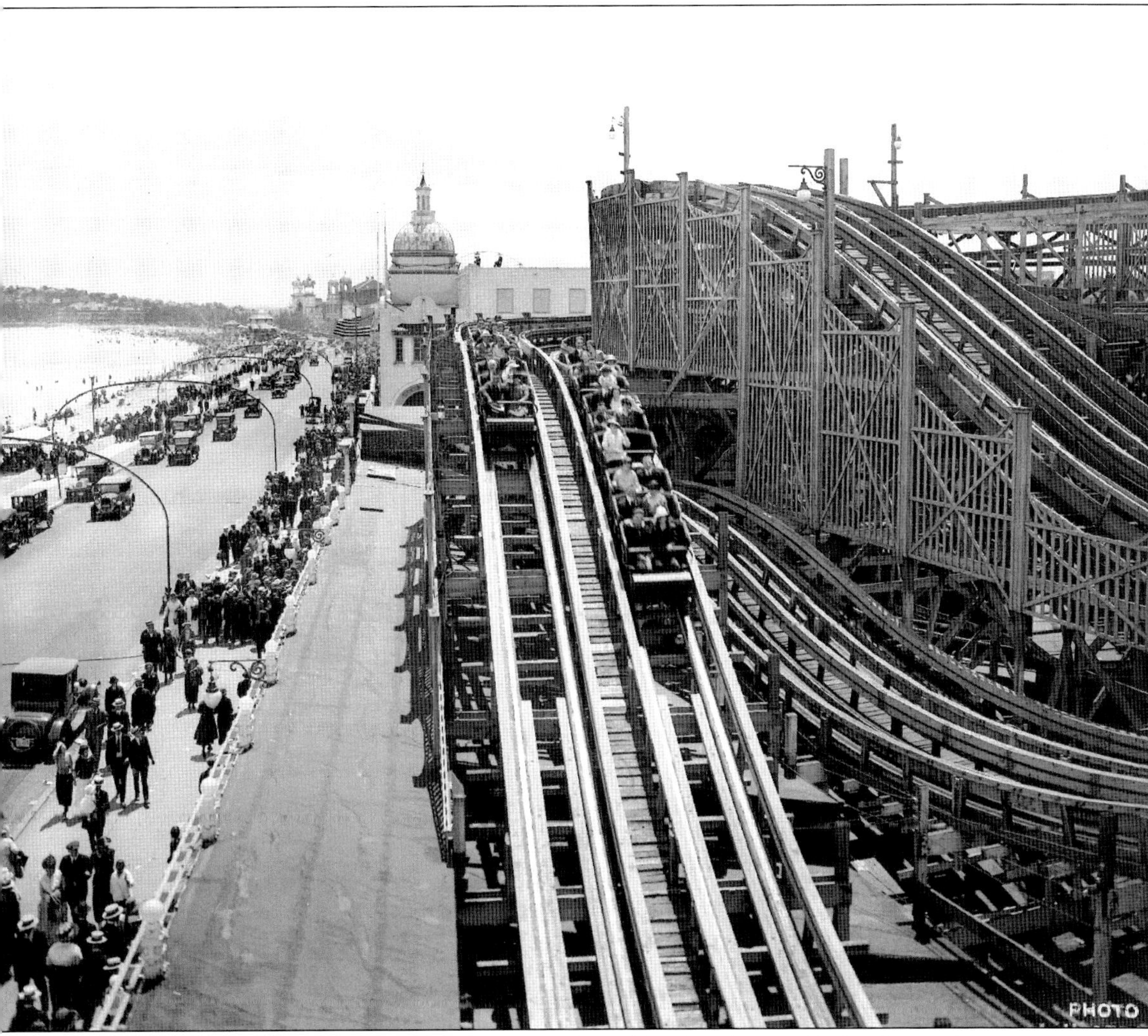

Freelance photographer Leon Abdalian captured on film the famous Derby Racer during an outing to Revere Beach in 1920. The wildly popular, double-tracked coaster operated until 1937 and featured parallel tracks on which ran two cars that would ascend a moderately steep incline via cable power. From the top they would plunge downward at approximately the same time. Ride attendants operated separate breaking systems, enabling one car to lead before being overtaken by the other in thrilling semblance of a race. Favored by intermediate thrill seekers, Louis Bopp's innovative and centrally located coaster also provided a considerable potential for danger. In fact, three fatalities occurred on the ride between 1911 and 1917, culminating in the horrific death of Louis Kadeveski of nearby Lynn on Sunday, July 15, 1917. While attempting to retrieve his wind-snatched hat, Kadeveski was struck and dragged 35 feet by the second car, breaking nearly every bone in his battered body. Accidents such as this resulted in increased safeguarding measures, including the implementation of additional protective devices. (Courtesy Boston Public Library, Prints Department.)

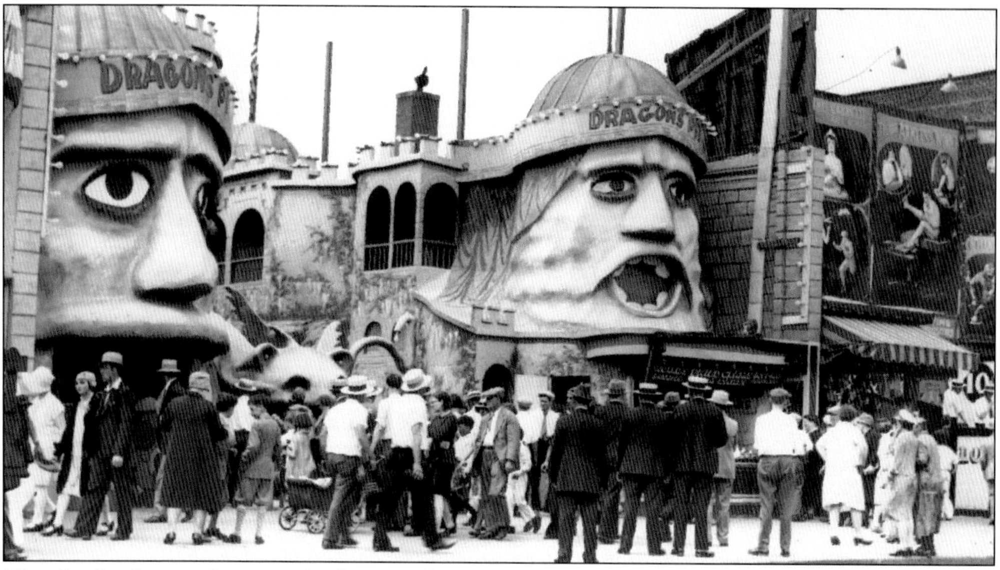

This Leslie Jones photograph depicts the intriguing attraction known as the Dragon's Pit. Created by the McGinnis family, the fun house contained recreational inventions patented by Mr. McGinnis. The elaborately crafted facade featured two enormous faces placed on either side of a central dragon figure. On the reverse of this photograph is enigmatically written: "Do you remember? This was a scene at Revere Beach 1929—no one seemed to be afraid." (Courtesy Boston Public Library, Prints Department.)

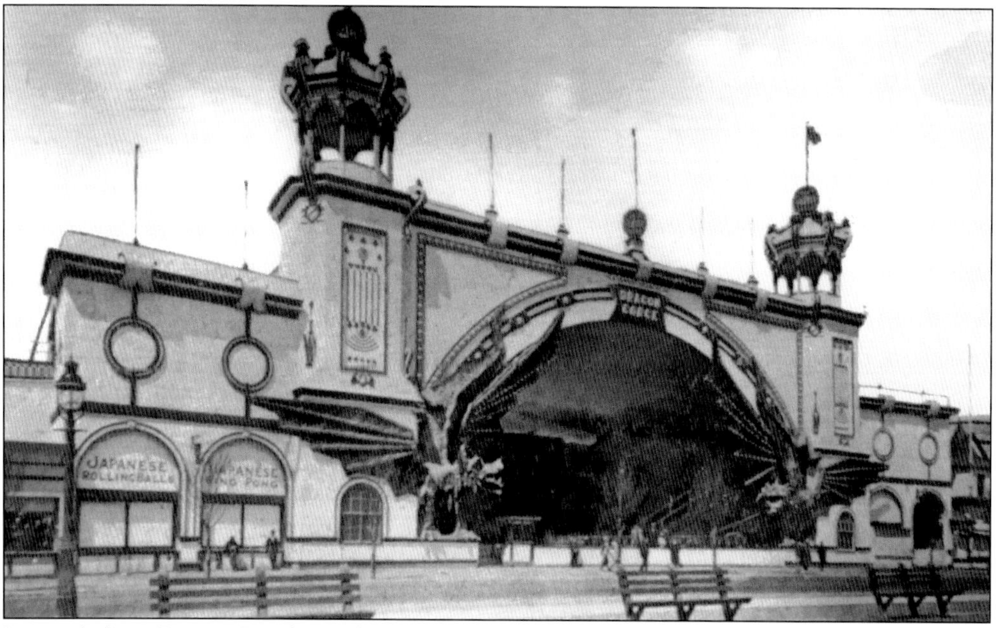

Located along Revere Beach Boulevard's southerly end, Dragons Gorge was a popular scenic railway attraction. The facility also contained Japanese-themed amusements, which reflected America's continued fascination with the mysterious Orient. The lavish exterior featured two fearsome dragons stationed at opposing sides of an enormous convex entrance and was topped by two crowning towers. The building encompassed 40,000 square feet and extended over eight lots. (Courtesy Lynn Museum.)

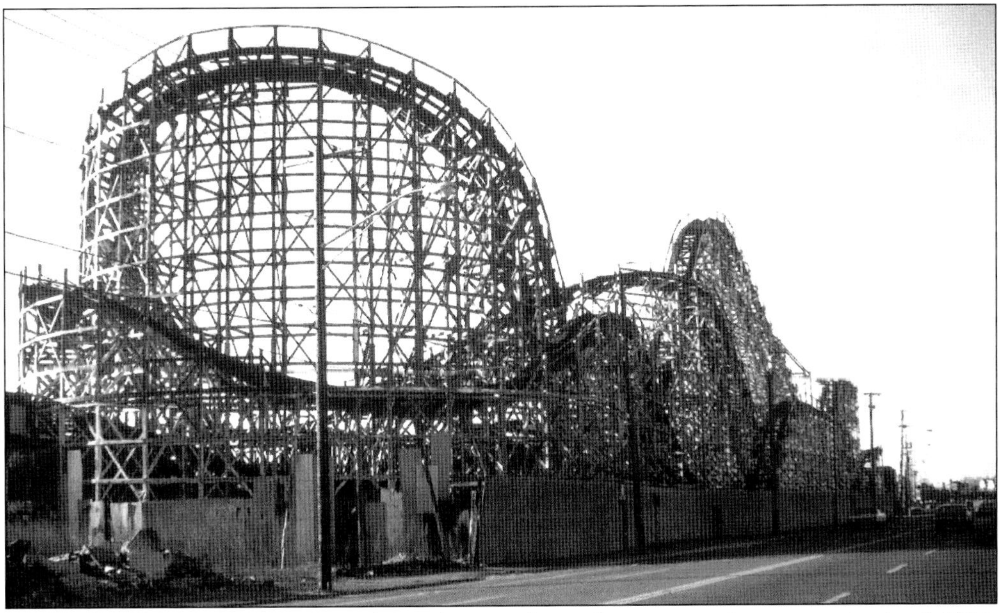

The mighty Cyclone roller coaster looms large and proud prior to its destruction in April 1974. Owned by the Shayeb family, it was built in 1925 for $125,000 and was reportedly the world's fastest and largest coaster. Speeds exceeded 45 miles per hour, and the ride featured 3,600 feet of interlocking safety track. The Alba Corporation purchased the property in May 1973 for $400,000. (Courtesy Jack Cook.)

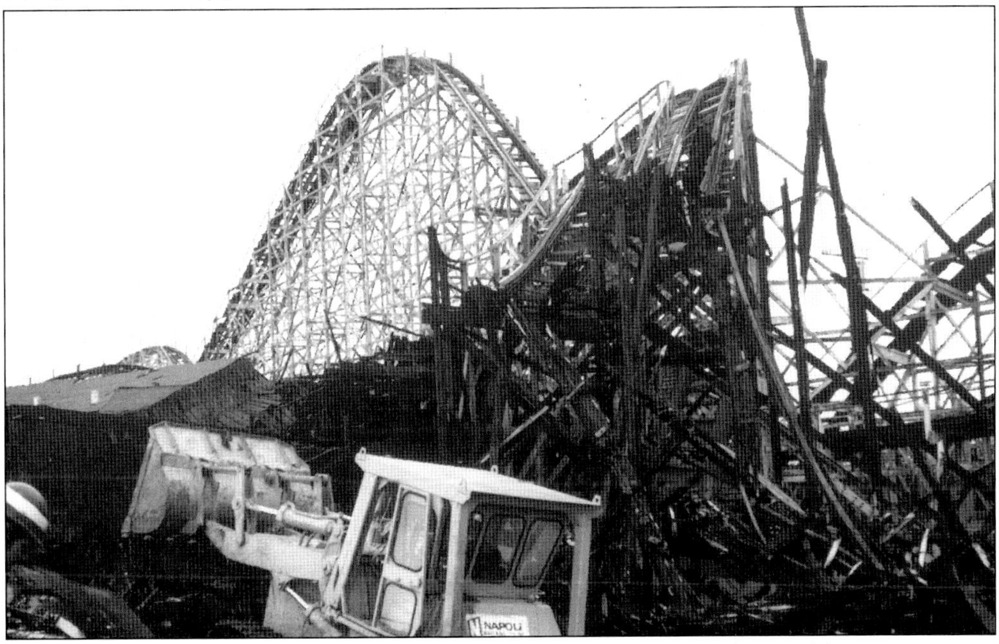

As the 1974 demolition process continues, the great wooden behemoth resembles an enormous, undulating serpent poised to strike the machinery that is destroying it. In its heyday, the Cyclone operated up to 14 hours per day and its cars, which were controlled by a 100-horsepower motor, were able to accommodate 24 riders at once. The beloved coaster ceased to operate in 1969 due to soaring maintenance and insurance costs. (Courtesy Jack Cook.)

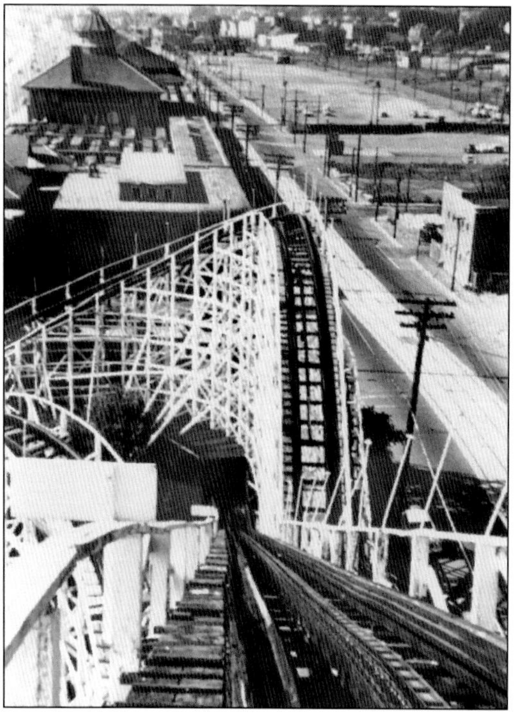

Photographed from high aloft the wooden skeleton of the Cyclone is the dizzying drop that propelled riders at great speed into the enclosed tunnel below. From this height Ocean Avenue is clearly visible, running past the city public works yard (right center) and the expansive vacant lots that would later be occupied by Wonderland Station's aft parking lot followed by Water's Edge Condominiums. (Courtesy City of Revere.)

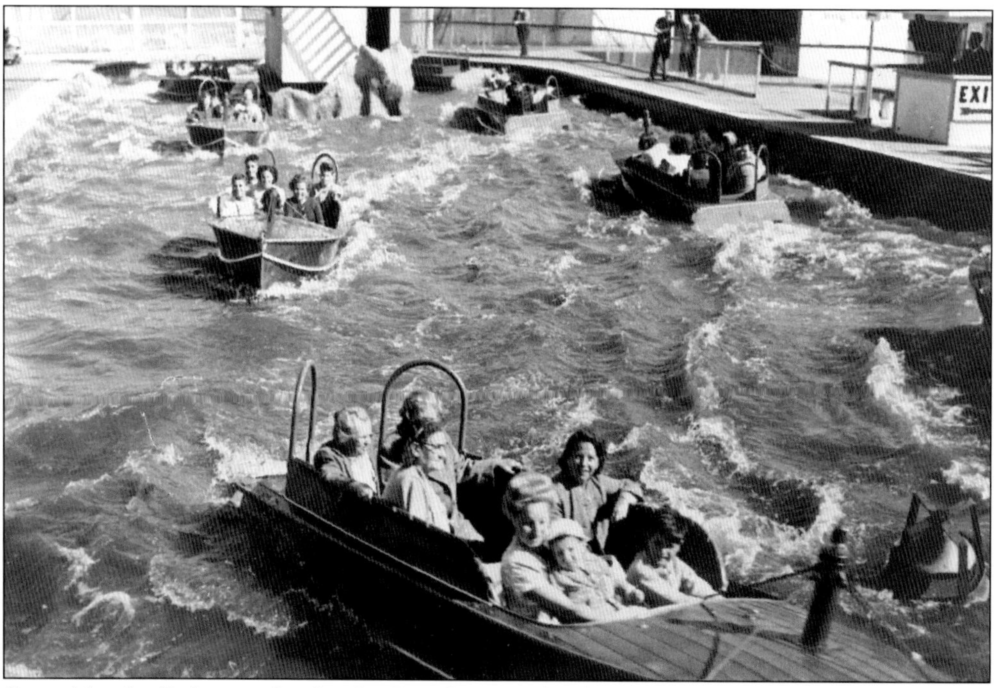

Owned by the Ridgeway family, the Rapids was a family-friendly aquatic amusement located south of Shirley Avenue. Occupying the former site of the Lightning roller coaster, the attraction featured boats that navigated within a sizable wave-fraught pool around a contrived island containing a small-scale lighthouse and keeper's residence. The favored ride operated during the 1950s and 1960s. (Courtesy City of Revere.)

Six

ALONG THE BOULEVARD

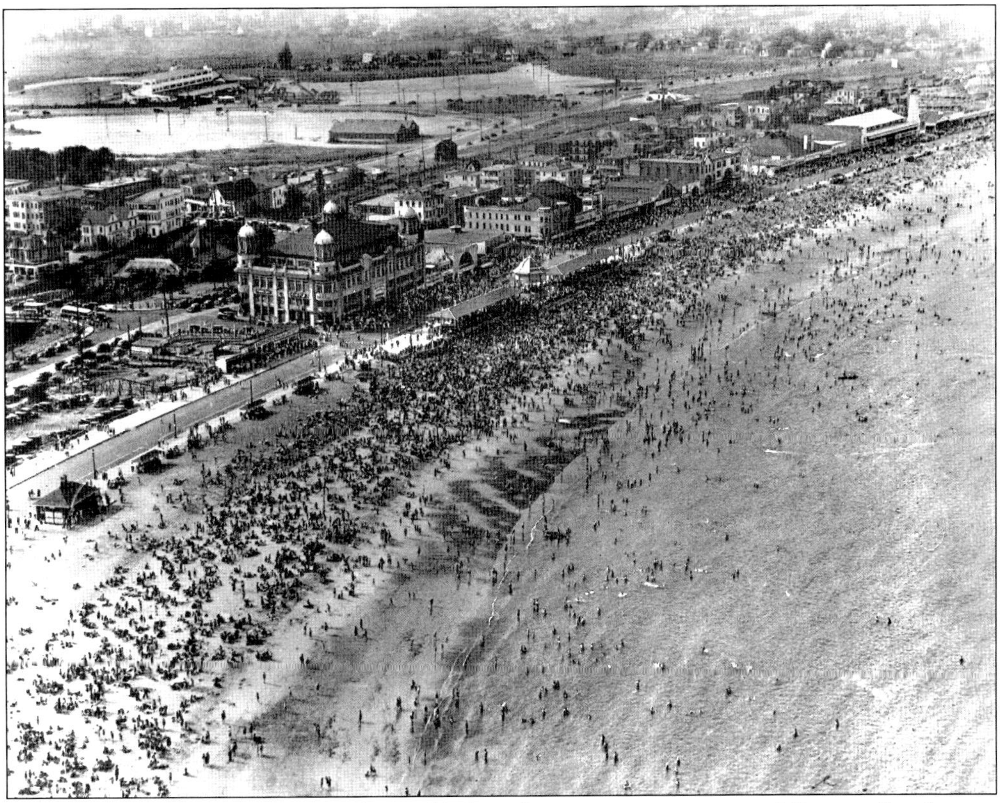

This mid-1930s aerial view firmly establishes the preeminent status of Revere Beach as a veritable New England seaside resort. To the left of center is the magnificent Crescent Gardens and Ballroom, located adjacent to the beachside bandstand. Onshore, innumerable bathers dot the sand and gentle surf. This photograph easily captures the gracious curve of the delicate shoreline, which is nicely complemented by the parallel placement of Revere Beach Boulevard. (Courtesy Winthrop Public Library.)

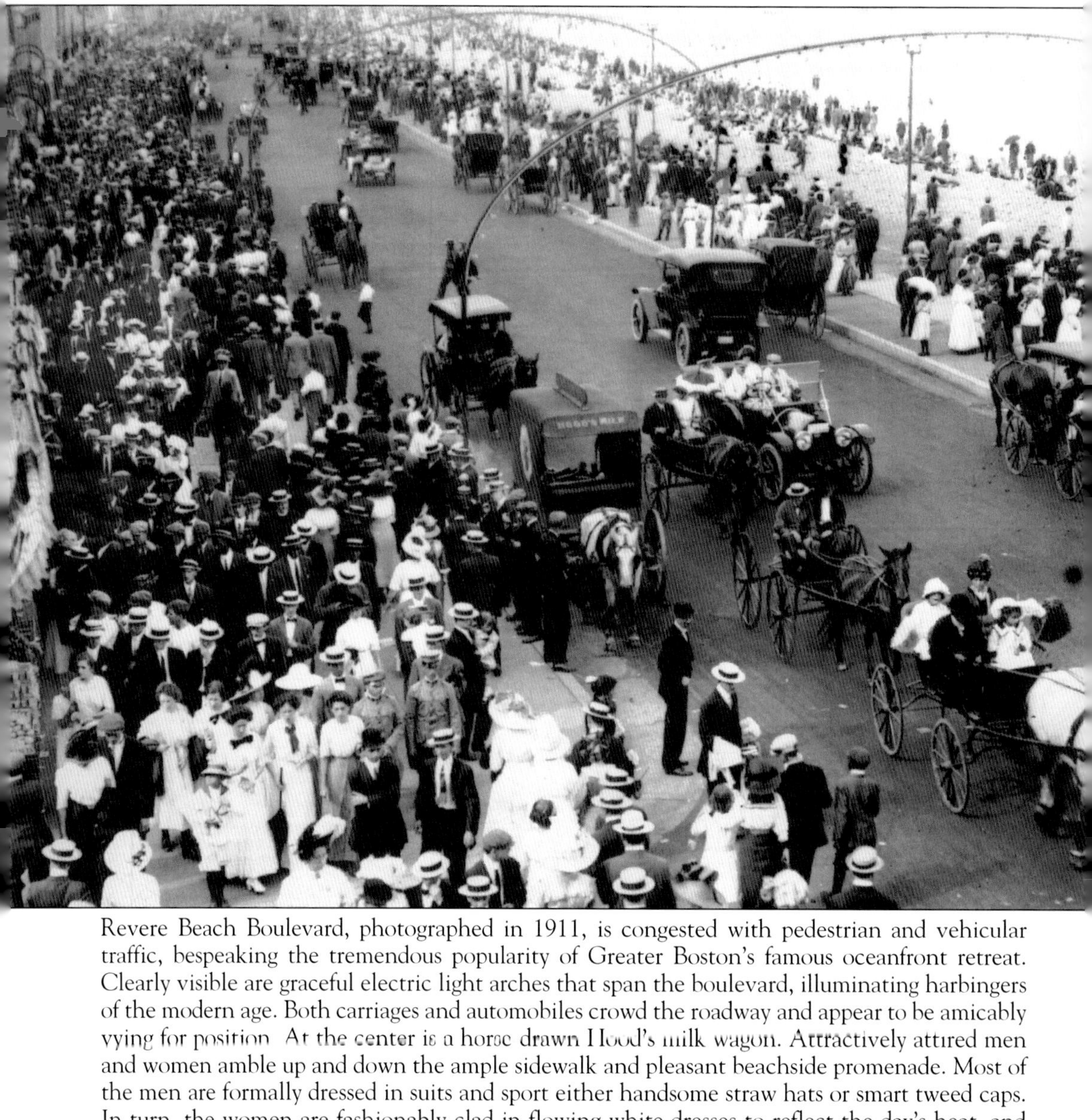

Revere Beach Boulevard, photographed in 1911, is congested with pedestrian and vehicular traffic, bespeaking the tremendous popularity of Greater Boston's famous oceanfront retreat. Clearly visible are graceful electric light arches that span the boulevard, illuminating harbingers of the modern age. Both carriages and automobiles crowd the roadway and appear to be amicably vying for position. At the center is a horse drawn Hood's milk wagon. Attractively attired men and women amble up and down the ample sidewalk and pleasant beachside promenade. Most of the men are formally dressed in suits and sport either handsome straw hats or smart tweed caps. In turn, the women are fashionably clad in flowing white dresses to reflect the day's heat, and many female heads are concealed from view by swank sun hats. A few young women are further sheltered from the sun by stylish parasols. Close inspection reveals a mixed ethnicity evident among the visitors photographed here, providing additional credence to the designation of Revere Beach as the "People's Beach." (Courtesy Boston Public Library, Prints Department.)

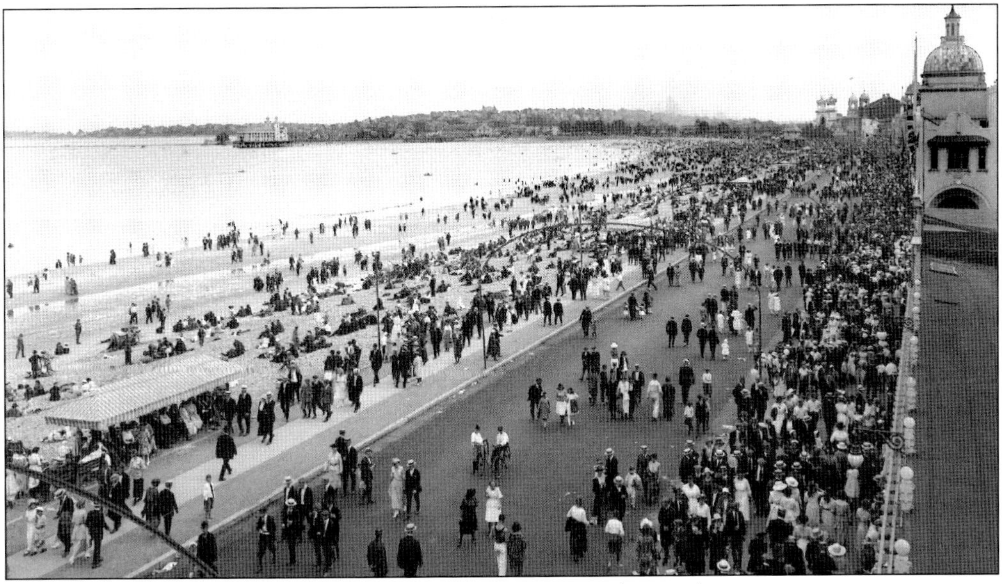

Revere Beach and accompanying beachside driveway are alive with activity on a warm summer afternoon in 1920. Photographed by Leon Abdalian from an elevated position on the Derby Racer, throngs of people are pictured walking directly on the driveway, a permissible activity only after 1:00 p.m. on Sundays in season. At the left, visitors dawdle beneath a striped, canopied sun shelter. The regal spire rising at the right graces the neighboring Nautical Garden. (Courtesy Boston Public Library, Prints Department.)

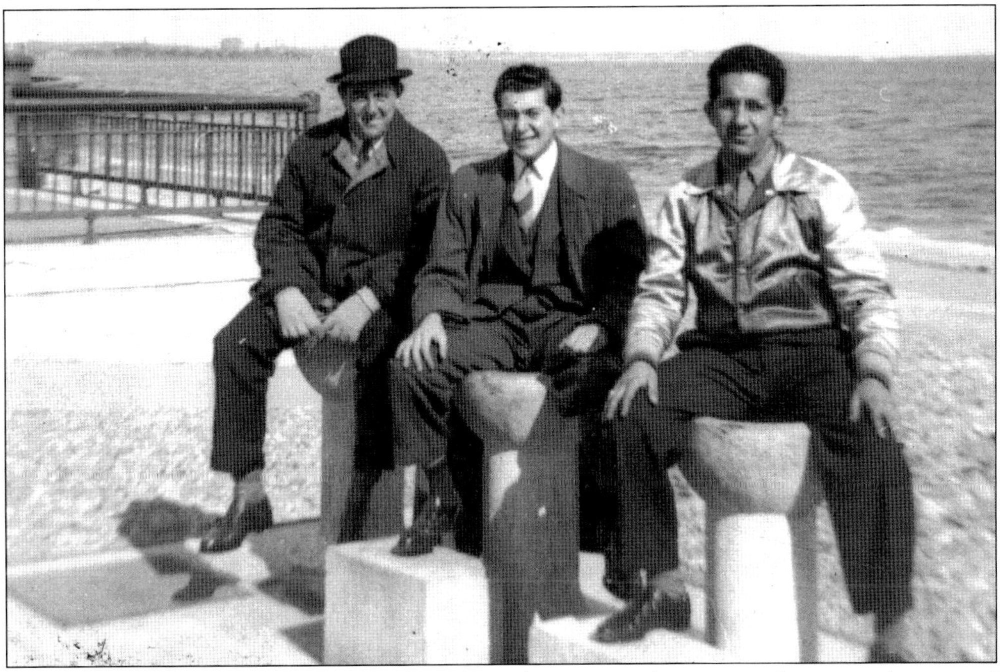

Sited near the centrally located Bandstand Pavilions were three water fountains that served as pedestals in support of these dapper men one afternoon in 1940. From left to right are Jack Kaplan, Jack Cook, and Max Ruben. In the distance behind the young men, the coastline of Lynn and Nahant is clearly visible. (Courtesy Jack Cook.)

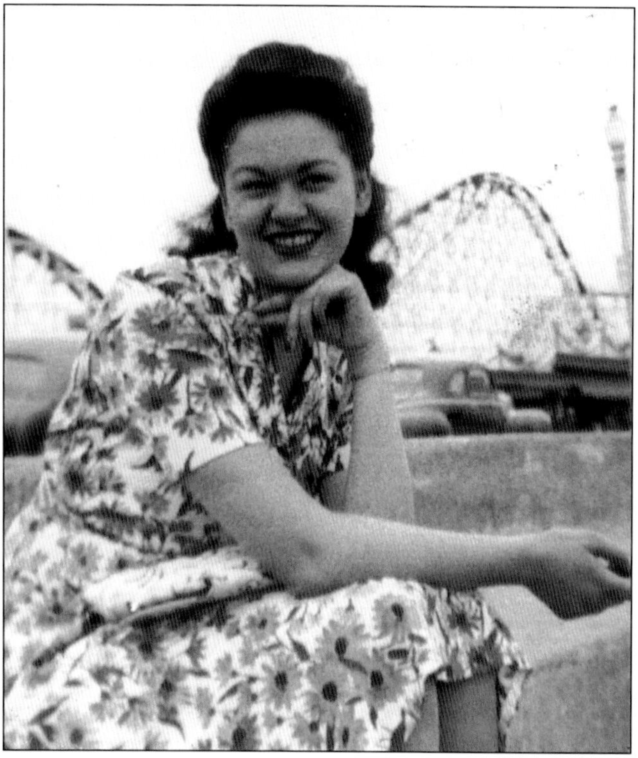

The irrepressible bloom of true love illuminates the youthful face of Miriam Port, who coyly poses for her fiancé, Jack Cook, during a visit to Revere Beach in 1941. Behind her ascend the calculated arches of the Cyclone coaster, a favorite attraction among the more adventurous thrill-seeking visitors to the renowned crescent-shaped beach. (Courtesy Jack Cook.)

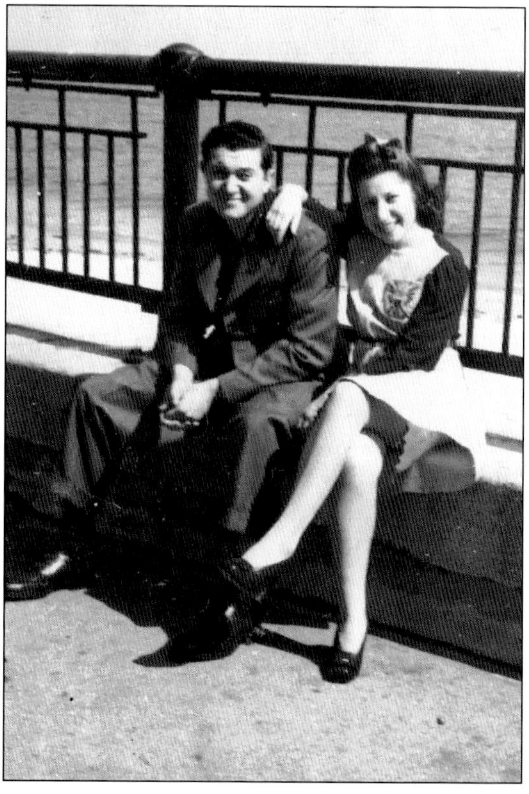

The amicable Jack Cook poses with his stylish sister Sylvia in 1941 in front of the iron railing that stretched protectively along the beachside promenade. The Cook siblings grew up in Revere and resided on Campbell Avenue. An avid photographer, Jack Cook relished his role behind the camera. This playful photograph places the photographer before the lens that appears to have captured in him a shy yet compliant subject. (Courtesy Jack Cook.)

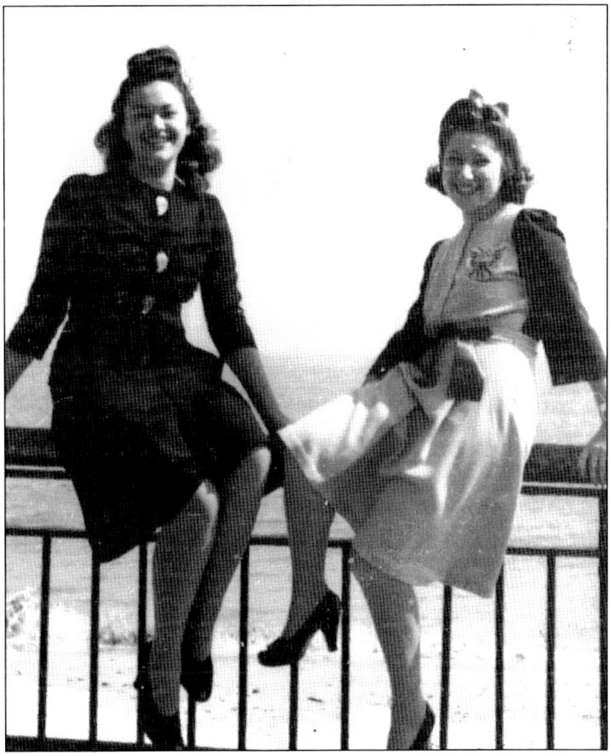

Miriam Port and her future sister-in-law Sylvia Cook smile charmingly for photographer Jack Cook as they balance carefully on a cast-iron railing toward the southerly end of Revere Beach Reservation. The fashionable Revere residents appear quite content as the sun warmly illuminates their faces and the gentle surf rolls in behind them. (Courtesy Jack Cook.)

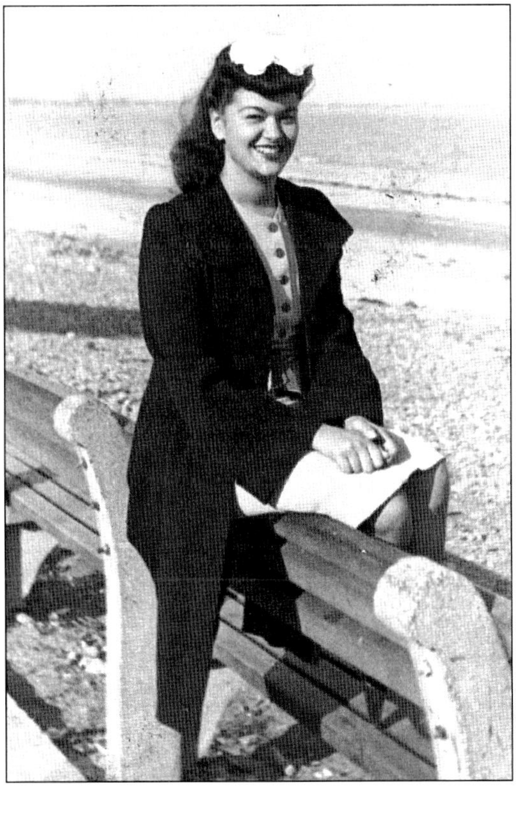

As war rages in the Pacific, the elegant and meticulously attired Miriam Port appears perfectly poised and calm before the camera during an outing to Revere Beach in 1941. She is seated atop one of several cement-based wooden benches that dotted the driveway and whose existence encouraged visitors to repose while witnessing the encompassing beauty of Greater Boston's northern shore. (Courtesy Jack Cook.)

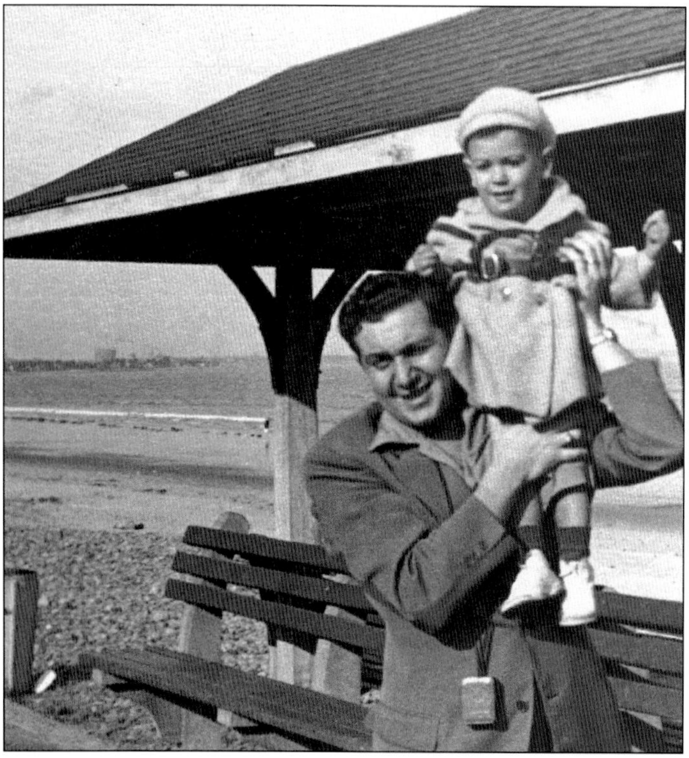

Photographer Jack Cook relinquishes his post behind the camera to elevate his young nephew Ronald Wayne Feldman atop his left shoulder. The smartly attired fellows are standing in front of one of many sun shelters constructed along the southerly stretch of shore. Benches were positioned so that those who employed them could elect to view Revere Beach Boulevard or the beach itself. (Courtesy Jack Cook.)

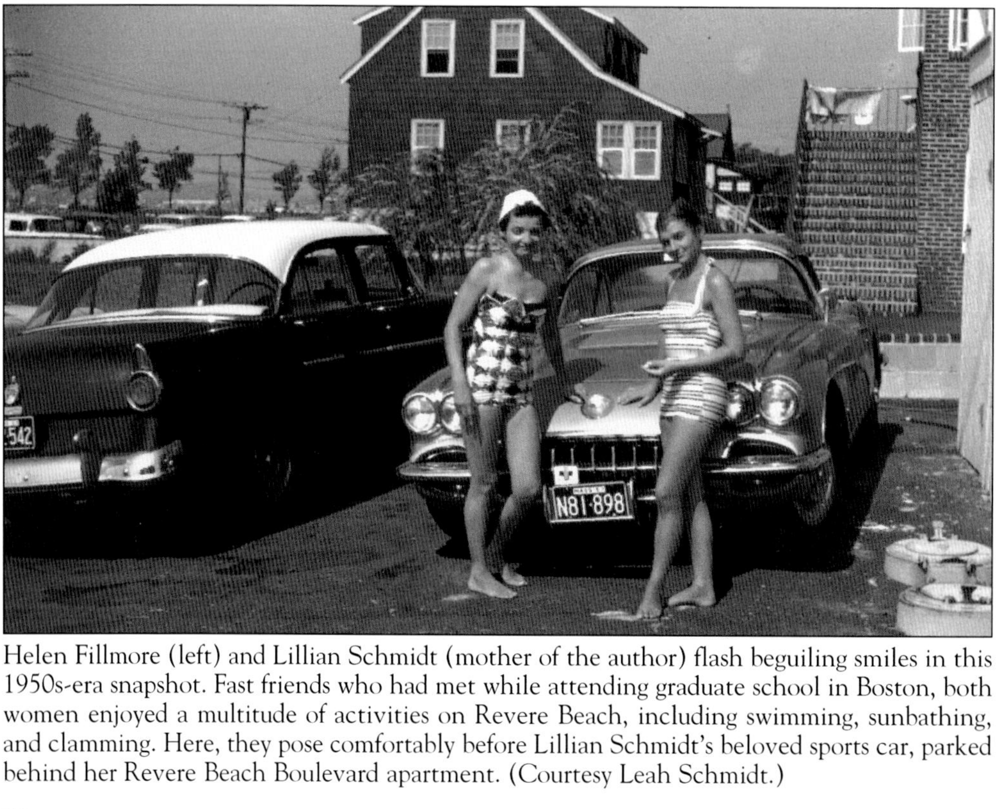

Helen Fillmore (left) and Lillian Schmidt (mother of the author) flash beguiling smiles in this 1950s-era snapshot. Fast friends who had met while attending graduate school in Boston, both women enjoyed a multitude of activities on Revere Beach, including swimming, sunbathing, and clamming. Here, they pose comfortably before Lillian Schmidt's beloved sports car, parked behind her Revere Beach Boulevard apartment. (Courtesy Leah Schmidt.)

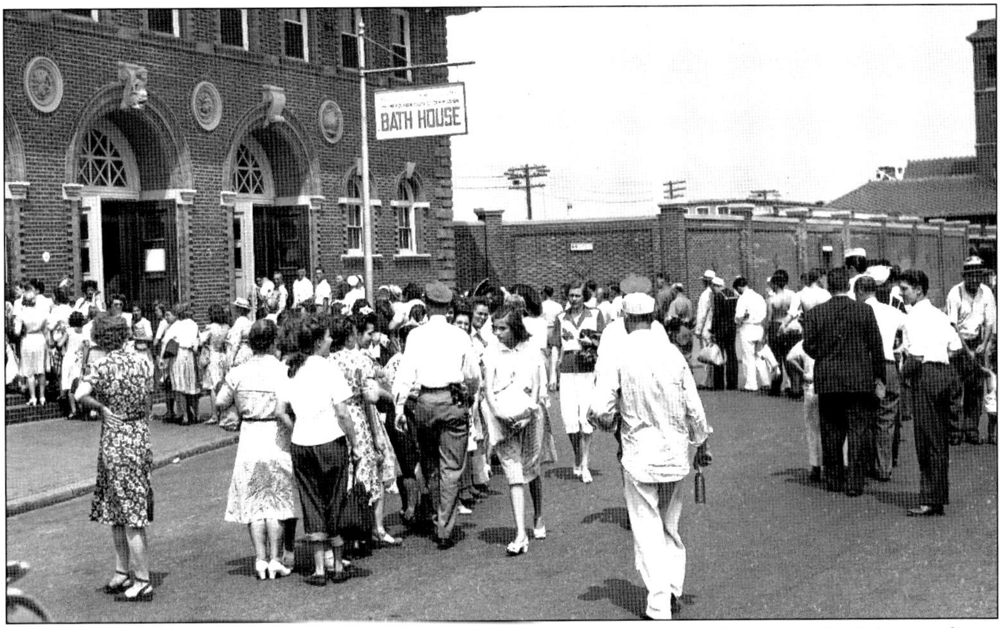

Long lines of patient visitors seeking swimsuits pour out of open doors to the Metropolitan District Commission Bath House and flood the street in this photograph dated August 14, 1944. Atop the detailed central entrance is the statuette of a child riding a fantastic dragonlike creature reminiscent of classic Greek statuary. Such craftsmanship contributed greatly to the overall grandeur of the stately landmark, which presided over the popular beach for 65 years. (Courtesy City of Revere.)

In this c. 1950 photograph, an unidentified bespectacled man, arms extended, stands before the high pedestal base of the ornate post clock that graced central Revere Beach Boulevard. The remarkable clock, manufactured by E. Howard & Company of Boston, surmounted a Corinthian-columned substructure and stood between the gracious Bath House Pavilions. When the Metropolitan District Commission facility was taken down in 1962, the clock was removed. Its fate is unknown. (Courtesy City of Revere.)

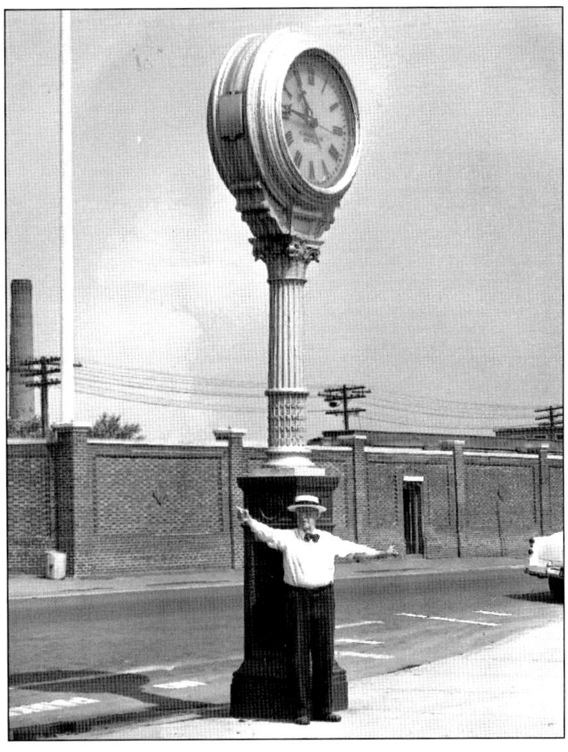

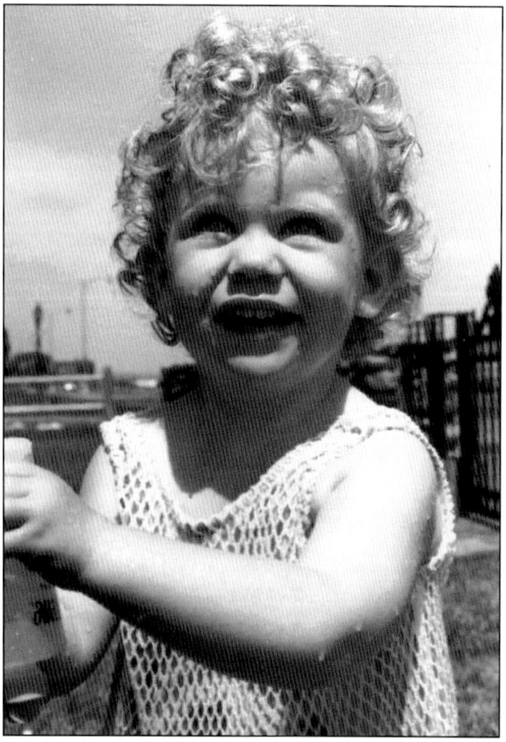

This 1964 picture depicts two-year-old Marlayna Schmidt laughing with unabated glee after dousing herself with refreshingly cool water on a sweltering summer day. Photographed in the front yard of her 640 Revere Beach Boulevard home, mirth animates the child's features and a gentle breeze tousles her curly blond hair. At the right, the Art Deco–inspired wrought-iron gate gracefully divides the stone wall that fronts the residential property. (Courtesy Leah Schmidt.)

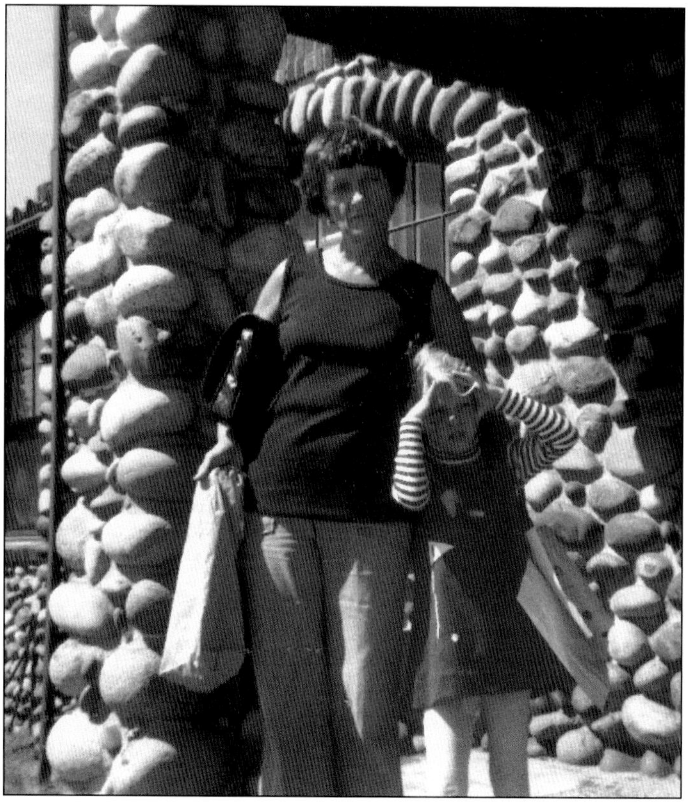

Six-year-old Leah Schmidt is photographed with her mother, Lillian Schmidt, on the front porch of their northerly Revere Beach Boulevard home in 1976. Arms raised to shield her face from the sun's glare, the anxious child gazes toward Carey Circle in anticipation of the arrival of the school bus on her first day of elementary school. Built in 1920, the stone-and-brick home looms protectively behind mother and daughter. (Courtesy Leah Schmidt.)

Seven

Entertainment and Lodging

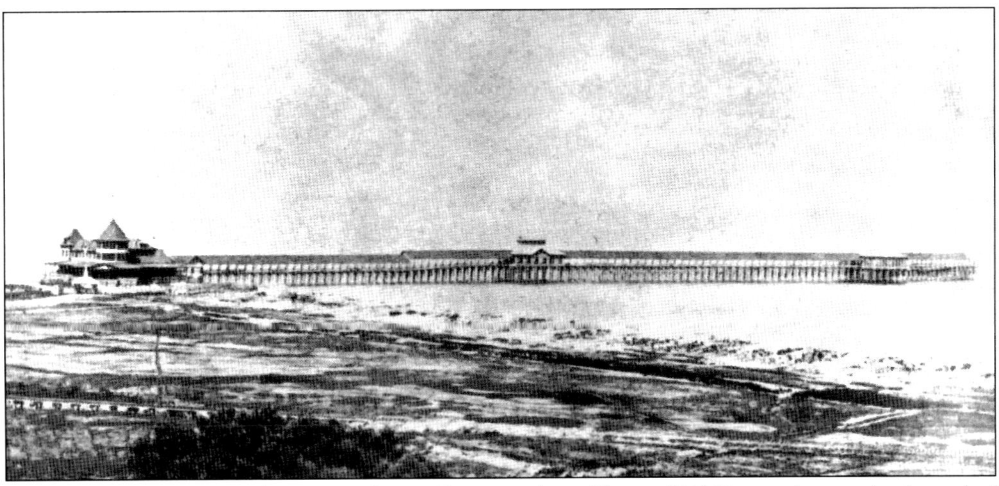

Photographed in 1883, the Great Ocean Pier stood on Cherry Hill Bar at the southerly end of Revere Beach. Built in 1881 by the Boston Pier and Steamboat Company, the pier extended 1,700 feet over the Atlantic, was 22 feet wide, and contained two large halls that housed a ballroom, a roller-skating rink, and an ample 500-seat café. In 1893, the impressive landmark was dismantled and sold in sections. (Courtesy Revere Public Library.)

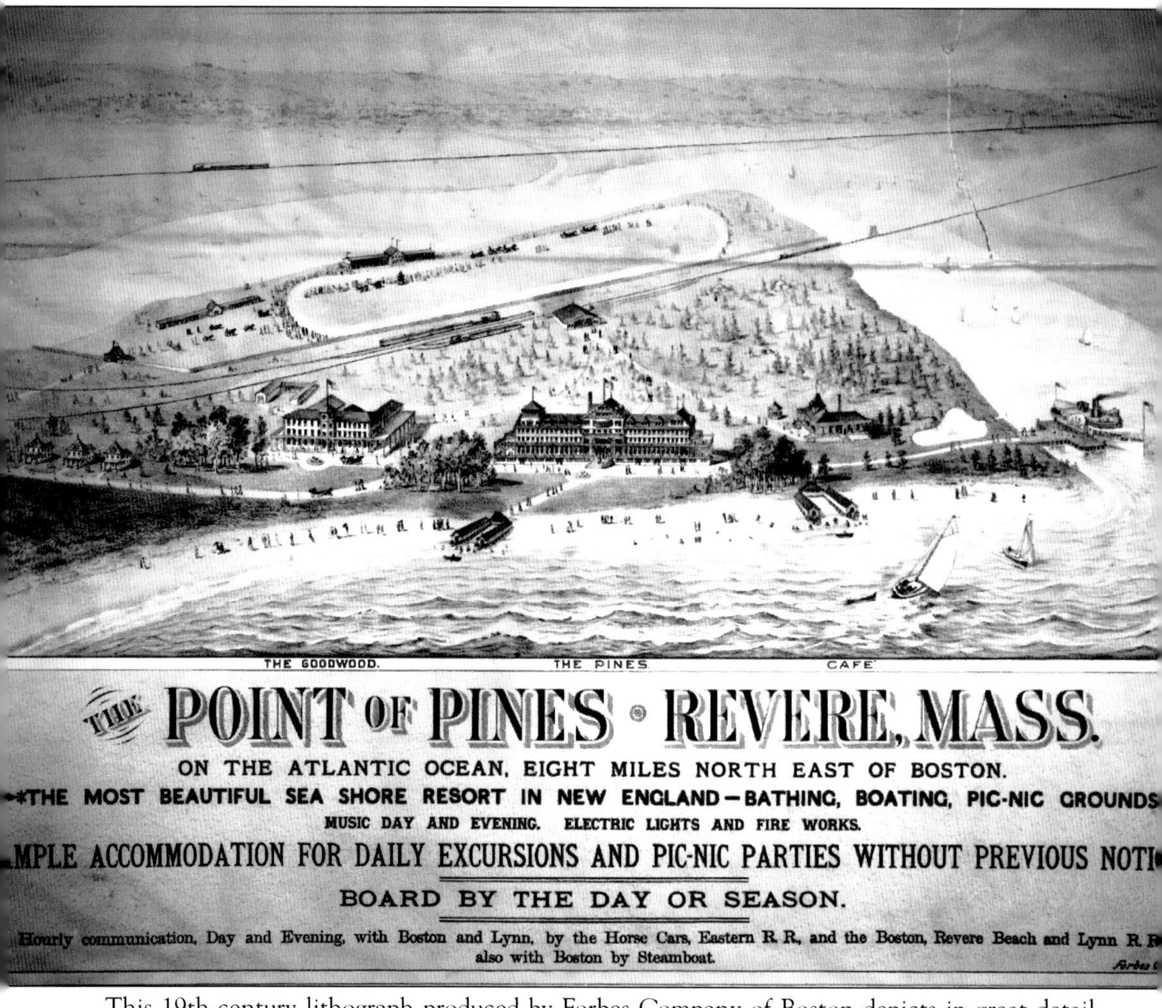

This 19th-century lithograph produced by Forbes Company of Boston depicts in great detail the northerly section of Revere Beach known as Point of Pines. This area featured some of the earliest local amusements and encompassed approximately 200 acres of recreational shoreline. At the left, the Hotel Goodwood was constructed for $20,000 in 1857 and originally operated under the name Ocean House. The facility and grounds, which stood near the Pine's southerly entrance, housed an eating and drinking establishment, stables, a bowling alley, and a bathhouse. The facility operated successfully until 1889, when it was razed. At the center is the prominent Point of Pines Hotel. Col. Theodore Roosevelt campaigned for the presidency here in August 1912, speaking from the gracious veranda to a crowd consisting of more than 2,000 supporters. The grand hotel closed in 1913 and was taken down the following year. During its heyday, the Point of Pines operated a tremendously popular cafe (at the right), hosted dramatic fireworks displays and elaborately staged events, contained a roller-skating rink, and even boasted an on-site horse track. The former resort area is now an upscale residential community. (Courtesy Boston Public Library, Prints Department.)

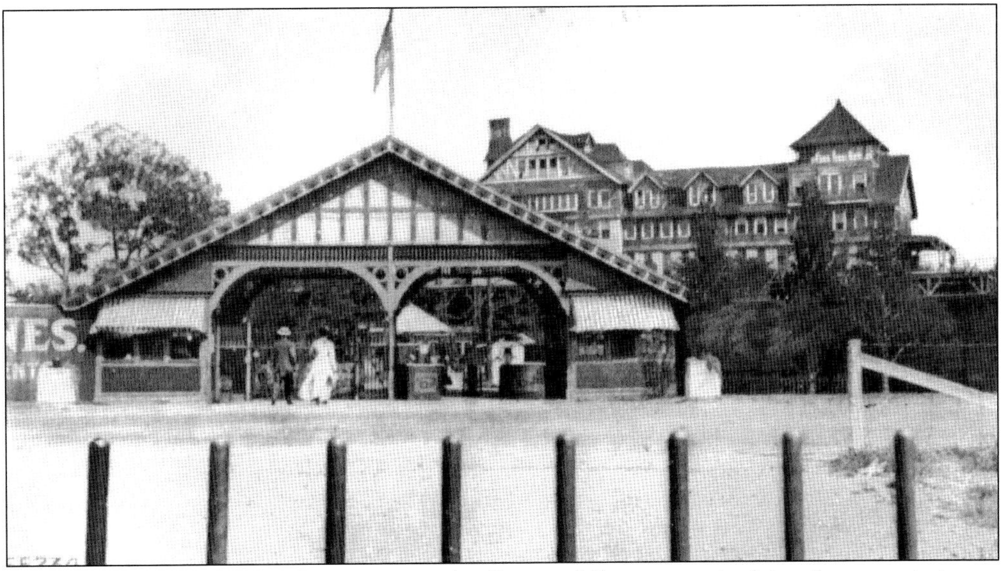

The large double-entranced gateway to the Point of Pines was sited in close proximity to the Boston, Revere Beach & Lynn Railroad tracks along the Lynnway near Revere Beach Reservation's northernmost location. The handsome wooden structure, whose postcard image circulated frequently during the early 20th century, was topped by Old Glory and contained concession and ticket booths. Behind the Victorian Eclectic entrance looms the gracious Point of Pines Hotel. (Courtesy Lynn Museum.)

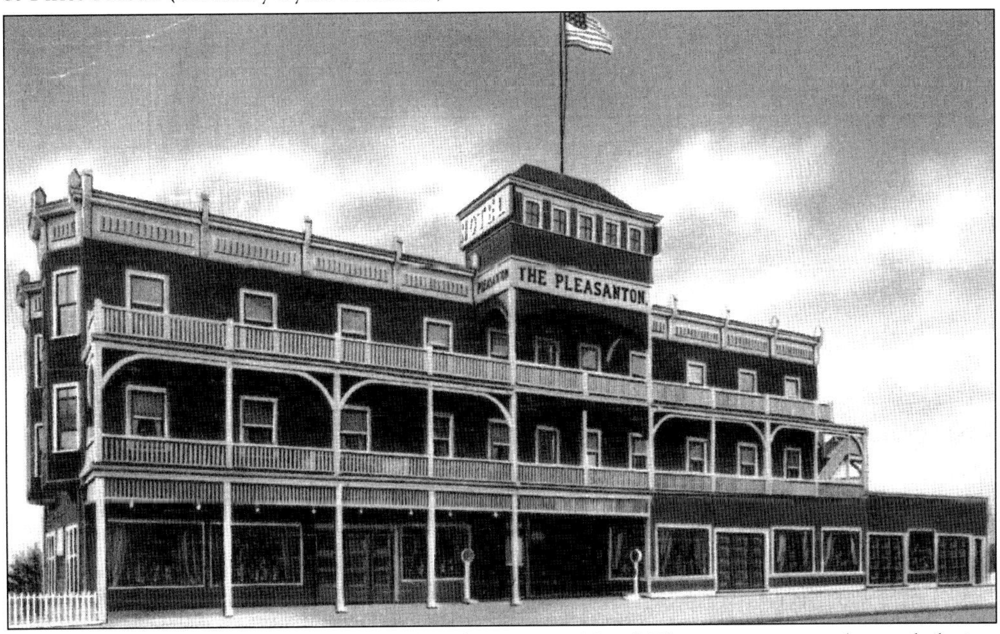

Originally located near Bath Street, the three-story Hotel Pleasanton was relocated during the fall of 1924 to 45 Revere Beach Boulevard. Managed for many years by Arthur Kirby, the wooden landmark featured 40 guest rooms, on-site dining and dancing, and free overnight parking in its own "private locked garages." Believed to have been built in 1875, the historic structure sustained significant fire damage on January 11, 1940. (Courtesy Boston Public Library, Prints Department.)

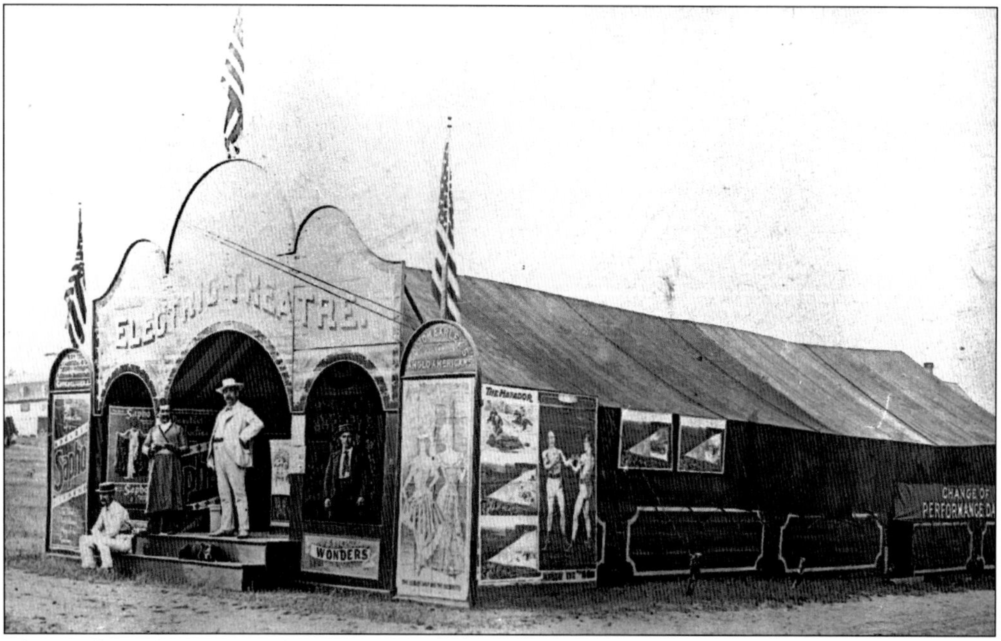

This early-20th-century photograph depicts the Electric Theatre, an early motion picture facility owned by local amusement pioneer J.J. Hurley. Sited on an expansive lot of land along Ocean Avenue, the tentlike structure prominently featured promotional posters for performers, including the Matador and Sapho. Standing below the flag-adorned entrance are four well-dressed employees. On the steps, a reclining canine casts an inquisitive glance toward the camera. (Courtesy City of Revere.)

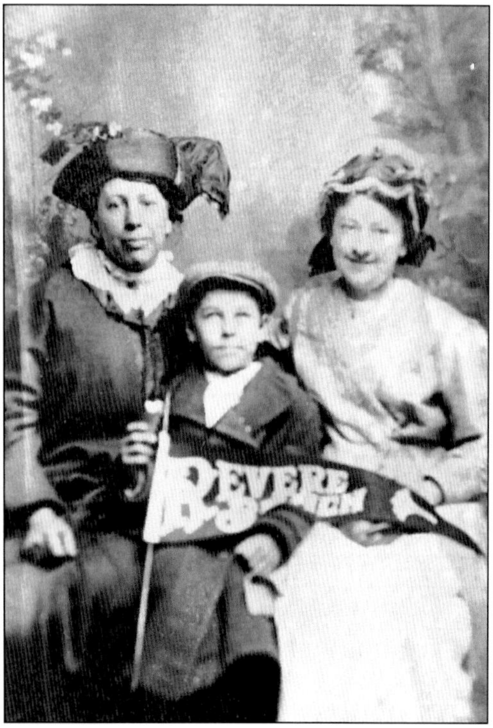

In addition to amusement rides, ballrooms, and fun houses, yet another stake in the lucrative visitor industry thriving along Revere Beach was claimed by the photography studio, which first appeared locally c. 1900. In this undated photograph, three smiling family members pose for a formal portrait in an unspecified studio to commemorate their visit to the destination emblazoned across the conspicuous pennant at the center. (Courtesy City of Revere.)

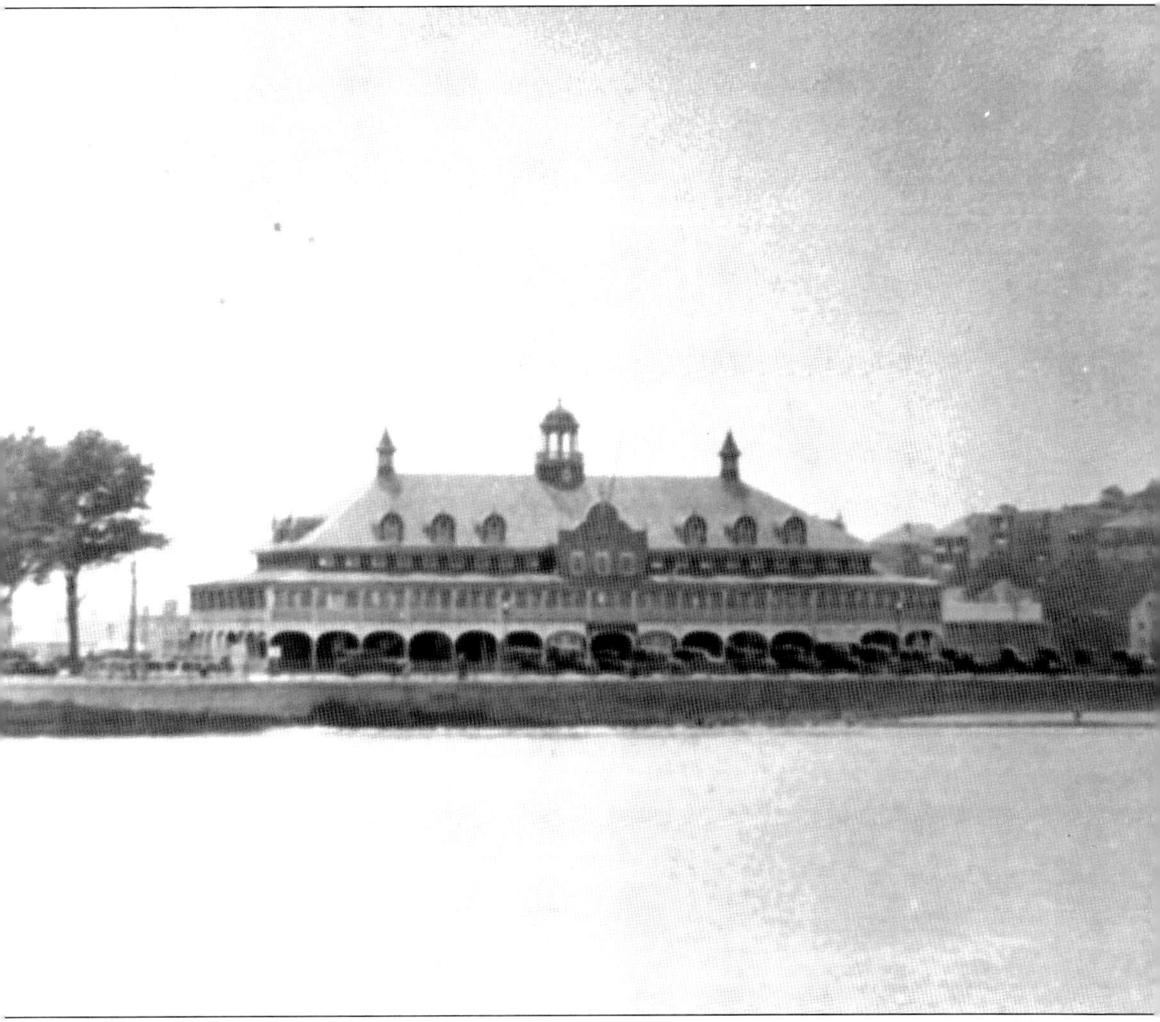

The gallant ballroom located at the southerly end of Revere Beach Reservation was named for its owner J. Condit and opened on June 17, 1904. Built for approximately $20,000, the gracious facility was operated by Condit for more than 20 years until his death in 1926. As Condit's, the ballroom featured first glide and then modern dancing, hosting weekly modern-dance contests beginning in 1915. By the mid-1920s, the respected facility had changed its name to Beachcroft and had gained legendary fame as the first ballroom in New England to introduce a live jazz orchestra. The facility was known for featuring nationally recognized musicians and hosted the *Boston Advertiser's* Miss New England Pageant in 1924. Four years later, the ballroom was transformed into Spanish Gables under the careful direction of Herbert Ridgeway, who introduced Spanish-inspired atmospheric changes. The facility enjoyed tremendous popularity through the 1930s, and period promotional material proclaimed the ballroom to be "the largest and most lovely in New England." After World War II, the facility operated as the Oceanview until fire destroyed the historic structure in December 1959. (Courtesy City of Revere.)

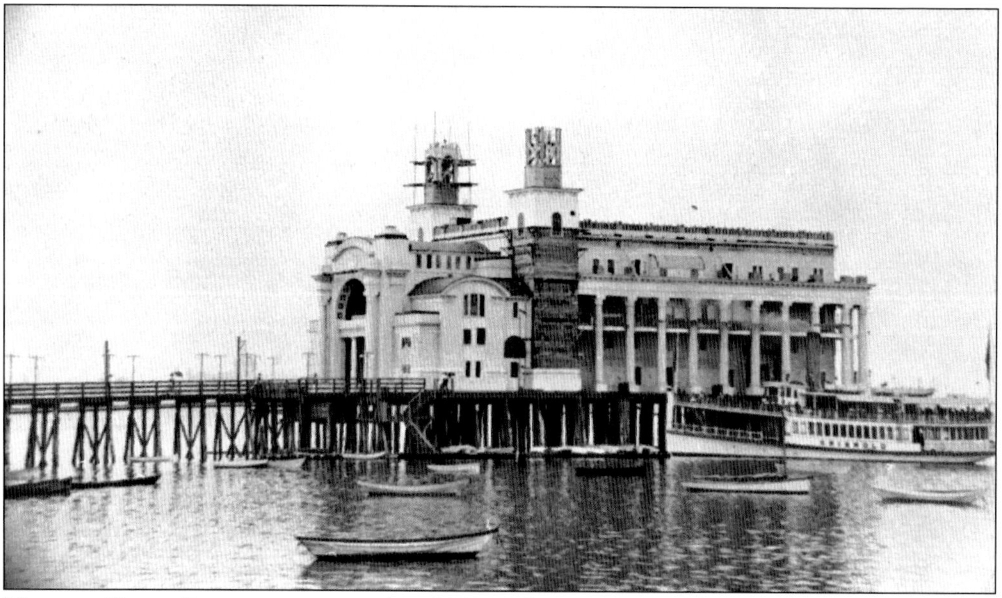

The new Ocean Pier was constructed in 1911 at the approximate location of the Great Ocean Pier that was dismantled in 1893. The recently constructed 1,200-foot pier contained a dance hall, restaurants, and a nightclub and was serviced by Ocean Pier Line passenger ferries, including the 105-foot *Griswold*, which plied the waters between Revere Beach's southerly location and Bass Point in Nahant. The boats easily accommodated several hundred passengers and ran every 15 minutes, greatly increasing the number of visitors to both shore locations. Pictured above is the palatial building dominating the eastern end of the pier. Resting at its berth beside the enormous structure, the crowded *Griswold* appears minute in comparison. Below, small pleasure boats occupy the serene water between pier and shore, and children play peacefully near the rocky shallows in plain view of the impressive structure. (Courtesy City of Revere.)

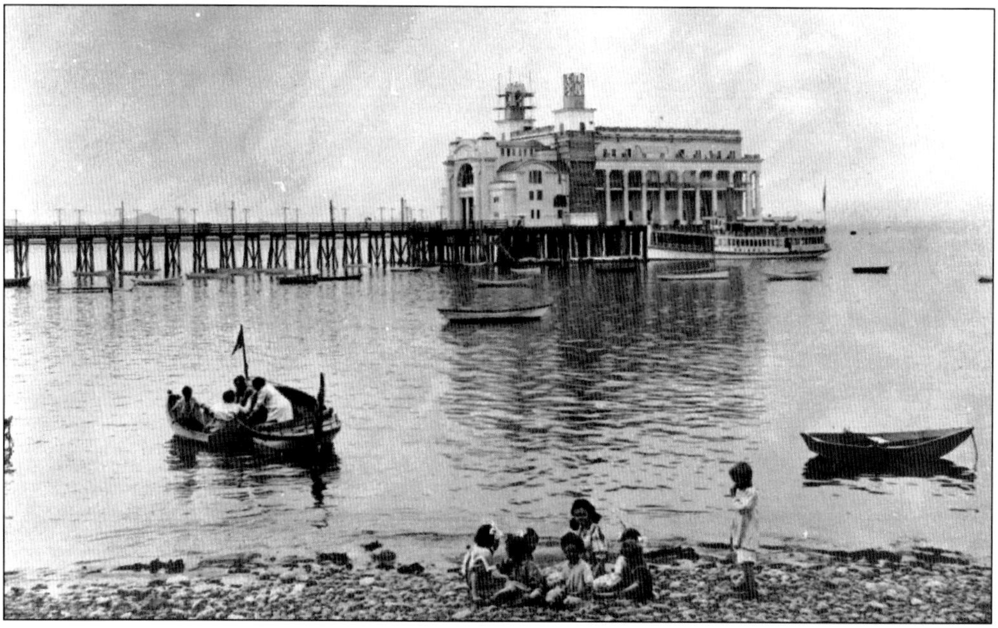

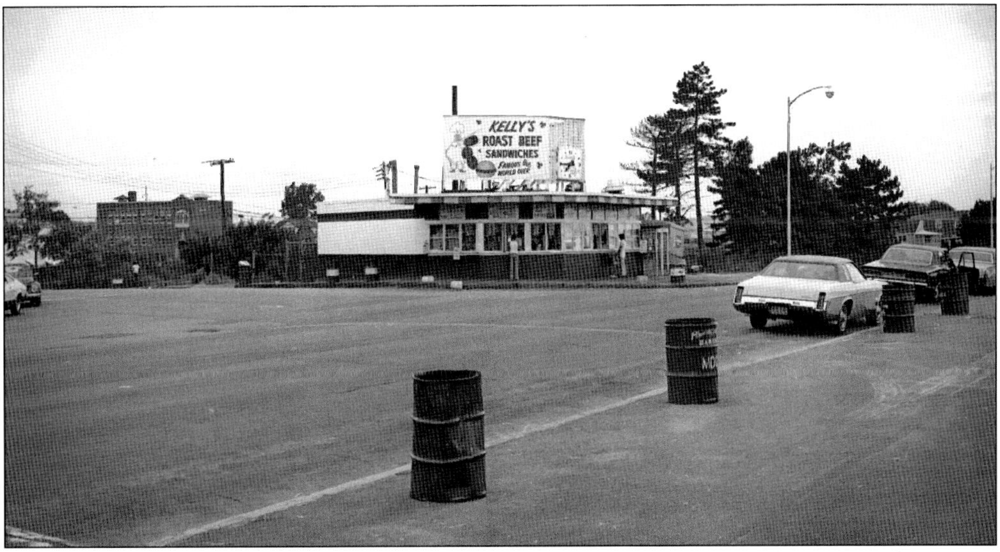

Kelly's Roast Beef has been a Revere Beach favorite for over 50 years. Started by Raymond E. Carey, a former restaurant manager, and chef Frank V. McCarthy, the family-owned takeout facility, located on the corner of Oak Island Street opposite the northernmost paired pavilions, introduced the original roast beef sandwich to the American public. The popular establishment has since opened several additional restaurants in Greater Boston suburbs. (Courtesy Brian McCarthy.)

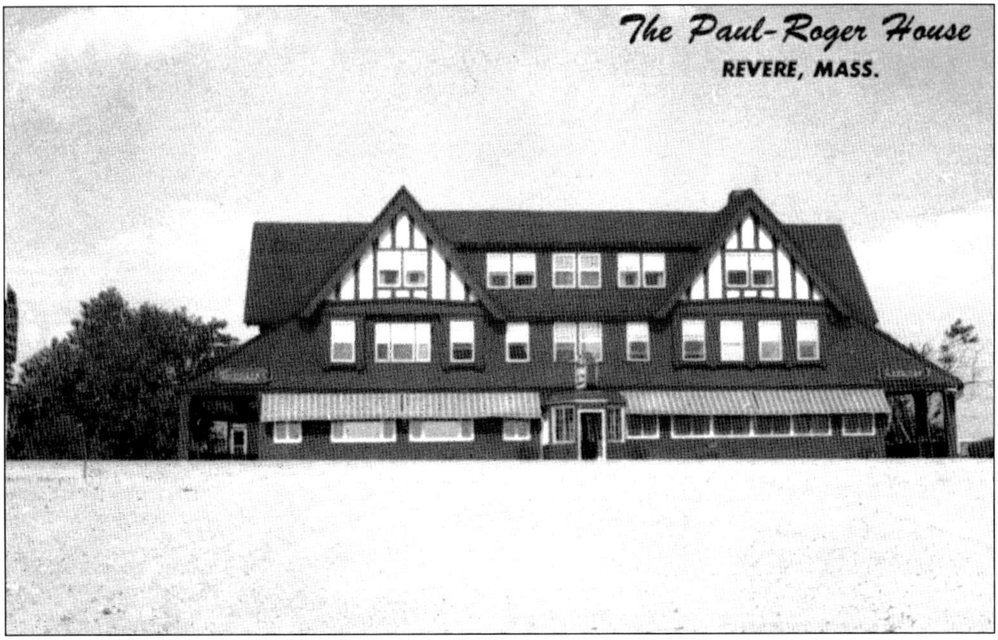

The Paul-Roger House was located near the corner of Oak Island Street. Owned and operated by Mayor Carey's family, the modified Tudor building served as a successful inn, featuring a full-service restaurant and an inviting cocktail lounge. Originally built by the Episcopalian Church as a retreat center known as Mother's Rest, the hospitable facility was often filled to capacity with weary mothers and energetic children from numerous urban parishes. (Courtesy Jack Cook.)

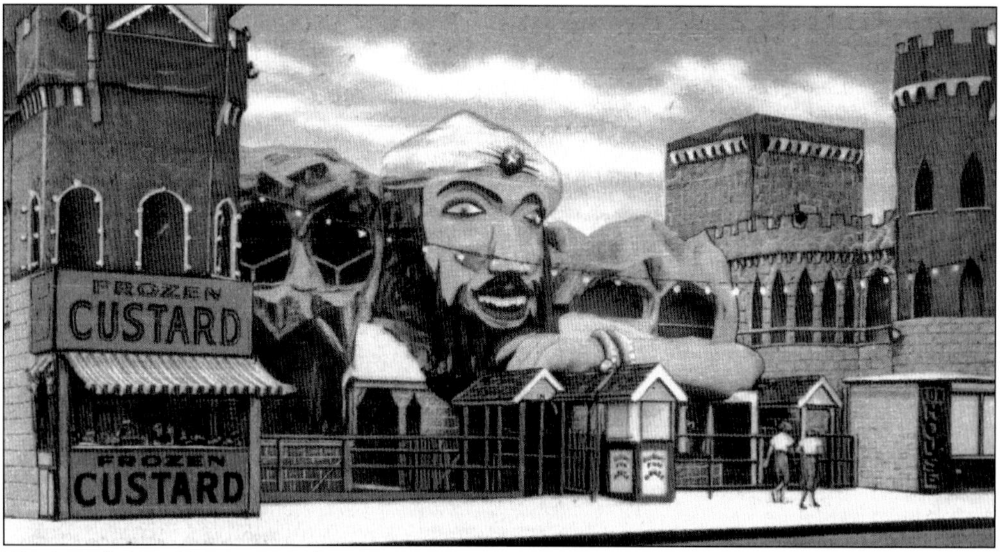

Bluebeard's Fun House was a later amusement incarnation owned by local businessman Victor Shayeb. Named for an infamous rogue, the amusement was a favorite destination for many low-to-moderate thrill seekers. It was located toward Revere Street immediately between the Virginia Reel and the Thunderbolt coaster. This postcard, which shows the curious facade featuring an enormous bejeweled head and forearm, circulated during the mid-20th century. (Courtesy Boston Public Library, Prints Department.)

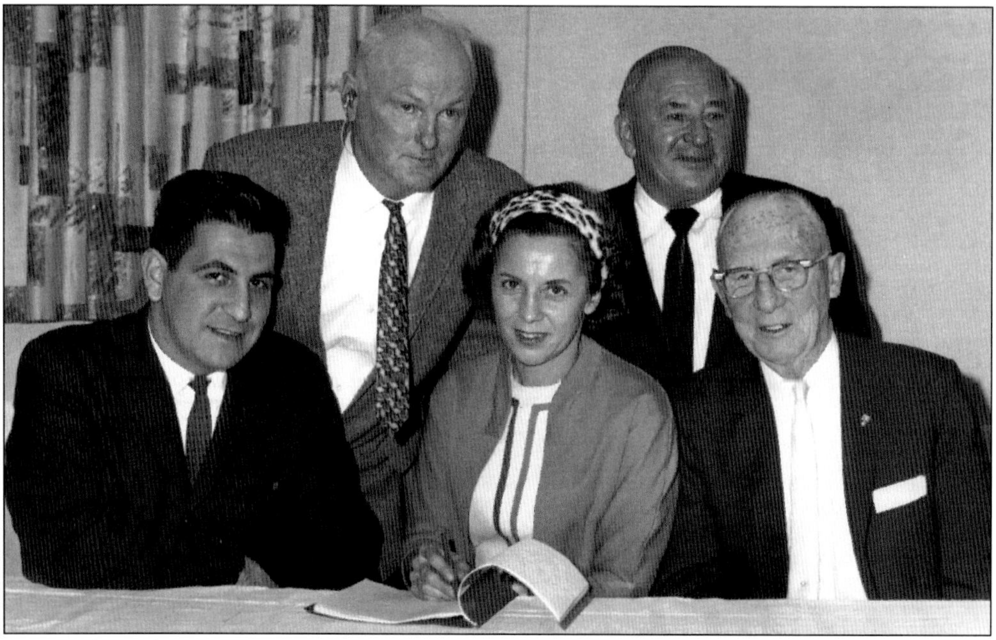

During the early 1960s, several Revere Beach business leaders met at a luncheon to discuss their unified stance against urban development. The luncheon was held at the General Edwards Inn, located opposite Northern Circle along the residential end of the beach. Pictured from left to right are the following: (front row) Joe C. Dicarlo, Mildred Hurley, and Raymond Carey; (back row) Clement Hurley and Harry Prince. The photograph and accompanying article ran on December 9, 1962. (Courtesy Boston Public Library, Prints Department.)

Eight

DESTRUCTIVE FORCES OF NATURE

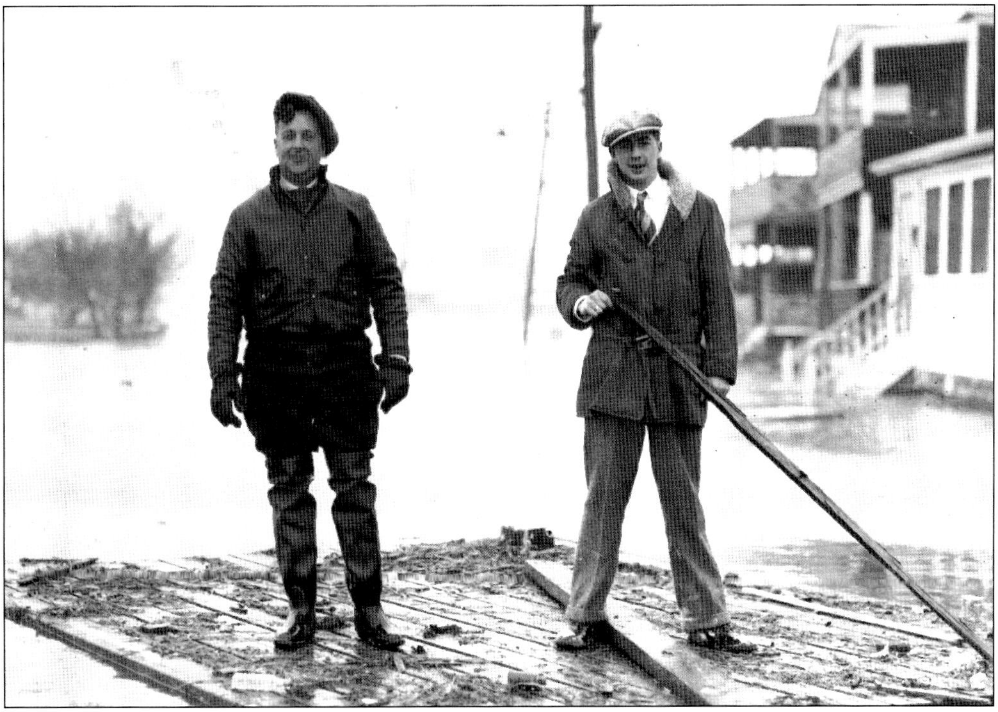

In a scene reminiscent of a Mark Twain novel, two unidentified men stand upon a makeshift wooden raft while one of the fellows carefully navigates their passage through an unspecified street at Roughan's Point in Beachmont, the community that borders Revere Beach Reservation immediately to the south. This early March 1931 storm caused severe flooding and incalculable damage to many residential and commercial properties in the area. (Courtesy Winthrop Public Library.)

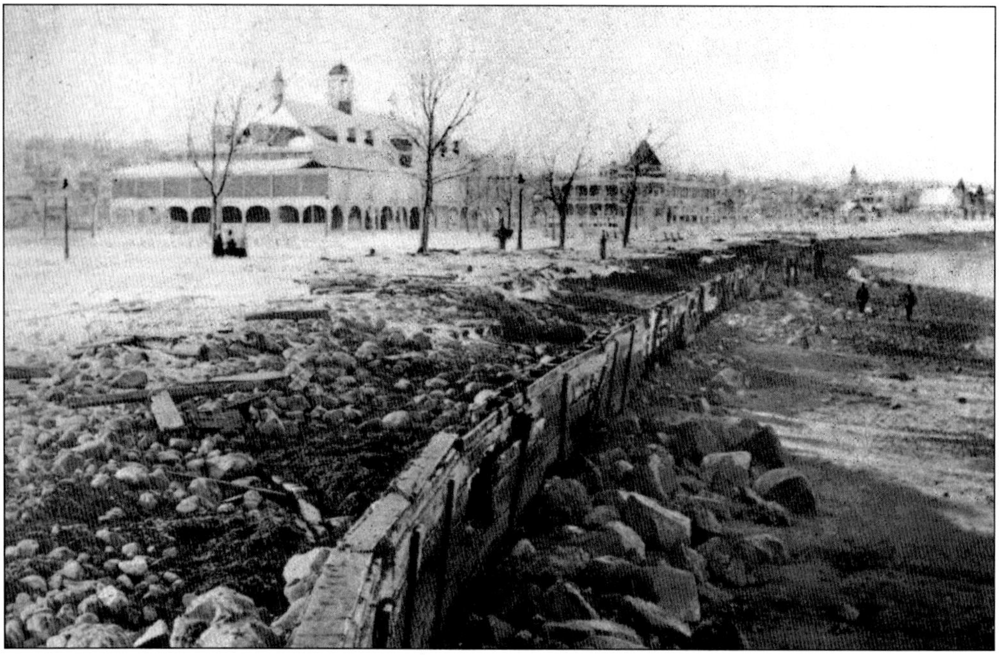

In 1910, a construction contract worth $15,610 was awarded to W.H. Ellis of Boston to build a concrete sea wall 800 feet in length along the southerly section of Revere Beach Reservation. Construction was completed the same year and replaced a storm-ravaged wooden bulkhead (above) dating from the 19th century. The new concrete shore fortification included a circular center section with an iron railing (below) that conformed to the layout of the parallel roadway. Both photographs were taken during the off-season, evidenced by the thin layer of snow blanketing the shore, creating a tranquil seascape rife with natural beauty. At the left in both images stands the courtly dance pavilion, which operated during this time period under the ownership of J. Condit. (Courtesy MDC Archives, Boston.)

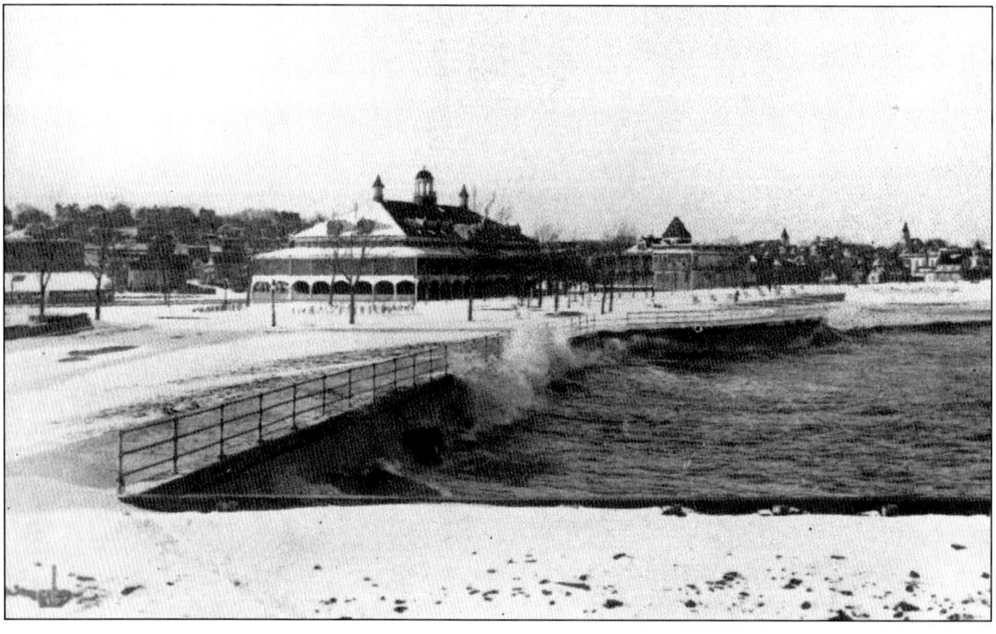

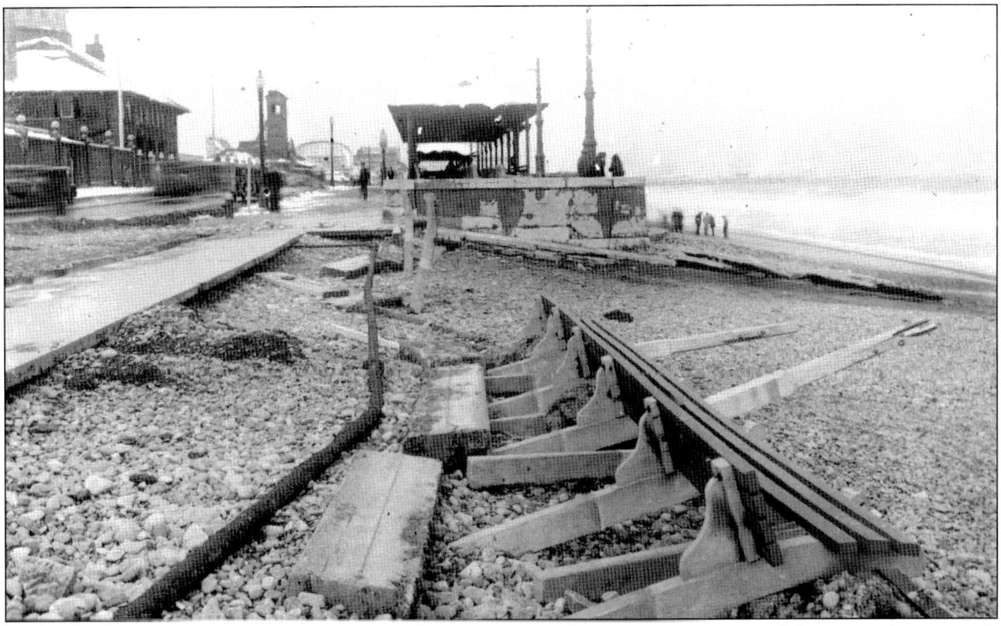

Nature unleashed her fury on the Revere coast in the form of a powerful storm that struck during the winter of 1933. A state official recorded on film the significant damage wrought by the storm, including these collapsed concrete-based wooden benches located just south of the State Bath House. In the background, a concrete walkway leading onto the beach has suffered tremendous damage as well. (Courtesy Massachusetts Archives.)

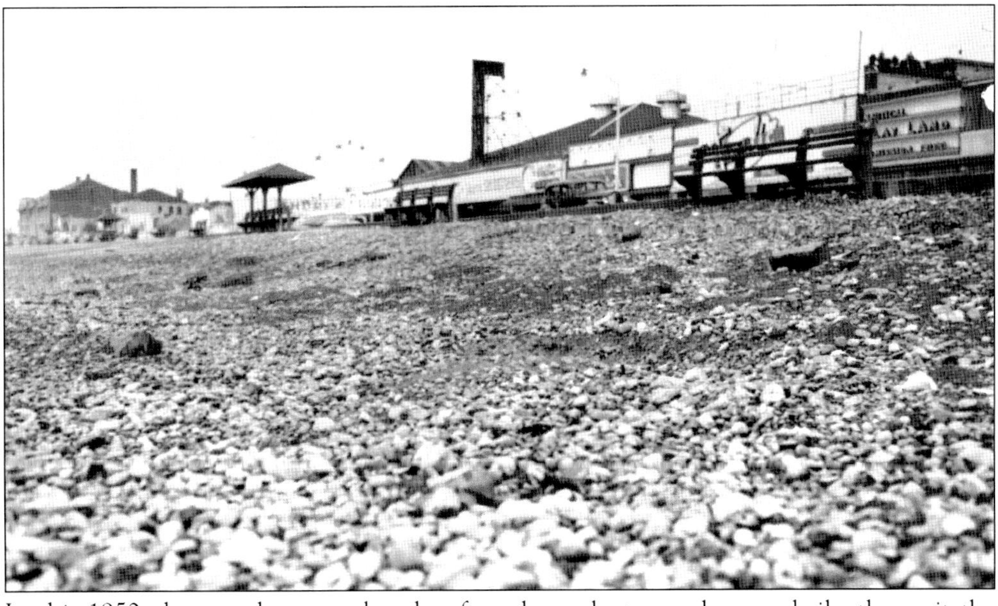

In this 1950 photograph, empty benches face the rock-strewn shore and silently await the arrival of warm-weather visitors. Behind the benches stand several entertainment properties, including the renowned Frolic, at 155 Boulevard. From this prominent nightclub, the famous trumpeter Louis Prima and his talented orchestra made national broadcasts during the 1940s. Other celebrities who reportedly performed here include Dinah Washington, Barbara Streisand, and Sammy Davis Jr. (Courtesy Massachusetts Archives.)

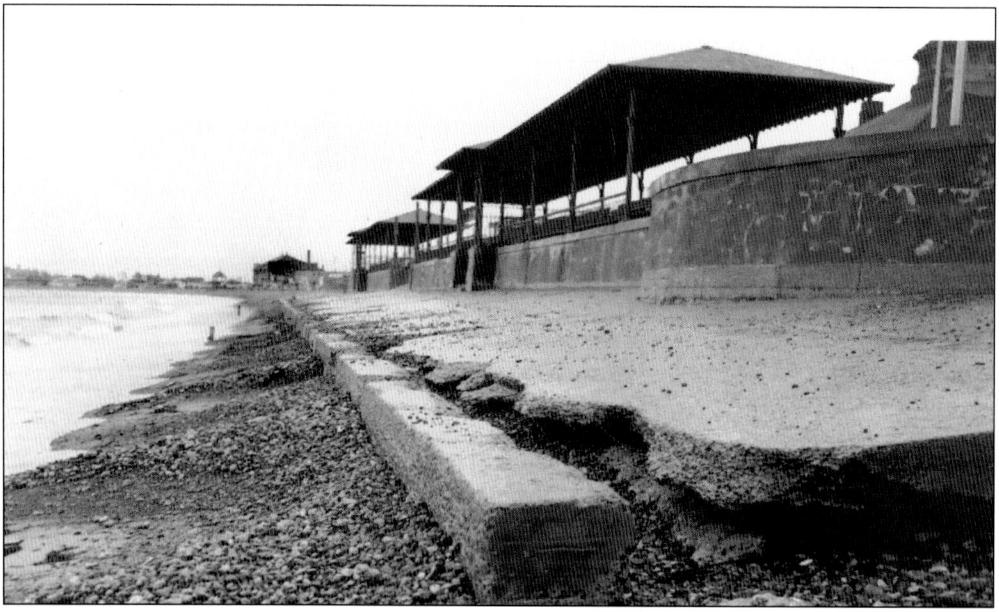

This photograph was taken in 1950 to detail the evident erosion along Revere Beach Reservation. A 1938 Works Progress Administration project constructed 576 linear feet of 7-foot-tall sea wall and poured concrete over existing terraced steps to form a ramp on the seaward side of the Bath House Pavilions. In little over a decade, pounding waves and cascading rocks have undermined the base of the ramp. (Courtesy Massachusetts Archives.)

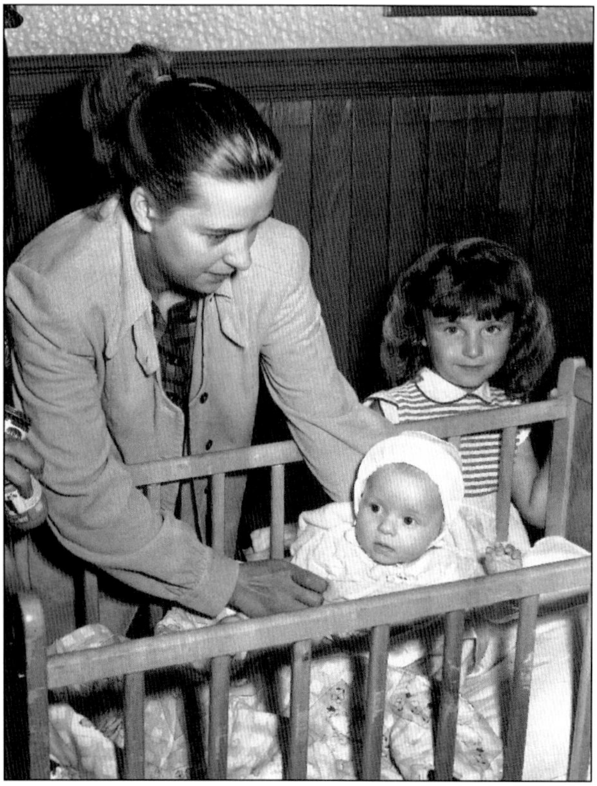

Hurricane Carol produced extensive wind- and flood-related damage along the Revere seacoast in early September 1954. Many residents sought escape and solace within designated storm shelters throughout the community. *Boston Herald* staff photographer Dan Murphy snapped this picture within the Red Cross shelter at Our Lady of Lourdes Church of Mrs. Leo Hurley tenderly attending her infant son Paul while daughter Lee, 4, shyly looks on. (Courtesy Boston Public Library, Prints Department.)

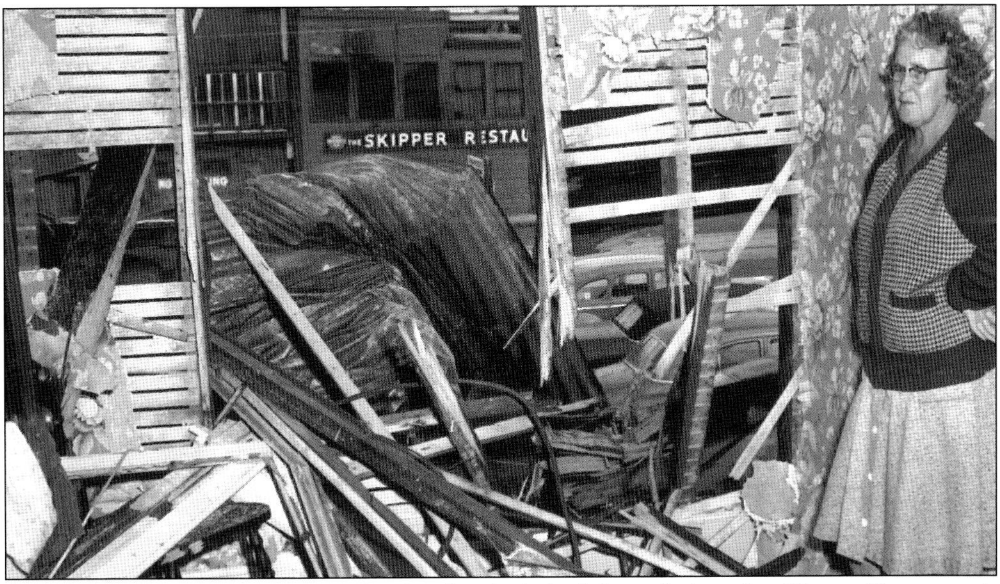

Girders torn from a nearby Ferris wheel violently slashed through the side of Emma Shaugnessy's house during Hurricane Carol, which ravaged the seaside community in September 1954. Professional photographer Dan Murphy took this picture detailing the twisted wreckage at the 157 Baker Street residence while the distressed homeowner contemplates the cluttered debris at her feet. In the background, the Skipper Restaurant presides over a silent, storm-desecrated street. (Courtesy Boston Public Library, Prints Department.)

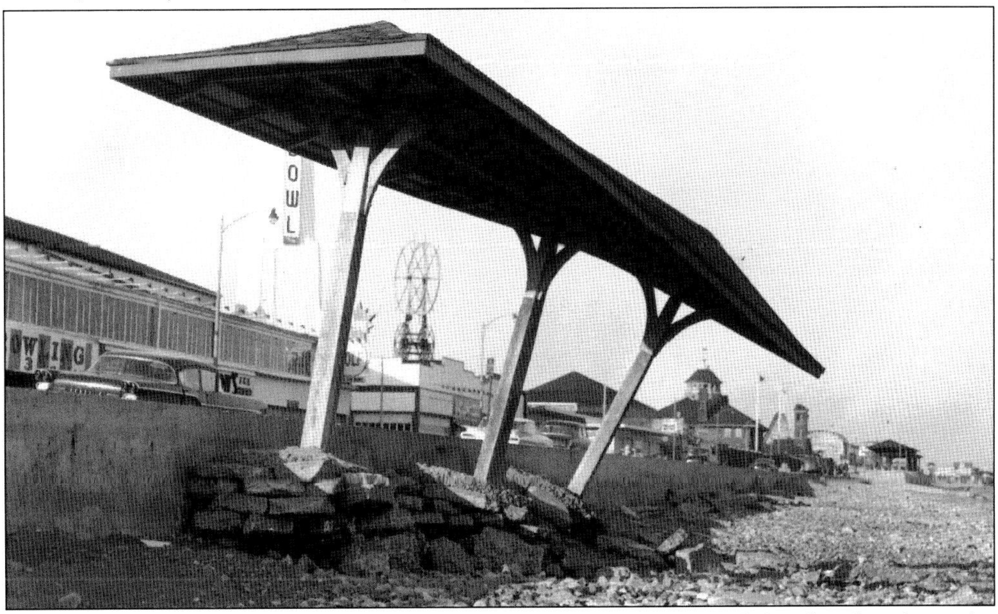

Dark slate topped the graceful hip-roofed sun shelters that existed for decades along the seaward side of Revere Beach Boulevard. Photographed in 1959 by Jim Phelan, erosion and age have undermined the unstable base of this structure, which leans precariously toward the uncompromising rocks below. Across the street stands the Nautical Amusement Center, featuring 32 bowling lanes. The popular Nautical entertained generations of visitors and operated until 1978. (Courtesy MDC Archives, Boston.)

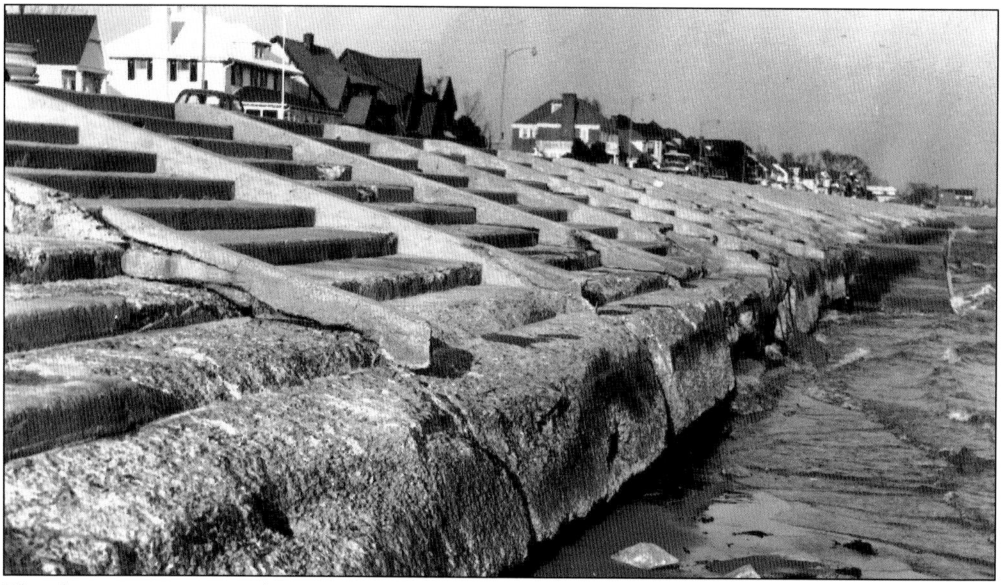

Bleacher-type concrete shore protection, built 30 feet wide, stretched for 1,500 feet along the northerly section of Revere Beach Reservation and appears greatly deteriorated in this 1959 photograph by Jim Phelan. The protective steps were constructed between 1914 and 1915 by M.J. McGawley and, along with the convex breakwaters sited below, valiantly defended the residential properties located along Revere Beach Boulevard for over 75 years. (Courtesy MDC Archives, Boston.)

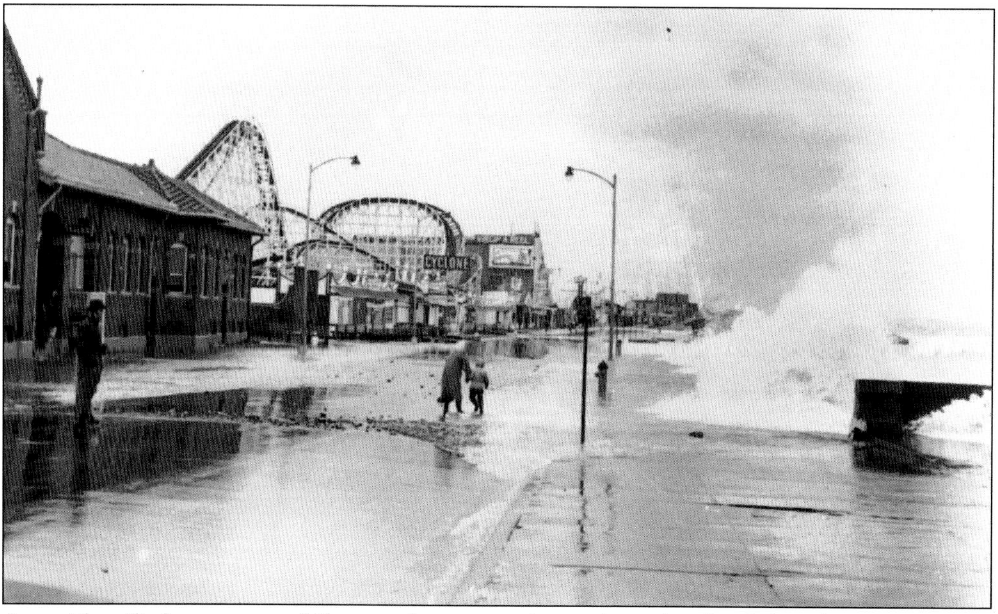

An unidentified woman carefully steers her young charge through a flooded, rock-strewn Revere Beach Boulevard while a lone bystander looks on. This dramatic photograph shows the strong storm surge that defied restraint on December 29, 1959. From left to right are the Metropolitan District Commission Police Station, the Cyclone, and the Virginia Reel—three Revere Beach landmarks that sustained damage during this perilous holiday week storm. (Courtesy MDC Archives, Boston.)

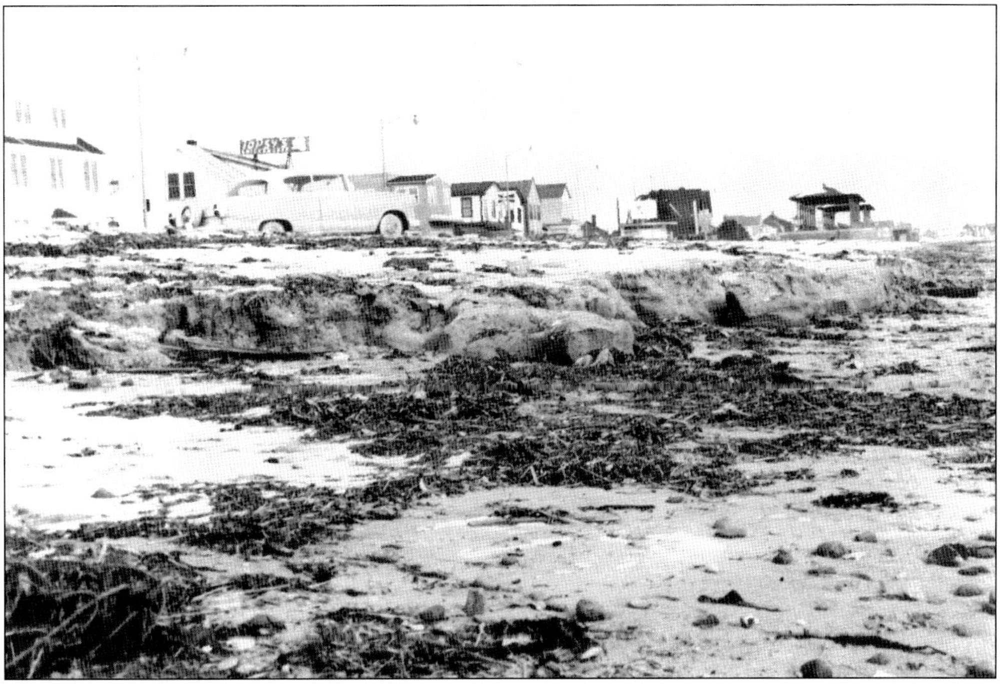

These photographs taken between the Oak Island and Revere Street Pavilions reveal the great extent to which the sand has been naturally resculptured following a monumental storm in 1959. In the above image, a lone car appears to be perched directly on the elevated strata of sand adjacent to Topsy's Chicken Coop, at 377 Revere Beach Boulevard. Opposite the Oak Island shelters stands Kelly's Roast Beef. The photograph below details a debris-strewn expanse of shore stretching southward opposite Revere Beach Boulevard fast-food establishments, which offer varied menu items, including ice cream, pizza, and chop suey. Several of the buildings at the center are still standing. (Courtesy MDC Archives, Boston.)

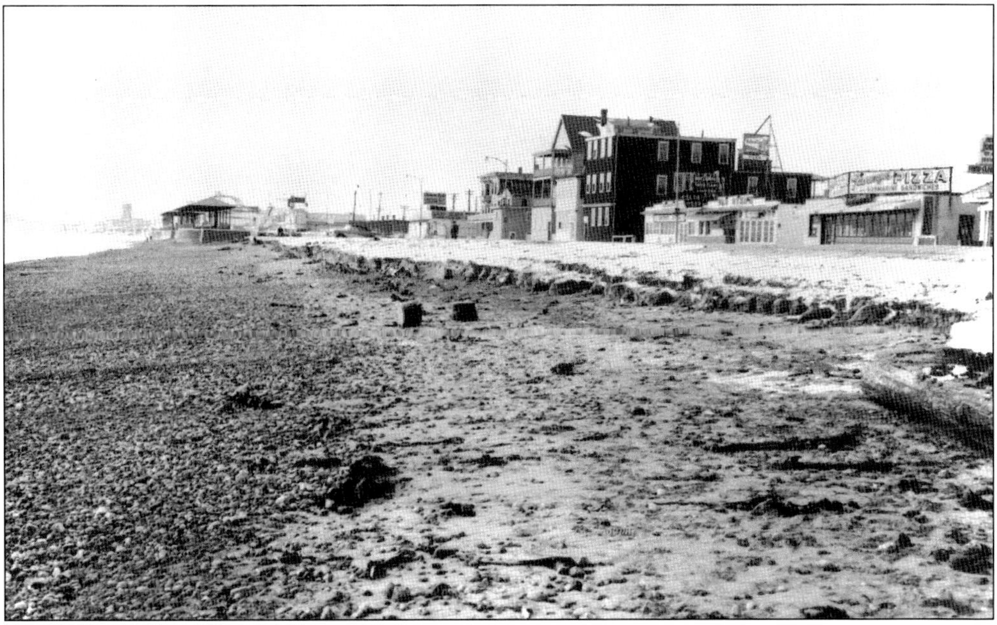

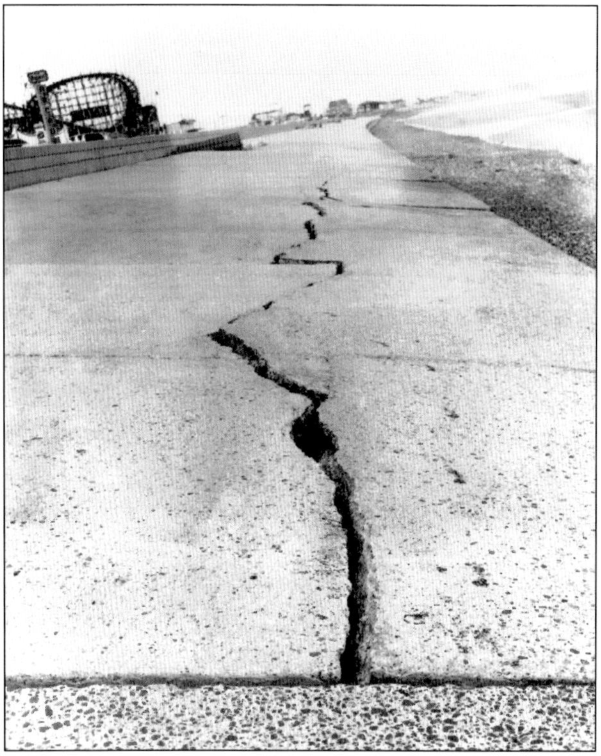

A lengthy fissure born of aquatic assault and age bisects the concrete shore protection stretching northward in the vicinity of the Metropolitan District Commission Police Station. At the left along the roadway are an arcade and the prominent Cyclone coaster. At the right, the placid surf belies nature's tremendous capacity for destruction. This photograph was taken during the 1960s to document the structural disrepair evident along the seaward side of Revere Beach. (Courtesy MDC Archives, Boston.)

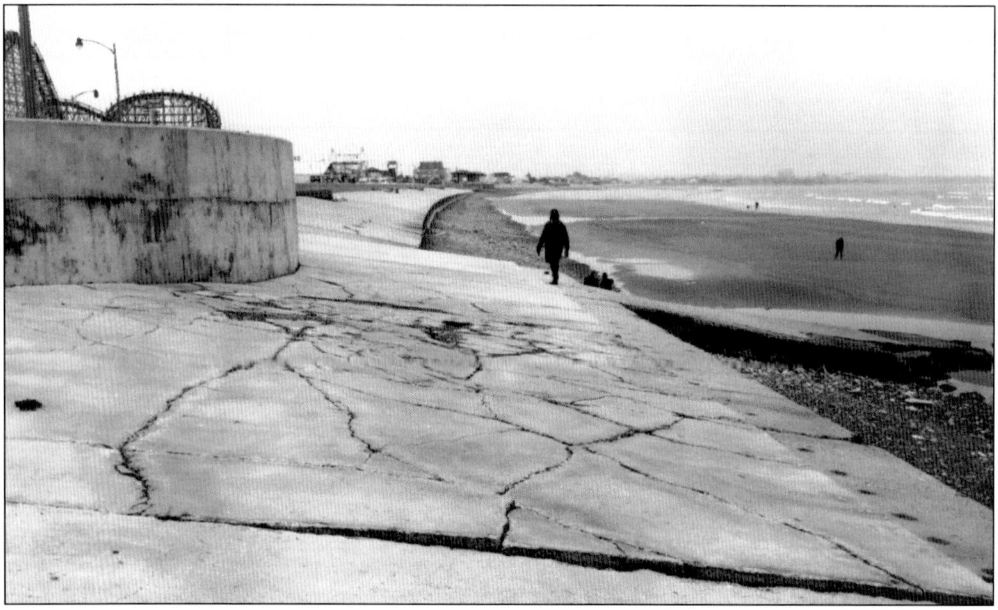

This off-season photograph was taken during the 1960s and clearly illustrates the enormous cracks in the concrete shore protection that emerged after years of exposure to storm-driven tides. Clearly visible at the center right is a vehicular ramp created as part of a Works Progress Administration project in 1938. The beneficial ramp was constructed opposite the Metropolitan District Commission Police Station. At the left rise the dramatic wooden arches of the Cyclone. (Courtesy MDC Archives, Boston.)

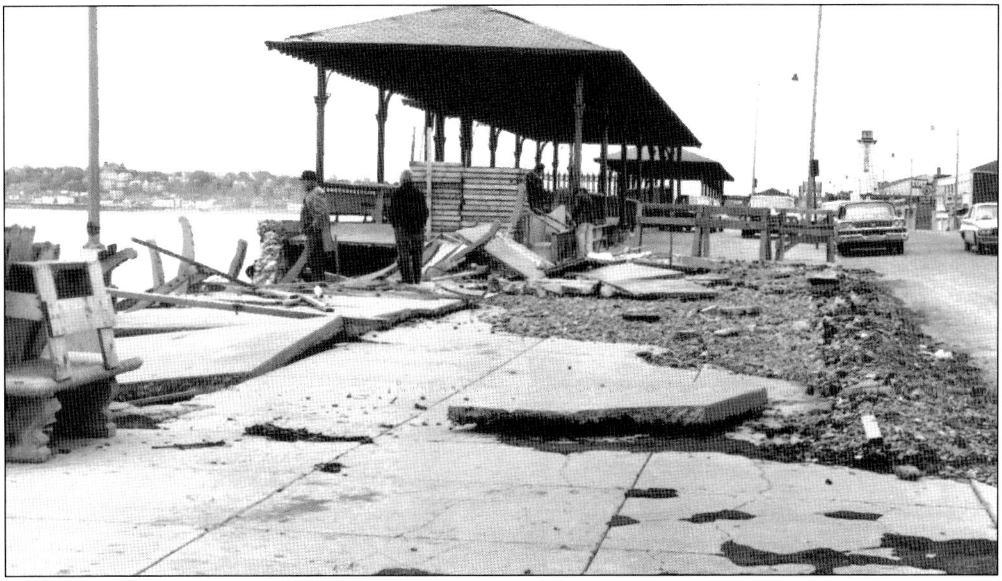

Damage wrought by a severe storm necessitated reconstruction of the sidewalk adjacent to the Bath House Pavilions, near present-day Chester Avenue. Photographed by R. Horrigan on the morning of May 27, 1967, the debris-laden sidewalk was soon to be replaced, as evidenced by the abundant building materials stored within the forward pavilion. The classic hip-roofed structure has itself sustained damage, indicated by the absence of several roof slates. (Courtesy MDC Archives, Boston.)

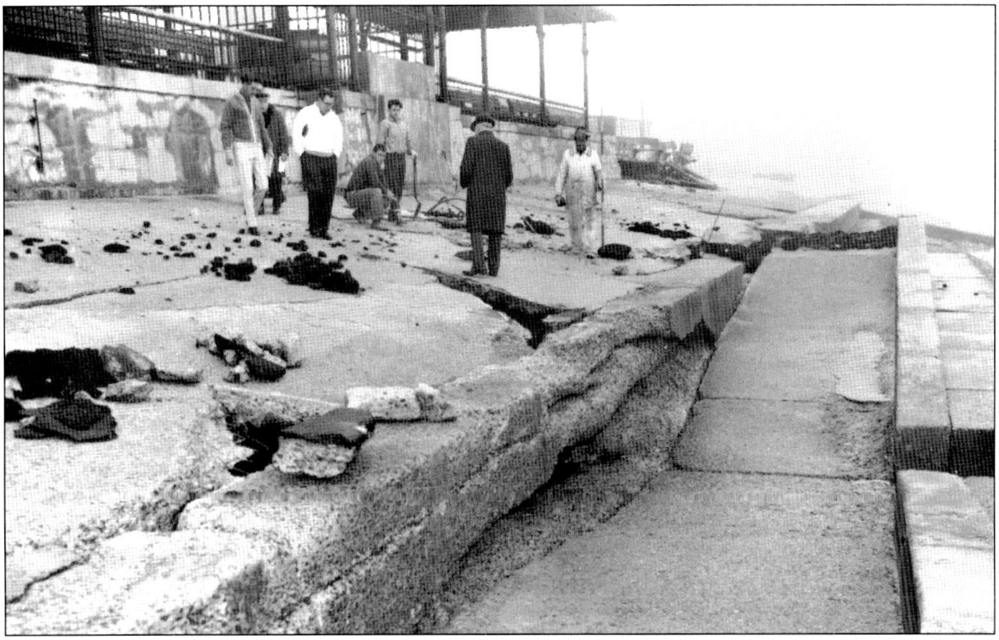

This photograph was taken by Officer Hardigan on a May morning in 1967. An informally clad work crew and several men in business attire appear to be assessing the disrepair evident along the fortification sited below the elegantly detailed Bath House Pavilions. Morning fog envelops the shoreline north of the damaged stretch of storm-assaulted concrete, while extricated debris clutters the work site and attests to difficult labor ahead. (Courtesy MDC Archives, Boston.)

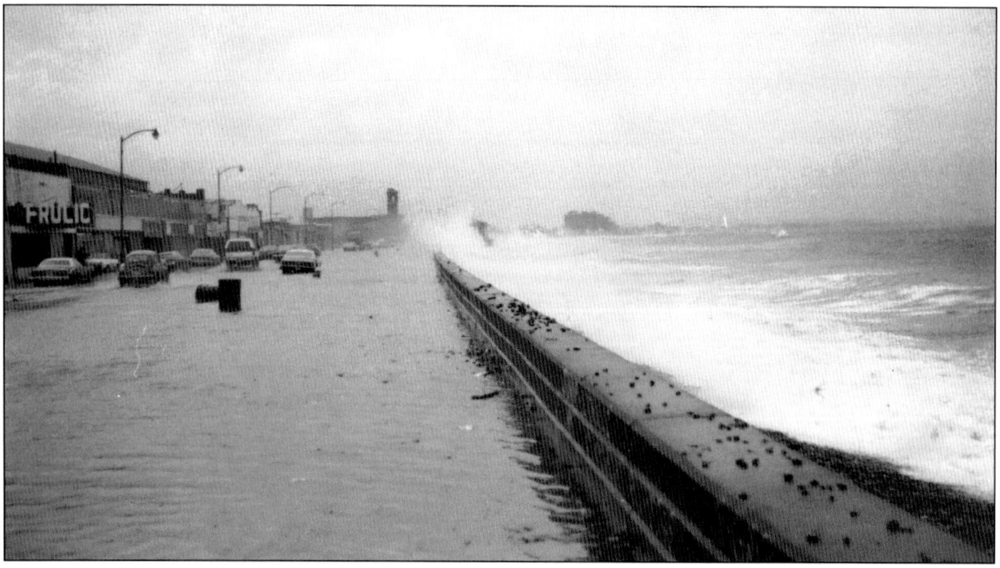

Several cars navigate the flooded roadway along central Revere Beach Boulevard in this February 1978 photograph. At the center, the concrete sea wall extending the entire length of the reservation barely separates land from sea. Pebbles, sand, and other shore debris litter the wall and submerged parking area. Relentless waves break angrily against the shore barrier and white froth explodes in visible testament to the potent power of nature. (Courtesy MDC Archives, Boston.)

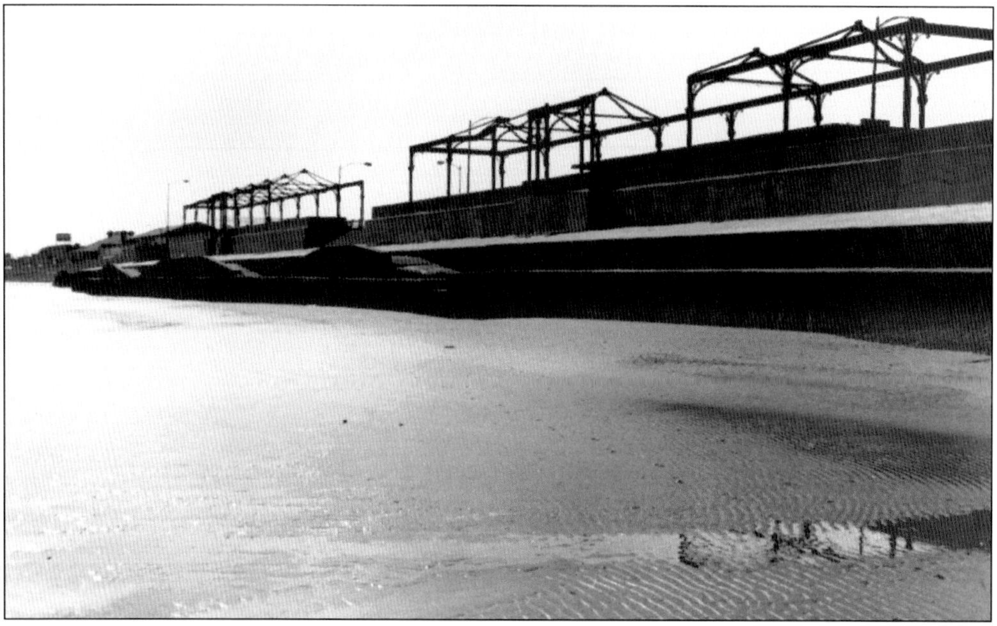

The calamitous storms that struck the East Coast during the early months of 1978 rendered millions of dollars worth of damage along Revere Beach. Pictured here at dead low tide, extensive concrete shore protection was unable to shelter these once grand pavilions from the unbridled fury of wind and waves. Stripped bare of their roofs and ornamental dignity, these skeletal structures silently await forthcoming repair and, later, complete restoration. (Courtesy MDC Archives, Boston.)